D1531157

Ronsard
and the Age of Gold

RONSARD
AND THE AGE OF
GOLD

ELIZABETH ARMSTRONG

CAMBRIDGE

AT THE UNIVERSITY PRESS

1968

Published by the Syndics of the Cambridge University Press
Bentley House, 200 Euston Road, London, N.W.1
American Branch: 32 East 57th Street, New York, N.Y.10022

Library of Congress Catalogue Card Number: 68–11279
Standard Book Number: 521 04056 6

Printed in Great Britain
at the University Printing House, Cambridge
(Brooke Crutchley, University Printer)

To
my parents
JOHN OCTAVIUS TYLER
and
ANNETTE TYLER
in grateful memory

Contents

✤ ✤

Contents

Illustrations

✣ ✣

PLATES

between pages 80 *and* 81

ix

Illustrations

Preface

❈ ❈

The research on which this book is based was begun with the help of a Grant from the Vaughan Cornish Bequest in 1959, a Grant from the Leverhulme Trust in 1960, and a term's leave of absence granted in 1960 by my College.

I am grateful to Professor Jean Seznec for advice and encouragement at the outset; to Professor Isidore Silver for generously placing at my disposal his own notes on the occurrences of the Age of Gold theme in Ronsard's poetry; to Dr W. G. Moore for discussing with me the paper which formed the starting-point of chapters 1 and 5; to Miss Rosemary Syfret for reading chapters 1 and 2 in their earliest form; and to Dr Christina Roaf for answering numerous questions. Many friends, colleagues and pupils interested in the sixteenth century have contributed something to the result, in so far as it is sound.

I should like to thank also the authorities and staff of the libraries where I have worked, especially the Bodleian, the Ashmolean and the Taylorian, in Oxford; the British Museum and the Warburg Institute, in London; and the Bibliothèque Nationale, in Paris.

ELIZABETH ARMSTRONG

Somerville College
Oxford
8 May 1967

Acknowledgements

The author and publishers are grateful to the following for having granted permission to reproduce photographs: Archives Photographiques, Paris (Pl. 6); the Bodleian Library (Figs. 1, 2, 6, 7, 8); the British Museum (Figs. 3, 4, 5, 10); the Conservateur au Cabinet des Dessins, Louvre, Paris (Pl. 3); J. Combier, Macon (Pl. 4); the Nationalbibliothek, Vienna (Pl. 2).

Abbreviations

NOTE

In quoting sixteenth-century texts, I have expanded contractions, adopted the modern usage as regards the use of 'i' and 'j', 'u' and 'v', etc. and occasionally modernised the punctuation where this seemed necessary to clarify the sense.

Introduction

✣ ✣

The Age of Gold in Renaissance symbol and ceremonial

'Ce fut ung renouvellement du temps de Saturne, tant il fut faict alors grand chère.' Thus Rabelais, writing in 1532, summed up the rejoicings at the triumphal entry of his hero, the giant-prince Pantagruel, into the city of the Amaurotes whom he had liberated.[1] The association of ideas was becoming a familiar one to most sixteenth-century readers.

The Age of Gold, a legendary era of human happiness, ruled by Saturn (before he was dethroned by Jupiter), and sanctified by the presence among men of Astraea, the virgin goddess of Justice, had been succeeded by an Age of Silver, an Age of Brass, and finally an Age of Iron. Whether it had been an age of simple civilised life favoured by ideal conditions, or an even earlier phase when Nature supplied every need unbidden, the provision of 'good cheer' for everyone was a constant feature of the reign of Saturn. That the cycle of the years might one day bring it back again was an ancient belief, consecrated by Virgil, the most respected of all the poets of antiquity: the occasion would be (according to Book VI of the *Aeneid*) the reign of Augustus, or (according to the Fourth Eclogue) the birth of a mysterious child.

Renaissance poets, orators and pageant-masters, called upon to celebrate an accession or a marriage, the birth of an heir or the signing of a treaty, could do no less than promise the same to their patrons. First fully exploited in Italy, this device became equally popular in northern Europe.[2] It was particu-

---

[1] *Pantagruel*, ed. V.-L. Saulnier (TLF), chap. XXI, p. 166.
[2] See Frances Yates, 'Queen Elizabeth as Astraea', *JWCI*, x (1947), 27–82, and E. H. Gombrich, 'Renaissance and Golden Age', *ibid.* XXIV (1961), 306–9, and *X Congresso Internazionale di scienze storiche: Rassunti delle communicazioni* (1955), VII, 304–5.

larly prominent in the ceremonial Entries of rulers into cities on some occasion of public festivity.

It could, on such occasions, be made to stand for more sectional interests. The show or 'tableau vivant' contributed to the Entry of the Archduke Charles (the future Charles V), as Count of Flanders, into Bruges in 1515, by the Franc or Vrij, the

Figure 1. Astraea and the Age of Gold from *Le siècle doré* of Guillaume Michel
Paris, 1521, 4°, woodcut on title-page and at end

rural area lying round Bruges, thus used the Age of Gold to symbolise the country as against the town. Whereas most of the other shows along the processional route naturally glorified various crafts and trades, the 'tryumphe des seigneurs du Franc' showed Charles's father Philippe le Beau, who had in 1501 restored the status of the Franc as the Fourth Member of Flanders, handing the charter to a group of knights kneeling on his left, while on his right Saturn holding his sickle presided over the divinities of field and forest and over a group of shepherdesses dancing in a ring. The author of the illustrated published account (which was printed at Paris) explained that 'in the first Age and archaic crudeness of the human race, under the rule of the gods and goddesses represented in this enclosure, men lived in huts and cottages, entirely, and peacably, on agriculture and stock-raising, for they sought no gain nor fruit save from the earth and from the brute beasts', and claimed that the building of cities and states had been the downfall of the 'bienheureux ciercle aurain du glorieux Saturne' and of the simple virtues for which it stood.[1]

In contrast to this, one author made an imaginative attempt to show that the Age of Gold as the ideal society into which a nation could be turned were the Three Estates—clergy, nobles and people—persuaded to abandon 'mauvaise coûtume' and live according to piety and reason, each citizen contributing his share of work and good will to the community. This was the allegorical story, part verse, part prose, by Guillaume Michel, entitled *Le siècle doré, contenant le temps de Paix, Amour & Concorde*,[2] published in 1521. The moral earnestness with which the author pleaded for honesty and unselfishness had indeed nothing ascetic about it. The perfect society would be the affluent society. The elegant Astraea in the illustration on the title-page and back page of the book is being apostrophised by a figure symbolising the *siècle doré*: the figure is that of a fashionably dressed young man.[3] The same figure appears, in an illustration

---

[1] Rémy du Puys, *La tryumphante entrée faicte sur le nouvel advenement de Charles prince des Hespaignes en la ville de Bruges* (1515), ff. F4ᵃ–F5ᵇ. A nearby show staged by the tailors' guild reflected a different concept of it: here an allegorical figure of Bruges lamented the decline of her economy, speaking of her 'golden time and age' turning to silver as the merchants deserted her (f. F3ᵇ).

[2] The Bodleian copy has the mark of ownership on the title-page of Louise de Bourbon-Vendôme (1495–1575), Abbess of Fontevrault, which suggests that the work attracted some attention at the time. B. Weinberg, in his article in *BHR*, XI (1949), argues on stylistic grounds that Michel was responsible for the 'modernised' version of the *Roman de la Rose* published at Paris in 1526, and lists his works (pp. 75–6). See also below, p. 149, n. 5.

[3] See Fig. 1.

near the end, seated in his house counting piles of money at a table, while in the background stands a dresser (the traditional show-place for the family silver) loaded with splendid plate: only the ears of corn and sprays of vine which deck his hat remind us that he is an allegorical figure, symbolising the plenty of the Age of Gold which would follow if the Three Estates

Figure 2. The Age of Gold enjoying the Benefits of Peace, Love and Concord, from *Le siècle doré* of Guillaume Michel
Paris, 1521, 4°

decided to heed the preaching of 'divine sapience'.[1] There is, it is true, a reference to a legendary Age of Gold in the past when even the greatest were content to live on Nature's bounty, on acorns and wild fruit. This is mentioned with scorn by Mauvaise Coutume, who asks rhetorically: 'fault-il revoir en ce monde la

[1] See Fig. 2.

4

souffisance de nature qui jadis contentoit par sa chiche face les plus grands et parfaitz du glan des bois & forestz de Dodonne, de pommes, poires, labrusques et aultres fruitz sauvaiges? me contenteroie bien de cela? nenny, certes!'[1] It is not, however, the material conditions of such an Age of Gold which the author seeks to re-establish, in defiance of Mauvaise Coutume, but the spirit of moderation and contentedness which it symbolised. The greatest obstacle to a happy society seemed to him that 'evil habit' of desiring gain as an objective in its own right. It was rare for the Age of Gold to be used, as in this work, as an equivalent to an age of social justice, compared ⌈for instance with its use to denote the revival of learning.[2]

Frequently it stood, however, for peace, as opposed to war or civil strife (the Age of Iron was particularly notorious as an age of war). Deploring the wars between Charles V and Francis I, Jacques de Pape, an outspoken humanist poet of Ypres, repeatedly used this image,[3] and, welcoming the prospect of the treaty of 1529, wrote:

> Marte soporato redeant saturnia nobis
> Tempora, felices et sine lite dies.
> Aurea sedato bellorum saecla tumultu,
> Iam reduci veniant saepe vocata pede.[4]

With this ideal of peace might be associated ideas of religious revelation and revival.

Jean Raulin, whose life had been devoted to reform of the French Church and especially of the monastic orders, and whose letters and treatises were published posthumously in 1521, was very fond of this image. In an *Oratio* delivered in the Collège de Navarre on the feast-day of St Louis, he described how a *gens aurea* might spring up under the rule of a good king, which would so overcome malice by their virtue that swords should

---

[1] G. Michel, *Le siècle doré: contenant le temps de Paix, Amour, et Concorde*, f. F3ᵃ.

[2] E.g. 'Haec sunt vere aurea tempora, in quibus bonarum literarum studia multis annis neglecta refloruerunt'. Jo. Trithemius, *Epistolae familiares* (Hagenau, Petrus Brubach, 1536, 4°), p. 175, letter dated 24 June 1506.

[3] *Elegiae Jacobi Papae Hyprensis, edidit Jacobus Meyerus, Elegia Tertia*, pp. 7 ff.

[4] *Ibid. Elegia Septima*, p. 13, lines 3–6.

be beaten into ploughshares, etc.[1] He applied the term *gens aurea* too to the golden age of monasticism in the past (contrasting it with the decadence he saw around him) regarding that as the fulfilment of the oracle of Virgil in *Eclogue* iv.[2]

Clément Marot, on the other hand, hoped in 1536 for an era of evangelical truth which might spring from endurance of the current religious persecutions:

> Viens veoir de Crist le regne commencé,
> Et son honneur par tourmens avancé!
> O siecle d'or le plus fin que l'on treuve,
> Dont la bonté dedans le feu s'espreuve![3]

There is here, it would seem, an allusion to 'the fiery trial which is to try you' which St Peter warned his flock to expect before the glory of Christ should be revealed.[4] Marot assimilated St Peter's words to the image found in the Old Testament of God trying his people as gold is tried in the fire.[5] The passage occurs in his Eclogue ii, an 'Avant-naissance' in honour of the expected third child of his patroness Renée de France, Duchess of Ferrara.

Direct imitation of the Fourth Eclogue for a state occasion does not seem to have been attempted in French poetry until his *Eglogue sur la naissance du filz de Monseigneur le Daulphin* in 1544.[6] A long-standing tradition—a tradition familiar to English readers still, through Milton's allusion to it in the Nativity Ode—had connected the sibylline prophecy, evoked by Virgil, with the birth of the Messiah, and only a very solemn event in the life of the French nation could justify to a poet like Clément Marot the application of it to a secular purpose. The birth of the long-awaited heir of the Dauphin (the future

---

[1] 'Nam sub generoso principe saepissime surgit gens aurea mundo, quae pacis ineundo consilia adeo sua virtute maliciam vincit, ut convertat gladios in vomeres... O quis aureum illud saeculum heroico carmine describere posset.' Jean Raulin, *Epistolarum opus*, (1520–21), f. 146ᵃ.

[2] 'O secula aurea super aurum, et lapidem preciosum desyderabilia, quando de claustri latibulo iuxta Maronis oraculum surgebat gens aurea mundo. O felix nimium prior illa aetas...' *Ibid.* f. 158ᵇ (in *De perfecta religionis plantatione*, an address to an assembly of his order at Cluny).

[3] *Œuvres lyriques*, ed. C. A. Mayer, pp. 341–2, lines 59–62.

[4] I Peter iv, 12–13.   [5] Zechariah xiii, 9.

[6] *Œuvres lyriques*, ed. C. A. Mayer, p. 354. The child was the future Francis II.

Henry II) and of his wife Catherine de' Medici seemed such an event.

By that time, the theme of the Age of Gold had been pressed into service in one of the most spectacular occasions of the period, the celebrations organised for the marriage of Duke Cosimo I de' Medici to Eleanor of Toledo at Florence in 1539. In particular, it had figured in the Third Interlude in the comedy *Il Commodo*, presented on Wednesday, 8 July 1539: here the god Silenus, surprised (as in the Sixth Eclogue of Virgil) by shepherds, had ransomed himself by a song, in this case a *canzonetta* beginning, 'O begli Anni del Oro, ò secol divo'. The words, by Gio. Batista Strozzi, recalled a time when there had been neither scythe nor rake nor snare nor cruel iron nor poison; when the rivers ran milk and the oaks exuded honey, for the benefit of the nymphs and shepherds; and the possibility that such an idyllic world might once more return was referred to with nostalgia.[1]

The accession of Henry II and Catherine de' Medici occurred when memories of this festival were still vivid. Not surprisingly, a prologue and interludes on this theme, performed in the interludes of the comedy *Calandria*, featured prominently in the entertainment devised by the Florentine colony in September 1548 for the Entry of the king and queen into Lyons.[2] The Age of Gold, in a sumptuous golden costume, appeared after Act IV, accompanied by Peace (in white), Justice (in silver and black) and Religion (blue and white), announcing herself to the king with the opening words:

> L'età mi chiamo Aurata, & vengo à voi
> Gran Re, per esser vostra...

[1] Pier Francesco Giambullari, *Apparato et feste nelle noze dello Illustrissimo Signor Duca di Firenze, e della Duchessa sua consorte, con le sue Stanze, Madriali, Comedia et Intermedii, in quelle recitati* (1539), p. 125. Cf. A. M. Nagler, *Theatre Festivals of the Medici 1539–1637* (New Haven and London, 1964), pp. 5–12.

[2] 'Particolare descritione della comedia fatta recitare in Lione la Natione Fiorentina à richiesta di sua Maestà Christianissima', in *La magnifica et triumphale entrata del re Henrico secondo fatta nella città di Lyone* (1549). This supplement, not included in the French edition (also printed by G. Roville), begins on f. M1ᵃ.

7

After the last Act of the play, she was brought back by Apollo and left alone on the stage in the presence of the king, to whom she recited a long poetic address, afterwards presenting the queen with a golden lily weighing twenty marks.[1] Not to be outdone, the city fathers of Rouen (when Henry II made his Entry, 1 October 1550) decorated the town gate as a triumphal arch representing the Age of Gold: it was crowned with a gilded statue of Saturn, standing on a silver crescent moon (the king's personal emblem) supported on either side by a Sibyl. Saturn held a tablet inscribed with the lines:

> Je suis l'aage d'or
> D'honneur revestu,
> Je suis en vertu,
> Et seray encor,

while the following quatrain appeared on the arch:

> L'aage d'or, qui fut florissant,
> Avant l'argent, le fer & cuyvre,
> Par un Roy, en vertu croissant,
> Au monde recommence à vivre.[2]

As to their gift to the queen, this was a gold figurine of Astraea, standing one and a half feet high, 'élégante Image emaillée sur le nud d'incarnation', holding in her right hand the sword of Justice and in her left 'une sphere de félicité', a symbol of Heaven.

The Entry of Henry II into Paris (16 June 1549)[3] used other symbols of prosperity: the organisers no doubt wished to avoid even the semblance of copying the shows put on the previous year at Lyons. But the theme was none the less in people's

---

[1] An almost exactly similar scheme was adopted over a century later by Saint-Aignon as part of the entertainment offered by Louis XIV to his guests at Versailles called *Les plaisirs de l'Ile enchantée.* The dramatic interlude on 7 May 1664 introduced Apollo and the Four Ages, and represented the Age of Gold professing her confidence in the king's power to revive her. The verses for this were written by Molière.

[2] *C'est la deduction du sumptueux ordre et magnifiques theatres dressés par les citoiens de Rouen à Henry second,* ff. M2ᵇ–M3ᵇ. See also f. Q4ª.

[3] See V.-L. Saulnier, 'Sébillet, Du Bellay, Ronsard: L'entrée de Henri II à Paris et la révolution poétique de 1550', *Les fêtes de la Renaissance,* 1, ed. J. Jacquot (Paris, 1956), 31–59.

minds. Ronsard's ode on the prospect of the Entry, the *Avant-entrée du roy treschrestien à Paris*,[1] one of his earliest works, predicted boldly that the goddess Astraea (who had ruled the Age of Gold and was the last of the immortals to abandon the human race) would make her entry with the king:

> J'oi arriver ton Roi qui t'apporte
> La vierge Astrée, & sa belle sequelle,
> Qui s'envolla de ce monde avec elle...

sang the poet, addressing the city of Paris:

> Ne la voi-tu comme elle prend sa place
> A son retour dans le sein & la face
> De nostre Roine...?[2]

Over twenty years later, when Ronsard was the favourite poet of the sovereign, Charles IX, and a national figure, he was commissioned by the city of Paris to assist in planning the scenario and writing the verses for an equally splendid occasion, the Entry into the capital of the king on the occasion of his marriage (1571).[3] In this, though in a subordinate position, the Age of Gold was actually represented among the decorations along the processional route.[4]

It would be natural to expect that any poetry that he wrote on the Age of Gold theme during the intervening period, or indeed afterwards, would similarly treat it as a symbol of splendour, prosperity and culture under a just and enlightened prince. The reality is quite different.

[1] The publication of this ode may have contributed to the mistaken belief that Ronsard helped to provide poems for the *official* programme of the Entry—see V.-L. Saulnier, *op. cit.* p. 34.
[2] Lau. I, p. 18, lines 10–15.
[3] See F. A. Yates, 'Poètes et artistes dans les entrées de Charles IX et de sa reine à Paris en 1571', in *Les fêtes de la Renaissance*, I, ed. J. Jacquot (Paris, 1956), 61–84.
[4] See below, p. 45.

1

❀ ❀

The Age of Gold in Ronsard's Poetry[1]

FROM THE BEGINNING TO
'LES ISLES FORTUNÉES' (1553)

Ronsard's first specific mention of the Age of Gold speaks of

> L'age d'or precieus,
> Où le peuple ocieus
> Vivoit aus bois sans peine
> De glan cheut & de feine.[2]

These are the concluding lines of a versified prayer, *A Dieu, pour la famine*, written in the name of the people of France (according to Laumonier, in the famine of 1546). The manner of the poem is imitated from certain of Marot's metrical French version of the Psalms. If Ronsard, in such circumstances, prayed for the return of the Age of Gold, and pictured it as a life of idleness in the woods, sustained by acorns and beechnuts, his words must be intended at least as seriously as those in the *Avant-entrée du roi*. It can scarcely have been a return to such a life as this which Ronsard and his fellow-citizens wished to characterise the new reign: to be tolerable, let alone desirable, it would require provision of a climate infinitely milder than any to be had in Europe as we know it.

And it was as an era of Eternal Spring, an era long since banished for ever from the earth by gods jealous of human happiness, that Ronsard next celebrated the Age of Gold, in his Ode entitled *Avant-venue du printens* (1550). After that era, men became subject to the rigours of heat and cold. Henceforth

---

[1] A chronological table of the poems discussed in this chapter will be found at the end of the book (*Appendix to chapter 1*).

[2] Lau. II, p. 186, lines 61–4. The poem was published in the *Bocage*, a small collection of juvenilia appended by Ronsard to *Les quatre premiers livres des Odes* (1550).

they began to build ships and to forge weapons, learnt the arts of bloodshed and of poisoning; the coffer—Pandora's box is meant—unloosed upon the world its contents of evil, and the rocks felt the effects of thunderbolts:

> Mais la main des dieus jalose
> N'endura que telle chose
> Suivist son train coutumier,
> Et changeant le premier vivre
> Fist une saison de cuivre
> En lieu du bel or premier.
>
> Lors le printems donna place
> Au chaut, au vent, à la glace,
> Qui renaissent à leur tour.
> Et le sapin des montaignes
> Galopa par les compaignes
> Qui nous baignent alentour.
>
> On ouit sonner les armes,
> On ouit par les alarmes
> L'acier tinter durement,
> Et les lames assérées,
> Sur les enclumes férrées
> Craqueter horriblement.
>
> On inventa les usages
> D'empoisonner les bruvages
> Et l'art d'épandre le sang:
> Les maus du cofre sortirent,
> Et les haus rochers sentirent
> La foudre desus leur flanc.[1]

If Ronsard thus believed the Age of Gold to be irrevocably lost, he did not wholly renounce the convention by which friends or patrons might be credited with the power to symbolise or even revive its virtues. He praised Jacques Bouju (who had recommended his poetry to the king's sister Margaret, afterwards Duchess of Savoy) in another Ode of the 1550 collection:

[1] Lau. I, pp. 152–4, lines 85–108.

> Pour estre de nostre France
> L'un de ceus qui ont defait
> Le villain monstre Ignorance
> Et le siecle d'or refait.[1]

Margaret herself seems about to receive a similar tribute in an Ode of the Fifth Book, two years later. The poet apostrophised her as:

> Vierge dont la vertu redore
> Cest heureux siecle qui t'adore...

But his compliment is turned in a direction somewhat different from that expected by the reader. The princess is an example of magnanimity unparalleled in *any* age in the past and certain to remain so in the future, *even* were the Age of Gold to come again: and for *that* to happen the present age would have to cease being the Age of Iron which it is. And as if to emphasise still further that this is a flight of fancy, it is all introduced by a rhetorical question, 'Shall I say that...?':

> Diray-je que les ans qui tournent
> De paz qui jamais ne sejournent,
> N'ont rien veu de semblable encor'
> A la grandeur de ton courage,
> Ny ne verront bien que nostre age
> Change son fer au premier or?[2]

In another Ode of the Fifth Book, he contrasted the restlessness of the present age with the contentedness of Golden Age humanity. Regretting the decision of his friend Claude de Ligneri to go to Italy, he expressed fears for him and for their friendship; how much happier men were before the era of travel:

> Telle saison fut bien dorée
> En laquelle on se contentoit
> De voir de son tect la fumée,
> Lors que la terre on ne hantoit
> D'un autre Soleil allumée.[3]

Chimney-smoke is decidedly not a traditional feature of the landscape of the Age of Gold. To be deprived of the sight of the

---

[1] Lau. II, p. 88, lines 9–12, and n. 2.   [2] Lau. III, p. 105, lines 133–8.
[3] *Ibid.* p. 175, lines 94–8.

smoke rising from one's own hearth is, on the other hand, a classic symbol of exile.[1] Remembering this, Ronsard treated modern man, who was not *content* with it, as unhappy, and contrasted him with the Age of Gold when (as he had already told his readers in the *Avant-venue du printens*) sea-faring was unknown.

Even pets are not what they were in the Age of Gold, reflected the poet, when in his *Folastries* (1553) he had occasion to reprove his dog for whining at the door behind which he was making love and so betraying him and his mistress:

> Au vieil temps que l'enfant de Rhée
> N'avoit la terre dedorée,
> Les Heroes ne dedaignoient
> Les chiens qui les accompagnoient,
> Fidelles gardes de leur trace...[2]

Had Jupiter *not* abolished the Age of Gold, he meditated in a more serious mood the same year, a host of other ills would have been spared mankind:

> Certenement la vierge Astrée
> N'eut point quitté nôtre contrée,
> Et les foudres tombés du ciel
> N'eussent accablé les montaignes;
> Toujours fussent par les campagnes
> Glissés les dous ruisseaus de miel.

> Le cheval au milieu des guerres
> N'eut point ronflé, ni les tonnerres
> Des canons n'eussent point tonné,
> Ni sus les bornes des provinces
> Le choc armé de deus grans princes
> N'eut point le pasteur étonné.

> On n'eut point emmuré les viles
> Pour crainte de guerres civiles,

---

[1] Cf. *Odyssey*, I, 57–9, and also Ovid, *Pont.* I, iii, 33–4. The symbol was to be used twice by Du Bellay in his *Regrets* expressing his longing for France while in Italy: *Œuvres*, ed. Chamard, II, 76–7 and 156–7.
[2] Lau. v, p. 35, lines 1–5.

Ni des étranges legions;
Ni le coutre de Pharsalie
N'eut heurté tant d'os d'Italie
Ni tant de vuides mourrions.[1]

There are features here which recall the *Avant-venue du printens*, and the similarities are emphasised by the choice of the same stanza form, the only metrical difference between the two odes being the substitution of 8-syllable for 7-syllable lines. The Age of Gold is again represented as a standing reproach to the present. Had it never ended, we should have remained innocent of war (whether typified by the war-horse or the cannon), and spared the need of defensive walls and the sad reminder of those slain in battle. The Ode, published in *Les Amours, nouvellement augmentées* (1553), is consecrated by the poet to his reconciliation with the reigning court poet Mellin de Saint-Gelais; the emphasis here given to the Age of Gold is appropriate to the occasion of 'burying the hatchet' with a rival and admitting the futility of anger. The theme of nature's benignity is, however, not omitted: if the *Avant-venue du printens* celebrates the era of eternal Spring, the Ode to Saint-Gelais sings of streams which ran with honey.

The very next poem printed in the same collection, *Les Isles Fortunées*,[2] is a still fuller treatment of the theme. It is a free imitation of the Sixteenth Epode of Horace, in which the Roman poet had summoned his friends to leave war-ridden Italy vowing like the Phoceans never to return to their city, and to sail with him to the Blessed Isles where the Age of Gold lived on. Ronsard addresses a similar exhortation to his friends, headed by Marc-Antoine Muret, the classical scholar whose commentary graced the volume in which the poem first was printed and whose portrait there appeared with Ronsard's own.

Ronsard stresses the abandonment not so much of his own land as of his own continent. It is not France, it is Europe which

[1] Lau. v, pp. 169–70, lines 73–90 (*A Melin de Saint Gelais*).
[2] *Ibid.* pp. 175–91.

14

is irremediably polluted by the Age of Iron,[1] and which he
exhorts his friends to exchange for the kinder shores of 'an
Isle so long unknown'.

It was in fact no longer possible to dismiss the Blessed Isles
as a semi-mythical place on the western rim of the world;
geographical reality had been made of them, by accounts of
islands in the New World where eternal spring reigned indeed,
and the identification had the authority of Columbus himself.
This is not to say that the *Isles Fortunées*, as imagined by
Ronsard, are notably exotic. The settlers expect to find there,
as Horace had done, a flora which included corn and vines, and
the fauna is rich in Ronsard's favourite creatures: the deer, the
nightingales and even the naiads. We might be in the Loire
valley. What is exotic, is the relationship there between man
and Nature. He and his fellow-colonists will live on nature's
bounty, which will supply in plenty all their needs. Engaged in
endless play—sporting or learned as the fancy takes them—they
will at most exert themselves from time to time to the extent of
founding a city, but even this is not a serious suggestion of urbanisation. They will not be the exploiters of the island, but its
guests:

> Là, nous vivrons sans travail, & sans peine.
> Là, là, toujours, toujours, la terre est pleine
> De tout bonheur, & là toujours les cieus
> Se montreront fideles à nos yeus:
> Là, sans navrer, comme ici, nôtre aïeule
> Du soc aigu, prodigue, toute seule
> Fait herisser en joïeuses forets
> Parmy les chams, les presens de Cerés.[2]

---

[1] Puisqu'Enyon d'une effroïable trope
Piés contremont bouleverse l'Europe,
La pauvre Europe...   (*Ibid.* p. 175, lines 1–3.)

Au port heureus des Isles bien-heurées,
Que l'Ocean de ses eaus asseurées,
Loin de l'Europe, & loin de ses combas,
Pour nous, pour nous emmure de ses bras...
                                       (*Ibid.* p. 182, lines 89–92.)

La pauvre Europe, Europe que les Dieus
Ne daignent plus regarder de leurs yeus...
                                       (*Ibid.* p. 191, lines 263–4.)

[2] *Ibid.* p. 182, lines 93–100.

The Age of Gold in Ronsard's poetry

Ronsard owed something of these descriptions to the passage in the *Aeneid* VI on the Elysian Fields,[1] and indeed the two themes are akin.

Some time between the publication of *Les Isles Fortunées* (May 1553) and the end of the year, Ronsard wrote the *Epitafe de Hugues Salel*,[2] one of his earliest poems written wholly in alexandrine couplets, and running to a hundred lines. This work celebrates the poet Hugues Salel who had translated the *Iliad* into French, and died during the summer of 1553. It contains no allusion to the Age of Gold, but uses features from the elegy of Tibullus (I, iii) on the Age of Gold to embellish a description of the Elysian Fields, just as he had borrowed from Virgil's picture of the Elysian Fields for certain features of the *Isles Fortunées*: it is thus some indication of what was going on in Ronsard's mind between *Les Isles Fortunées* and the poem called *Les Armes*[3] in which his characteristic elegiac evocation of the Age of Gold makes its first appearance. A few lines of the *Epitafe de Hugues Salel* will serve to show its relationship to descriptions of the Age of Gold:

> Là, sans jamais cesser, jargonnent les oiseaux
> Ore dans un bocage, & ore pres des eaus,
> Et en toute saison avec Flore y souspire
> D'un souspir eternel le gracieus Zephire.
> Là, comme ici n'a lieu fortune ny destin,
> Et le soir comme ici ne court vers le matin,
> Le matin vers le soir, & comme ici la rage
> D'acquerir des honneurs ne ronge leur courage.
> Là le bœuf laboureur, d'un col morne et lassé
> Ne reporte au logis le coutre renversé,
> Et là le marinier d'avirons n'importune,
> Chargé de lingos d'or, l'eschine de Neptune,
> Mais oisifz dans les prez toujours boivent du ciel
> Le Nectar qui distille, & se paissent de miel.[4]

It becomes clear that Ronsard lets his imagination dwell with pleasure not only on developing the theme of legendary natural fruitfulness, but on emphasising the beauty of inviolate Nature.

[1] Lau. v, p. 187, lines 193 ff. and p. 190, lines 231–52.
[2] Lau. VI, pp. 30–6. (*Bocage*, 1554.)   [3] See below, pp. 19–21.
[4] Lau. VI, pp. 34–5, lines 59–72.

To 'Les Isles Fortunées'

The thought came into his mind of a virgin land, an hitherto uninhabited island, where Nature had held sway for centuries in a climate of infinite benignity, unravished by human greed and restlessness:

> Là, comme ici, l'avarice n'a pas
> Borné les chams, ni d'un effort de bras,
> Avec grand bruit, les Pins on ne renverse,
> Pour aler voir d'une longue traverse
> Quelqu'autre monde: ains jamais decouvers
> On ne les voit de leurs ombrages vers,
> Par trop de chaut, ou par trop de froidure.[1]

The colonisers imagined by Ronsard, finding there the material conditions of the Age of Gold, are content to relive the ideal state of human society with which he peopled it; his 'peuple oisif' no longer have to fear the dreadful omens of war, or the tyranny of Prince or Senate, or the hardships of hunger or ill-health, or the evils of crime and error. Here, he concludes, is the refuge set aside by Jupiter for his own, when over the rest of the world he brought in the Age of Silver, and then the Age of Iron, now ruling Europe.

In these 268 decasyllabic lines of Les Isles Fortunées we have a picture of the Age of Gold which is frankly 'escape' or 'dream-world'. Although it owes its whole pattern and much of the detail to classical models, a distinctive emphasis of Ronsard's own can be detected in it of which there had been no more than hints before. Whatever his reasons for writing the poem in this way and at this date, it marks an important step in the development of his vision of the Age of Gold.

THE CENTRAL PERIOD OF THE THEME (1555–60)

From 1555 to 1560 inclusive,[2] Ronsard found continual inspiration in the Age of Gold theme, and celebrated it in a number of deeply-felt elegiac passages.

[1] Lau. v, p. 183, lines 115–21.
[2] Les Meslanges, which bears the imprint 1555, had in fact been printed by November 1554 (see Lau. vi, p. xi). Between August 1556 and August 1558 no new works of Ronsard were printed (see Lau. ix, pp. v–vii). Thus the interval 1556–7, for which my chronological table shows no mention of the Age of Gold, corresponds to an interval during which Ronsard wrote but did not publish any poetry at all.

2   **17**   ARA

He did not renounce using it on occasion in the conventional way. On the contrary his preoccupation with it perhaps brought it the more readily into his mind when he was required by pure politeness to turn a graceful compliment. In *Les Meslanges* he introduced an ode to François Charbonnier, an amiable elderly poet of the old school, with the words,

> Ta seule vertu reprend
> Le vieil Ascrean qui ment.

that is to say, that Charbonnier's virtues convicted Hesiod, the Ascrean poet, of falsehood in having declared that the Age of Gold was past, and that the present was an Age of Iron. And he concluded:

> Qui dira donq, Charbonnier,
> Que ce vieil siecle dernier,
> Où Dieu l'ame t'a donnée,
> Soit de fer, puisqu'aujourd'huy
> Par toy l'on revoit en luy
> La saison d'or retournée.[1]

Among a set of panegyrics to members of the royal family added to Book III in the third edition of the *Odes*, published also in 1555, the stock device of promising the return of Astraea is employed to conclude the Ode to the Dauphin:

> Tu feras égal aus dieus
> Ton regne, & par ta contrée
> Fleurir la paix, & des cieus
> Revenir la belle Astrée.[2]

On the other hand he wrote in the *Prière à la Fortune* a passage severely criticising the addiction of Christian princes to war, representing their disregard for peace by the image of them driving out Astraea:

> Puisque noz Roys espointz de trop de gloire,
> N'ont autre soing que par une victoire
> De quelque ville, ou d'un chasteau conquis

---

[1] Lau. VI, pp. 201–2, lines 1–2 and 13–18, and notes 1 and 2. Cf., for other instances of this, and its source, below, p. 31.
[2] Lau. VII, p. 55, lines 333–6.

> Hausser leur bruit par sang d'hommes aquis,
> Et puis qu'ilz ont de toute leur contrée
> Pour cherir Mars, chassé la belle Astrée,
> Et pour la Paix ont choysi le Discord...[1]

It was in a mood of disgust with war, too, that he embarked on the first full-scale description he had attempted of the Age of Gold as an era of lost happiness, and the first to find expression in the melodious alexandrine couplets of which he was now becoming a master. This is *Les Armes*, a poem of 128 lines, addressed to Jean Brinon, in *Les Meslanges* of 1555.

Brinon's friendship and patronage benefited a lively circle of young poets and scholars, before his early death in March 1555, and he evidently played some part in encouraging Ronsard exactly at the time when his elegiac inspiration was beginning to develop. As if recognising that Ronsard often worked best when confronted with a positive 'occasion' for a poem, he sent him at intervals a succession of presents, in this case a set of toy or ornamental weapons. Ronsard responded with a verse-epistle paradoxically deploring the invention of weapons, and especially of firearms. Opening with a frank imitation of an elegy of Tibullus (I, x), he began:

> Quiconque a le premier des enfers deterré
> Le fer, estoit, Brinon, lui mesme bien ferré...

and this train of thought led him in imagination to an age before war and greed—for him, the Age of Gold. This is how he described it:

> Que les siecles dorés à bon droit sont loüés
> Sur les siecles de fer, quand les glans secoüés
> Des chesnes nourrissiers, & quand la douce feine
> Paissoit le peuple oysif par les forés sans peine,
> Et quand dans les ruisseaux jusqu'à la rive plains
> Les hommes tiroient l'eau dans le creus de leurs mains.

[1] Lau. VIII, p. 107, lines 99–105. This poem, published in *Les Hymnes* in 1555, dedicated to Odet de Coligny, cardinal of Châtillon, is a different work from the *Complainte* [later, *Discours*] *contre Fortune* published in *Le second livre des Meslanges* in 1559, which is also dedicated to the cardinal of Châtillon. For another 1555 criticism of 'noz Roys' for refusing peace, cf. below, p. 25.

The Age of Gold in Ronsard's poetry

Alors on n'atachoit (pour les rendre plus seures)
Des portes aux maisons, aux portes des serreures:
Et lors on n'oyoit point ce mot de tien ne mien,
Tous vivoient en commun, car tous n'avoient qu'un bien.
De ce que l'un vouloit l'autre en avoit envie,
Et tous d'acord passoient heureusement la vie.[1]

The way is now open for a scathing denunciation of his own age, plagued with crime and dissension, and for an appeal to mankind to see where its true happiness lies. Despite the obligation to work in a friendly reference to Brinon and his gift, the poem ends in a solemn and sombre mood. Had iron, and weapons, never been discovered,

> Dieu n'eust detourné
> Son visaige de nous, & la paix violée
> N'eust point abandonné la terre desolée.[2]

The classical image, of peace or Astraea abandoning the earth when the Age of Gold came to an end, is here found combined with the Biblical one of God turning his face away from suppliant humanity in token of divine displeasure.[3] It is thus not surprising to find in the Age of Gold passage in *Les Armes* verbal echoes of the early ode *A Dieu pour la famine*.[4] In both poems, in the description of early Man, 'sans peine' rimes with 'feine', while 'le peuple ocieus' of the ode is echoed in 'le peuple oysif' of *Les Armes* and virtually repeated in 'au peuple oisif' of *Les Isles Fortunées* (line 138). And while in *Les Isles Fortunées* the endless leisure is variously spent on the sea-shore or in field or forest, in *Les Armes* Ronsard elaborates the purely woodland setting implied in *A Dieu pour la famine* with the

[1] Lau. VI, pp. 204–5, lines 1–2 and 9–20. On Brinon, see Lau. VI, p. 135, n. 1; P. de Nolhac, *Ronsard et l'humanisme* (1921), pp. 16–19, and E. Houth, 'Ronsard chez Jean Brinon à Médan', *Mercure de France*, CLXXIX (1925), 532–7. Ronsard wrote for him *Le Houx*, the earliest of his poems on a particular tree (Lau. VI, pp. 135–46), the *Elégie du verre (ibid.* pp. 165–71) on the gift of a wine-glass; *La Chasse (ibid.* pp. 231–42) on the gift of a dog, etc.
[2] *Ibid.* p. 211, lines 126–8.
[3] E.g. Psalms xii. 1: usquequo avertis faciem tuam a me? xxi. 25: Nec avertit faciem suam a me; xxvi. 9: Ne avertas faciem tuam a me; ne declines in ira a servo tuo, etc. (English Psalter xi, xx, and xxv).
[4] See above, p. 10.

food there to be found of nuts and acorns, adding that the streams supplied man's need for drink.

In *Les Armes*, too, Ronsard emphasises the absence of private property, suggested in *Les Isles Fortunées* by the words 'l'avarice n'a pas / Borné les chams' (lines 115–16), and indulges in picturing a world of mutual trust and sharing. This feature is prominent also in a passage of the *Hymne de la Justice* (published the same year as *Les Armes*), in addition to the abstention from sea-faring which we have already met in earlier odes and the abstention from agriculture in *Les Isles Fortunées*:

> Dieu transmist la Justice en l'âge d'or ça bas
> Quand le peuple innocent encor' ne vivoit pas
> Comme il fait en peché, & quand le Vice encore
> N'avoit franchy les bords de la boette à Pandore:
> Quand ces mots, *Tien* & *Mien*, en usage n'estoient,
> Et quand les laboureurs du soc ne tournmentoient
> Par sillons incongneuz les entrailles encloses
> Des champs, qui produisoient, de leur gré, toutes choses,
> Et quand les mariniers ne pallissoient encor'
> Sur le dos de Tethis, pour amasser de l'or.[1]

Ronsard was here adapting a narrative which he found in the *Phaenomena* of the Greek poet Aratus, expanding the tale (sketched by Hesiod) of Astraea the virgin goddess of Justice and her flight to Heaven, while changing Aratus' picture of the ideal human state to fit in with his own ideal of primitive bliss.[2] His poem was dedicated to Cardinal Charles of Lorraine, and he did not hesitate, to flatter this powerful patron, to conclude with the assertion that Jupiter had now sent Justice back to men miraculously embodied in the person of the Cardinal:

> Et lors le siecle d'or en France retourna,
> Qui sans se transformer depuis y sejourna,
> Faisant fleurir le Droict soubz nostre Prince juste.[3]

---

[1] *Les Hymnes* (1555). Lau. VIII, pp. 50–1, lines 49–58. The sailors are said to 'grow pale' on the ocean presumably either on account of the privations they endure or of the perils to which they are exposed.
[2] See below, pp. 56–9.
[3] Lau. VIII, p. 71, lines 533–5.

The *Hymne de la Justice* thus shows in the same work two quite distinct uses of the Age of Gold theme, the first elegiac, the second eulogistic, both developed at some length. The theme has left traces in other poems of the 1555 collection of *Hymnes*.

Le temple de messeigneurs le connestable, et des Chastillons is a eulogy of the Constable of France, Anne de Montmorency, and

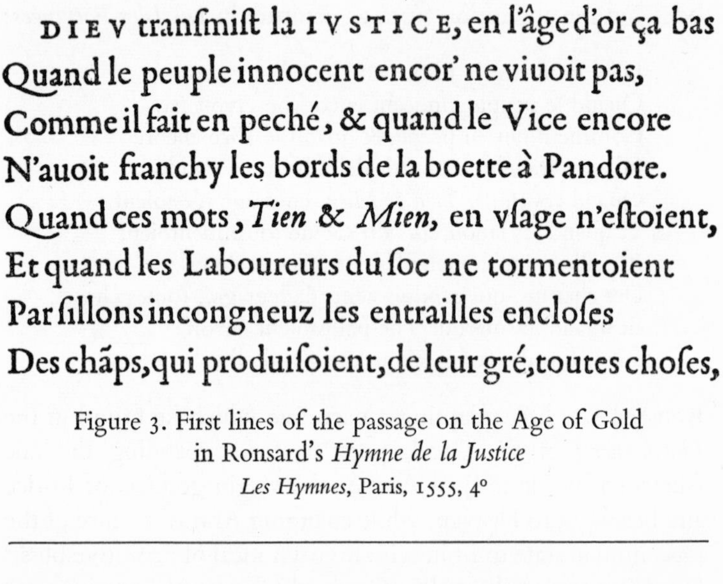

D I E V tranſmiſt la I V S T I C E, en l'âge d'or ça bas
Quand le peuple innocent encor' ne viuoit pas,
Comme il fait en peché, & quand le Vice encore
N'auoit franchy les bords de la boette à Pandore.
Quand ces mots, *Tien* & *Mien,* en vſage n'eſtoient,
Et quand les Laboureurs du ſoc ne tormentoient
Par ſillons incongneuz les entrailles encloſes
Des châps, qui produiſoient, de leur gré, toutes choſes,

Figure 3. First lines of the passage on the Age of Gold
in Ronsard's *Hymne de la Justice*
Les Hymnes, Paris, 1555, 4°

---

of his three nephews: Cardinal Odet de Châtillon (to whom the whole collection of the *Hymnes* was originally dedicated), Gaspar de Coligny, and François d'Andelot. The objects of Ronsard's praise are not, this time, credited with hastening the return of the Age of Gold, but the temple which he fancifully plans in their honour is to include allegorical figures of Truth, Faith, Hope and Love,

> Et toutes les Vertuz qui regnerent à l'heure
> Que Saturne faisoit au monde sa demeure.[1]

[1] Lau. VIII, p. 77, lines 101–2.

Central period of the theme

In the *Hymne de l'Or*, he followed the Roman satirists who had called their own epoch the Age of Gold in the most cynical sense, meaning an age which only valued money:

> D'autant que l'âge d'or regne encor aujourdhuy...[1]

but this somewhat hackneyed witticism led on to a more personal train of thought still connected with the Age of Gold.

For nowhere, he claimed, was the present age more blatantly an 'Age of Gold', in the sense of being ruled by money, than on the land, where sentimentalists might like to imagine some last survival of Astraea's reign. How unlike to that idyllic state are the realities faced by the practising farmer:

> Plus la terre aujourdhuy ne produist de son gré
> Le miel pour nourrir l'homme, & du chesne sacré
> (Lors que nous avons fain) les glandz ne nous secourent,
> Et plus de vin & laict les rivieres ne courent,
> Il faut à coup de soc, & de coutres trenchans
> Deux ou trois fois l'année importuner les champs,
> Il faut planter, enter, prouvigner à la ligne
> Sur le sommet des montz la dispenseuse vigne,
> Tout couste de l'argent, il faut achetter bœufz
> Pelles, serpes, rateaux, ou bien si tu ne peux
> En fournir ta maison, il faut que ta main aille
> Supplier ton voisin qu'à manger il te baille...[2]

The very contrast here drawn by Ronsard shows that his characteristic mental picture of the Age of Gold was an age not merely of rustic plenty and simplicity but an age before agriculture, when the natural products of the earth supplied all human needs. The *Hymne de l'Or* thus bears out the evidence afforded by *Les Armes* and by the *Hymne de la Justice*, all three poems published in 1555.

This harking back to the state of nature celebrated in *Les Armes* can also be detected in a passage of the *Hymne de la Philosophie*. Among the practical activities of Philosophy, the

[1] *Ibid.* p. 186, line 150. Cf. below, p. 71.
[2] *Ibid.* pp. 187–8, lines 173–84. For an interesting discussion of the poem as a whole, see J.-C. Margolin, 'L'Hymne de l'Or et son ambiguïté', *BHR*, XXVIII (1966), 271–93.

poet singles out her gift to mankind of Laws, but for which humanity would have in vain sacrificed its life of wild freedom in the woods and solitudes, to live together in cities:

> Car pour neant on eust quitté les bois,
> Et les desers, où le peuple sauvage
> Vivoit jadis, si l'on eust d'avantage
> Qu'entre les bois trouvé dans les citez
> Plus de pechez par faute d'equitez...[1]

Which of the two states was the happier—the state of nature, or civilised existence in cities—Ronsard might at times have difficulty in deciding, with the rational part of himself: which appealed most to his imagination, there could be no doubt.

Ronsard's readiness to show two sides of an issue is apparent in such a case as this. A more extreme case, like the antithesis between Peace and War, is equally well represented in his poetry by, for instance, the *Exhortation au Camp du Roy pour bien combatre le jour de la bataille* and the *Exhortation pour la Paix* of 1558.[2]

The idea of representing these contrasts was no stranger to a poet trained in the rhetorical tradition, and naturally versatile, than it was to Jean Goujon to be asked to carve in 1548 (to the specification of Pierre l'Escot, the architect of the new Renaissance quadrangle of the Louvre) an allegorical figure of War on one side of a window and Peace on the other.[3]

Besides this professional versatility, Ronsard was temperamentally capable of throwing himself into the mood or argument of the moment with passion: for the *Exhortation au Camp du Roy* he had no need to find a model but spoke out as a soldier's son and a lover of deeds and tales of valour, while as a scholar and an artist his practical preferences were all for

---

[1] Lau. VIII, pp. 95–6, lines 170–4.

[2] Lau. IX, pp. 1–26. Cf. James Hutton, 'Rhetorical doctrine and some poems of Ronsard', *The Rhetorical Idiom: Essays presented to H. A. Wichelns* (Ithaca, 1958).

[3] See P. du Colombier, *Jean Goujon* (Paris, 1949), pp. 87–9, and pl. XVIII. The adjacent pair, *La gloire du roi* and *La Renommée*, are alluded to by Ronsard in his *Elégie à Pierre l'Escot* (1560), claiming that the former was intended by L'Escot to symbolise the power of his verse to trumpet the king's fame abroad. Lau. X, pp. 306–7, lines 141–52.

peace. Similarly he could enlarge upon the blessings of peace—the beneficent pursuit of agriculture being one of them—while cherishing a private dream of a lost world where all forms of work were unknown.

Peace is indeed often associated in Ronsard's poetry with the pursuit of ordinary human life under happy conditions, and particularly with prosperity on the land: in the *Hymne de Henry II* (1555) he reproved Henry II and Charles V for spurning Peace,

> Que Dieu leur envoyoit, comme sa Fille esleüe,
> A fin que tous les ans le soc de la charrue
> Eust cultivé les champs, & que par les preaux
> Les troupeaux engraissés eussent de mille saux
> Resjouy le pasteur...[1]

And Peace, particularly when contrasted with War, is closely associated with the Age of Gold.

Modulation from one of these moods to another was so natural to Ronsard that he sometimes (consciously or not) effected it within the limits of a single poem.

The description of the Age of Gold in the *Exhortation pour la Paix*, published in 1558, is very close to the corresponding passage in *Les Armes*, occurring similarly in a poem denouncing war and weapons:

> Qu'heureuse fut la gent qui vivoit sous Saturne,
> Quand l'aise & le repos, & la paix taciturne,
> Bien loing de la trompette, & bien loing des soldars,
> Loing du fer & de l'or, erroit de toutes pars,
> Par les bois assurée, & du fruit de la terre
> En commun se paissoit sans fraude ny sans guerre.

And for the first time Ronsard adds a note of personal nostalgia:

> Helas! que n'ai-je esté vivant de ce temps là...[2]

Yet it is for having weaned mankind from such a wild and woodland life, by introducing flocks and herds, and the growing of corn and vines, that Peace is praised further on in the same

---

[1] Lau. VIII, p. 45, lines 749–53.   [2] Lau. IX, p. 23, lines 147–53.

poem. And the culmination of the blessings brought by Peace is said to have been that:

> Elle défaroucha de nos premiers Ayeux
> Les cueurs rudes & fiers, & les fist gracieux,
> Et d'un peuple vaguant es bois à la fortune,
> Dedans les grandz citez en fist une commune.[1]

That the reign of Peace should be imagined differently from the Age of Gold is not surprising: the two concepts may on occasion overlap but they need not be identical. That Peace should be commended for having rescued primitive man from conditions which are those of the Age of Gold as described thirty lines above is, however, more curious.

It is to an Age of Gold much more like the Reign of Peace in this eulogy that Ronsard must refer when he alludes to the *return* of the Age of Gold as desirable and imaginable; when he made the shepherds in his *Chant pastoral* for the wedding of Claude de France and Charles III of Lorraine (22 January 1559) anticipate happier times as a result of the royal marriage:

> Comme si l'age d'or vouloit recommencer
> A regner desoubs luy, comme il regnoit à l'heure
> Que Saturne faisoit en terre sa demeure,[2]

or when he credited Henry II by the Treaty of Cateau-Cambrésis (April 1559) with bringing back the Age of Gold:

> Qui, comme Auguste, apres la longue guerre
> As ramené l'aage d'or sus la terre,
> Themis, Astrée...

in his *Chant de liesse au roy*.[3]

But the woodland picture of early Man persisted. It was evidently nearer his heart at this period than facile promises of an Age of Gold which was simply a good time coming. In a new form, it inspired a striking episode in his autobiographical

[1] Lau. IX, p. 25, lines 209–12. For the elimination of this anomaly in a later edition, see below, p. 49.
[2] Lau. IX, p. 79, lines 74–6.   [3] Lau. IX, p. 132, lines 15–17.

poem, the *Complainte contre Fortune*, published in 1559 in the *Second Livre des Meslanges*.

Ronsard was now in a mood of disillusionment with his ambitions for worldly success. After a severe self-examination, he recognised failure as a punishment for having ceased to serve the Muses with his former single-minded zeal. Indulging for a moment in the thought of escape from the destiny he had called down upon himself, he dreamed of going overseas, and remembered the accounts he had heard of the French colony on the coast of Brazil. This dream he dismissed at once: his cares would follow him, he knew, wherever he went. But his imagination, once directed to the New World, began to picture what he had heard about the primitive yet happy existence of the Indians there. He saw their state as a living Age of Gold, and foresaw the day when they would curse the coming of the Europeans. He broke out into an appeal to Villegagnon, the leader of the expedition to Brazil, to renounce the plan of 'civilising' them, and to let them alone. And many of his assumptions about them, and even his phrases about them, echo what he had written in earlier poems about the Age of Gold. If they are not specifically wanderers in the forest, this may well be because the earlier part of the poem had already evoked this theme,[1] in the form of recollections of his own wanderings in the forest as a boy.

> Pauvre Villegangnon, tu fais une grand faute
> De vouloir rendre fine une gent si peu caute,
> Comme ton Amerique, ou le peuple incognu
> Erre innocentement tout farouche & tout nu,
> D'habis tout ainsi nu, qu'il est nu de malice,
> Qui ne cognoist les noms de vertu, ny de vice,
> De Senat, ny de Roy, qui vit à son plaisir
> Porté de l'apetit de son premier desir,
> Et qui n'a dedans l'ame, ainsi que nous, emprainte
> La frayeur de la loy, qui nous fait vivre en crainte :
> Mais suivant sa nature est seul maistre de soy :
> Soymesmes est sa loy, son Senat, & son Roy :

[1] See below, p. 186.

27

Qui à grands coups de soc la terre n'importune,
Laquelle comme l'air à chacun est commune,
Et comme l'eau d'un fleuve, est commun tout leur bien,
Sans procez engendrer de ce mot Tien, & Mien.[1]

If the colonists teach them to divide their land into private
properties, ambition to enlarge them will soon lead to disputes
and the Indians will become as wretched as Europeans,

nous autres pauvres hommes,
Qui par trop de raison trop miserables sommes.[2]

And there follows now the line (379):

Ils vivent maintenant en leur age doré,

and the remarkable prophecy of the hatred Villegagnon will
ultimately arouse as a result of his well-meant exertions.

The vividness of the picture he had imagined, and the
warmth of his own eloquence, carried Ronsard away, to the
point of directly greeting the Indians and frankly envying their
lot:

Vivez, heureuse gent, sans peine & sans soucy,
Vivez joyeusement: je voudrois vivre ainsi.

In the *Elégie à Robert de La Haye*, 'Si j'estois à renaistre au
ventre de ma mere', published a year later, in the first collected
edition of his works (1560), Ronsard seems to be pursuing still
further a similar train of thought or feeling.

The threefold wish to be born again as bird, fish or animal
(if invited to enjoy a reincarnation) rather than a man, though
it echoes a commonplace of moralists and satirists, is the
occasion for a sensual evocation of the delights of animal
existence, culminating in the picture of the stag:

J'aimerois mieux renaistre en un cerf bocager,
Portant un arbre au front, ayant le corps leger,
Et les argots fourchus, & seul & solitaire
Faire au-pres de ma biche à l'escart mon repaire,
Saulter parmi les fleurs, errer à mon plaisir,

[1] Lau. x, pp. 33–4, lines 353–68.
[2] For the continuation of this passage, see Fig. 4.

Central period of the theme

Et me laisser conduire à son premier desir,
Et la frescheur des bois & des fontaines suivre,
Que me veoir de rechef dans un homme revivre.[1]

The third couplet in this passage from the *Elégie à Robert de
La Haye* may be compared with the words in the *Complainte
contre Fortune* on the simple pleasures of the Indian,

LIVRE II. DES MESLANGES

Pource laiſſe les lá, ne romps plus(ie te prie)
Le tranquille repos de leur premiere vie :
Laiſſe les,ie te pry,ſi pitié te remord,
· Ne les tourmente plus, & t'en fuy de leur bord.
Las! ſi tu leur aprens à limiter la terre,
Pour agrandir leurs champs,ils ſe feront la guerre,
Les proces auront lieu,l'amitié defaudra,
Et l'aſpre ambition tourmenter les viendra
Comme elle fait icy nous autres pauures hommes,
Qui par trop de raiſon trop miſerables ſommes.
Ils viuent maintenant en leur age doré.
* Certes pour le loyer d'auoir tant labouré,*
De les rendre trop fins,quand ils auront l'yſage
De cognoiſtre le mal,ils viendront au riuage
Ou ton Camp eſt aſsis,& en te maudiſſant,
Iront auec le feu ta faute puniſſant,
Abôminant le iour que ta voile premiere
Blanchit ſur le ſablon de leur riue eſtrangere.
Pource laiſſe les lá,& n'atache à leur col
Le ioug de ſeruitude,ainçois le dur licol
Qui les eſtrangleroit ſous l'audace cruelle
D'vn Tyran,ou d'vn Iuge,ou d'vne loy nouuelle.
Viuez heureuſe gent,ſans peine & ſans ſoucy,
Viuez ioyeuſement:ie voudrois viure ainſi :

Figure 4. 'Ils vivent maintenant en leur age doré': Ronsard on
the Brazilians in the *Complainte contre Fortune*
Second Livre des Meslanges, Paris, 1559, 8°

---

[1] Lau. x, p. 316, lines 23–30.

> qui vit à son plaisir
> Porté de l'apetit de son premier desir.[1]

And as Ronsard had in the *Complainte* feared that ambition would torment the Indians like the Europeans,

> nous autres pauvres hommes
> Qui par trop de raison trop miserables sommes[2]

so he here blames man's much-vaunted faculty of reason for driving him to war or to sea or to mining, all (as we have seen) symptomatic in Ronsard's opinion of the Age of Iron:

> Cette pauvre raison le conduict à la guerre,
> Et dedans du sapin lui faict tourner la terre
> A la mercy du vent, & si luy fait encor
> Pour extreme mal'heur chercher des mines d'or.[3]

Fortunate therefore are the wild creatures in their lack of reason, wandering at their own sweet will, drinking pure water from the stream and living on nature's bounty for food:

> Au contraire les cerfs qui n'ont point de raison,
> Les poissons, les oiseaux, sont sans comparaison
> Trop plus heureux que nous, qui sans soin et sans peine
> Errent de tous costez où le plaisir les meine:
> Ils boivent de l'eau clere, et se paissent du fruict
> Que nostre mere grand d'elle-mesme a produict.[4]

While the phrase 'sans peine' in the emphatic position at the end of a line echoes *A Dieu, pour la famine, Les Isles Fortunées* and *Les Armes*, the verb 'errer' had been used to describe the movements of the human race under Saturn in the *Exhortation à la Paix* and of the Indians in the *Complainte contre Fortune*. The condition of this carefree existence—that they are content with food and drink provided for them by Nature—had come into all his alexandrine poems on the Age of Gold theme, in some even down to the use of the verb 'paître' which seems chosen to emphasise the 'happy animal' character of early man, beginning with line 12 of *Les Armes*, cf.:

[1] Lau. x, p. 34, lines 359–60.
[2] *Ibid.* lines 377–8.
[3] *Ibid.* p. 317, lines 45–8.
[4] *Ibid.* lines 55–60.

> erroit de toutes pars
> Par les bois asseurés et du fruict de la terre
> En commun se paissoit (*Exhortation pour la Paix*)

The happy state of the wild creatures thus amounts to living in the Age of Gold as Ronsard imagined it. They fulfil, in this poem, the *Elégie à Robert de La Haye*, the function allotted to the Indians in the *Complainte contre Fortune* of contrasting with the greed and corruption of 'civilised' man as well as providing a picture on which Ronsard's fancy can dwell (when he is in the mood) with positive and pleasurable envy.

When Ronsard eventually mentions the Age of Gold theme in this poem, it is in fact to pay his friend a compliment:

> Car, te voyant en terre ennemy de tout vice,
> Je ne puis confesser que la saincte Justice
> Soit remontée au ciel, & puis que ta vertu
> Ha du siecle de fer le vice combatu...[1]

This formula, which had provided a compliment to Charbonnier as far back as 1555,[2] had just done duty in a poem to Jacques Bourdin:

> Te voyant si preudhomme en faicts & en parler
> Qui est ce qui croiroit ce qu'Hésiode chante,
> Que la vertu, la honte & la foy innocente,
> Quittans le monde, au ciel ont deigné revoler?[3]

and Bourdin's brother in his turn was credited by Ronsard at the same period with having

> presque tout seul redoré
> Cest aage de fer où nous sommes.[4]

Ronsard's conviction that the Age of Gold was irrecoverable was often tempered, as we have seen, by his readiness to acknowledge the merits of his friends or patrons, merits which

---

[1] *Ibid.* p. 322, lines 149–52.   [2] See above, p. 18.
[3] Lau. x, p. 76, lines 5–8 of sonnet x. See, for the probable source of this device, Ausonius, to Probus, 'generi hic superstes aureo / satorque prolis aureae / conuincit Ascraeum senem / non esse saeclum ferreum', Ep. 16, lines 27–30.
[4] Lau. x, p. 270, lines 95–6.

stood out the more for manifesting themselves in what was otherwise an Age of Iron.

Even the homage of the poet to friend or patron did not always extend thus far: in a sonnet addressed to the Cardinal of Lorraine before October 1558, but published (like the *Complainte contre Fortune*) in the *Second Livre des Meslanges* of 1559, beginning 'Prelat, bien que nostre age aille tout de travers', Ronsard spoke of the age in which they lived as an 'Age vrayement de fer'.[1]

Such a designation of his own time as an 'age de fer' occurs also at this date in a particularly unexpected context—the preface to the King which he contributed to the collection of music published in 1560 by the King's Printer in Music, under the title *Livre de Meslanges*. Here Ronsard defended the inclusion in the miscellany of 'old' songs on the grounds that 'On a tousjours estimé la Musique des anciens estre la plus divine, d'autant qu'elle a esté composée en un siecle plus heureux, & moins entaché des vices qui regnent en ce dernier age de fer'.[2]

FROM THE 'RESPONCE AUX MINISTRES DE GENEVE'
TO THE 'ELEGIES, MASCARADES ET BERGERIE'
(1560–65)

The outbreak of the first civil war drew Ronsard into a series of increasingly acrimonious polemical poems against the Huguenots, whom he held responsible for the plight of France: the *Institution de l'adolescence du roi*, the *Discours des misères de ce temps* and its *Continuation*, and finally his reply to the enemies he had made by these attacks, the *Responce aux injures et calomnies de je ne sçay quels predicans et ministres de*

---

[1] Lau. x, p. 82.
[2] Lau. xviii, 2, p. 486, lines 103–7. Josquin des Prés is mentioned in the place of honour, followed by his disciples (as Ronsard calls them) Mouton, Vuillard, Richaffort, Janequin, Maillard, Claudin, Moulu, Jaquet, Certon, Arcadet (some of whom had set Ronsard's own songs to music) and 'le plus que divin Orlande', i.e. Orlando de Lassus. Ronsard was thus appreciative of 'old' composers but by no means grudging in his tributes to contemporary ones, whatever his views on the general corruption of his age.

Genève (1563). He was now concerned to point a contrast not
between civilised man and mythical or wild man but between
the present troubles of his country and its happy state before
the Reformation. Once indeed he went so far in his impatience
with his Protestant critics as to claim that the Age of Gold
would have reigned in France had all the 'Preachers' lived as
blamelessly and piously as he:

> Si tous les Predicans eussent vescu ainsi,
> Le peuple ne fust pas (comme il est) en souci,...
> Le laboureur sans creinte eust labouré ses champs,
> Les marchés désolés seroient plains de marchans,
> Et comme un beau soleil par toute la contrée
> De France, reluiroit le bel espy d'Astrée,[1]

the end of the last line being later (1567 edition) amended to
read: 'le vieil siècle d'Astrée'.

This is, I think, the only allusion to the Age of Gold in
Ronsard's *Discours*, and the evocation of the ploughman and
the merchant plying their trade under the auspices of Astraea,
goddess of Justice, shows that it here stands for normal civilised
human life lived under ideal conditions, as it did when Ronsard
credited Henry II with bringing it back to France. The dream-
world Age of Gold, idleness with plenty, in the shelter of the
forest, with all things owned in common, made one final
reappearance in his poetry as soon as the need to defend himself
and his party receded.

After the *Responce*, the culmination of his personal controversy with the Huguenots, later in 1563, he published a slender
collection of verse entitled *Les Quatre Saisons de l'an avecques
une Eglogue, une Elégie, l'Adonis et l'Orphée*; which became
Book One of *Les Trois livres du recueil des nouvelles poésies*. Here
in the first of the four seasons, the *Hymne du Printemps*, he
returned to the subject of the *Avant-venue du Printens*, not
specifically referring to the Age of Gold but to the belief

---

[1] Lau. XI, p. 148, lines 601-2 and 605-8. The 'bel espy' of the original text
refers to the 'épi' or ear of corn which was an attribute of Astraea. The
composition of the poem is dated by Laumonier in the first half of April
1563 (Lau. XI, Introduction, p. xvii).

(closely connected with it) that the earth once enjoyed eternal spring and brought forth corn of its own free will, distilled honey from the trees and poured milk into the rivers.[1] In the *Elegie* immediately following *Les Quatre Saisons*, he once more invoked the Age of Gold itself. This *Elegie* was addressed to Le Seigneur Baillon, 'Trésorier de l'Espergne du Roy', and conveyed the poet's request for a gift of money. As in *Les Armes*, he developed a theme paradoxical to his purpose, here declaring that money was the root of all evil. All ills are ascribed to the devilish inventions of mining and metal-working but in particular to the actual use of coins and currencies.[2] Wars, feuds and lawsuits have been the results; Justice and Modesty have fled; the pines have been felled to fashion ships and serve man's quest for gain, etc. How happy was the Age of Gold, which knew nothing of the use of gold as wealth:

> O bienheureux le siecle où le peuple sauvage
> Vivoit par les forests de gland et de fruitage!
> Qui, sans charger sa main d'escuelle ou de vaisseau,
> De la bouche tiroit les ondes d'un ruisseau...
> Les marchés n'estoient point, ny les peaux des ouailles
> Ne servoient aux contrats: les paisibles orailles
> N'entendoient la trompette, ains la Tranquilité,
> La Foy, la Preudhomie, Amour & Charité
> Regnoient aux cueurs humains, qui gardoient la loy saincte

---

[1] Lau. XII, p. 30, lines 41–6.

[2] A sonnet published in F. Grimaudet, *Des monnoyes*, seems to have been written in conscious protest against this or similar diatribes; it celebrates the recognition of 'meum & tuum', and the replacement of barter by money, as signs of progress:

> Lors que l'humaine gent premier dessauvagée
> Tien & mien establit en ce que fut commun:
> Quand pour mieux s'entr'aider elle convient en un...
> Son commerce elle fit par la chose changée;
> Qui dura jusqu'à tant qu'un moyen oportun
> De monnoye courante, approuvé de chacun
> Fit la communion des choses plus aisée...

The author of the book was 'avocat du roy au siege présidial d'Angers', and he dedicated it to René Crespin, 'président en la chambre des comptes à Paris', 24 March 1576.

To the 'Elégies, Mascarades et Bergerie'

De Nature & de Dieu, sans force ny contrainte.
L'ardante ambition ne les tormentoit pas:
Ils ne cognoissoient point, ny escus ny ducats...[1]

This passage is close in several respects to the corresponding portion of *Les Armes*, and has in common with it (unlike all the others) the detail that men drank direct from the streams, though now it is not even in the palms of their hands but with their mouths to the water. The emphasis on all things being in common, and the expression 'meum & tuum' (also found in the *Hymne de la Justice* and in the *Complainte contre Fortune*) is not found here, but the woodland life supported on raw food, the absence of markets and contracts and (of course) of war, points in the same direction. The use of the word 'sauvage' perhaps marks a further stage of Ronsard's thought on the Age of Gold, when the composition of the *Complainte* had brought together in his mind the Age of Gold people on the one hand and the real American Indians on the other, whom he had designated as 'farouche' while idealising their way of life. Before the *Complainte*, he had not faced the idea that men living as he described would in fact be savages or 'wild men', though the way of life, which men would in vain have given up but for the Laws given by Philosophy, is described in the *Hymne de la Philosophie* as 'sauvage'. With the *Complainte* there is also a verbal link, the line: 'L'ardente ambition ne les tormentoit pas' being reminiscent of the line: 'Et l'aspre ambition tourmenter les viendra' (*Complainte*, line 376). On the other hand, Ronsard had never before made such sweeping claims for the moral virtues of his Age of Gold people: that they kept both divine and natural law by instinct—that Faith, Honesty, Love and Charity reigned in their hearts. They had been happy, free, contented, innocent, living at peace with all; in the *Hymne de la Justice* it was said that they lived before sin and vice were at large in the world. As his judgement on his own age grew more severe, there seems to have been an increasing tendency to dwell on the Age of Gold as an ideal society leading the simple life amid simple virtues.

[1] Lau. XII, p. 90, lines 57–60, 65–72.

His conviction that his own time was an Age of Iron was expressed in the strongest terms in the *Compleinte à la royne mere du roy*, 'Royne qui de vertus passes Artemesie'. Walking alone and pensive by the Seine below the Louvre, he encountered a wizard with the face of his dead friend Rembure, to whom he confided his bitter disillusionment with the rewards received for his services to the royal family; Rembure rallied him for his naiveté in the following words:

> En quel age, ô bons dieux! ores pense tu estre?
> Pense tu que le Ciel pour toy face renaistre
> Encor le siecle d'or, où l'innocence estoit
> Sur le haut de la faux que Saturne portoit?...
> Ce beau siecle est perdu, & nostre age enroillée,
> Qui des pauvres humains la poitrine a souillée
> D'avarice & d'erreur, ne permet que le bien
> Aux hommes d'aujourdhuy vienne sans faire rien.[1]

Ronsard was quite aware that the Age of Gold of his dreams was incompatible with much that he admired in human life, such as pride of birth, knightly honour, and valour in war. In an *Elégie des Armairies*, composed to grace a MS genealogy of the Sanzay family and published in the *Recueil des nouvelles poésies*, Book II, he seems to have emphasised this dilemma. Relating the early history of mankind, he describes their way of life in terms very like those habitually used in his poetry to depict the Age of Gold, but only to point out its drawbacks. Men were created free and equal, and could live in idleness on acorns in the woods. This privilege was, however, dearly bought; it was at the price of knowing nothing of courage, skill or enterprise:

> Si est-ce, mon Sanzay, que sans faveur de race
> Les hommes sont yssus d'une pareille masse.
> Ils eurent sang pareil & pareil mouvement,
> Et furent tous egaux des le commencement,
> Sans point se soucier d'honneur ny de noblesse:

---

[1] Lau. XII, p. 186, lines 281–4 and 289–92. The poem, dated by Laumonier October 1563, was published in the Second Book of the *Recueil des Nouvelles Poésies*.

To the 'Elégies, Mascarades et Bergerie'

Ils estoient tous sans mestier, sans art & sans adresse,
Et vivoient par les bois, comme peu courageux,
De glans tombés menu des chesnes ombrageux.[1]

Ronsard was indeed never again to romanticise as the true
Age of Gold the way of life he described in *Les Armes* and the
other poems I have discussed, with its emphasis on the wandering
life in the woods, sustained by nuts and acorns and by the clear
streams, content in idleness; the *Elégie* to Baillon is its last
appearance. Within two years, the whole Age of Gold theme
was to fade from his poetry. But first it was, in a modified form,
to see him through the most active period of his connection
with the court, when (in the lull between the first and second
civil wars) Ronsard came into his own as the favourite poet of
the young Charles IX.

The theme of the *return* of the Age of Gold is much more
prominent in this last group of poems. It provides an episode
in the eclogue entitled *Daphnis et Thyrsis* published in 1563 in
the *Nouvelles Poésies*, Book II. Here the participants are to be
identified with Charles IX and with his brother, christened
Alexandre-Edouard, the future Henry III, and in the later
editions (1567 onwards) they are actually called Carlin and
Xandrin. Daphnis is made to ask whether the golden season
will never return when

la terre portoit, sans estre labourée,
Les bleds qui de leur gré par les champs jaunissoient?

and Thyrsis replies that hope springs eternal in the breasts of
living men, and maintains that the time will come when the
waters will once more run milk, the oaks distil honey, and
winter become spring.[2]

Most prominent of all, however, is the position of the Age
of Gold theme in the collection called *Elégies, Mascarades et
Bergerie* published in 1565. Here the principal single work is
the *Bergerie*, or first eclogue, commissioned for the royal
family's carnival revels at Fontainebleau in the spring of 1564.
This pastoral entertainment, which might almost be described

[1] *Ibid.* p. 240, lines 5–12.   [2] *Ibid.* p. 155, lines 157–64.

37

as a masque, was designed to be performed before Charles IX and his mother. Speaking parts were provided for the king's younger brothers, the Duke of Orleans (the future Henry III) and the Duke of Anjou, under the fancy-dress names of 'Orléantin' and 'Angelot'; for his sister Margaret ('Margot'), later the first wife of Henry of Navarre; for Henry himself ('Navarrin') and for another cousin, Henry of Guise ('Guisin'). Musicians and dancers (no doubt mainly professionals in the service of the court) would be required to fill out the entertainment with the recitations, songs and ballets making up the rest of the action. It is not known for certain to have been performed.[1] It is clear that Ronsard wrote as if it were to be performed and was on his mettle in composing it.

The opening chorus of the *Bergerie*, consisting of nymphs and shepherdesses, alluded flatteringly to the Queen Mother, Catherine de' Medici, in the lines,

> Si nous voyons le Siecle d'or refait,
> C'est du bienfait
> De la bergère Catherine...[2]

and invoked a blessing on their shepherd-prince 'Carlin' with the words,

> C'est ce Carlin promis des destinées
> Souz qui courront les meilleures années
> Du vieil Saturne & du bon Siecle d'or.[3]

The *second pasteur voyageur*, who takes part in the later episodes of the *Bergerie*, begins a description of his journey to Italy with an allusion to the belief that the reign of Saturn (equivalent to the Age of Gold) had been localised there, when mankind was content with innocence and a diet of acorns:

> l'Italie,
> Terre grasse & fertile, où Saturne habitoit
> Quand le peuple innocent de glan se contentoit.[4]

This is the only reference in the *Bergerie* which unequivocally implies the food-gathering and forest-dwelling people of Ronsard's characteristic Age of Gold.

[1] For discussion of this question, see Lau. XIII, Introduction, pp. xv–xvii.
[2] Lau. XIII, p. 79, lines 47–9.   [3] *Ibid.* p. 81, lines 84–6.
[4] *Ibid.* p. 120, lines 866–8.

To the 'Elégies, Mascarades et Bergerie'

But in a modified form—modified both by the pastoral convention inherent in the eclogue and by recourse to Sannazaro's *Arcadia*, a source not hitherto used for this purpose—the Age of Gold theme sustains two out of the five set speeches forming the heart of the work, the poetic contest. Of these one (assigned to 'Navarrin') hymns the wonders of the Age of Gold in the mythical past, while another (spoken by 'Guisin') alludes to a prophecy of its return in the future. The first particularly invites comparisons with Ronsard's earlier descriptions of the Age of Gold:

Que ne retourne au monde encore ce bel aage
Simple, innocent, & bon, où le meschant usage
De l'acier & du fer n'estoit point en valeur,
Honoré meintenant à nostre grand malheur !
Ha, bel aage doré, où l'or n'avoit puissance !
Mais doré pour autant que la pure innocence,
La creinte de mal faire, & la simple bonté
Permettoient aux humains de vivre en liberté !
Les Dieux visiblement se presentoient aux hommes,
Et pasteurs de troupeaux tout ainsi que nous sommes
Au millieu du bestail ne faisoient que sauter,
Aprenans aux mortelz le bel art de chanter.
Les bœufs en ce temps là, paissans parmy la plaine,
L'un à l'autre parloient, & d'une voix humaine,
Quand la nuict approchoit, predisoient les dangers,
Et servoient par les champs d'oracles aux bergers :
Il ne regnoit alors ny noise ny rancune,
Les champs n'estoient bornez, & la terre commune
Sans semer ny planter, bonne mere, aportoit
Le fruit qui de soymesme heureusement sortoit :
Les proces n'avoient lieu, la rancueur ny l'envie.
Les vieillars sans douleur sortoient de ceste vie
Comme en songe, & leurs ans doucement finissoient,
Ou d'une herbe enchantée ils se rajeunissoient :
Jamais du beau Printemps la saison emaillée
N'estoit (comme depuis) par l'hyver despouillée.
Toujours du beau Soleil les rayons se voyoient,
Et toujours par les bois les Zephires s'oyoient...[1]

[1] *Ibid.* pp. 101–2, lines 511–38.

The Age of Gold in Ronsard's poetry

Eternal spring; a fecundity in man's natural environment which made sowing and planting superfluous and the division of land-property unthinkable; the absence of iron and steel..., these are features already familiar in Ronsard's Age of Gold landscapes. Familiar too is the outburst of personal longing which was to follow:

> O saison gratieuse! Helas, que n'ay-je esté
> En un temps si heureux en ce monde aletté...[1]

Wholly new, however, is the emphasis on the friendliness which then reigned between gods and men, and between men and beasts, and on the happier fate of the old under Age of Gold conditions. Subsequent additions to this passage elaborated particularly the harmony between men and animals: the harmless sheep and oxen were never slain at this period for food, or even for sacrifice to the gods. And the underlying assumption is new, too: the Age of Gold is not an era of primitive food-gathering but of an idyllic pastoral society, to symbolise which milk is added to the acorns and wild-strawberries which an Age of Gold picnic might be imagined to enjoy in the woods:

> Chacun se repaissoit desouz les frais ombrages
> Ou de laict ou de glan, ou de frezes sauvages...[2]

The poet was drawing for the first time on a corresponding passage in Sannazaro's *Arcadia*, and was also for the first time obliged to adopt a pastoral setting and an Age of Gold of which it was feasible to desire the return. Even so, the shift of emphasis is notable.

The next speech, that of 'Guisin', draws openly on the prophecy of Virgil in the Fourth Eclogue, that the career of a particular child would bring back the rule of Saturn, the earthly presence of Astraea the virgin goddess of Justice, and the Golden Race of men. Here the prophecy is applied to the prospects for the reign of Charles IX, hitherto, during his minority, plagued by dissensions, but now, on his coming of age, to be blessed with peace and plenty. Ronsard foretells a

[1] Lau. XIII, p. 103, lines 549–50. [2] *Ibid.* lines 547–8.

40

miraculous change in nature, but he promises no reform of society or change of heart in man. He furthermore takes the precaution of having the prophecy spoken indirectly to the king by a character in the play, and even then as hearsay— 'on dit...'—as being words believed by the simple shepherds to have been spoken by the Fates at the birth of the 'grand pasteur Carlin'. The gods will once more sojourn on earth with men, and the earth itself will once more display the miraculous fecundity which alone can dispense men from labouring and travelling:

> La terre produira toute chose sans soing,
> Laquelle ne sera comme devant ferüe
> De rateaux bien dentez, ny du soc de charüe;
> Car les champs de leur gré, sans toreaux mugissans
> Souz le joug, se voirront de froment jaunissans.
> Les vignes n'auront peur de sentir les faucilles,
> De leur gré les sommetz des arbres bien fertilles
> Noirciront de raisins, & le clair ruisselet
> Ondoira par les fleurs & de vin & de laict...[1]

Once at least in the slighter verses printed in the *Elégies, Mascarades et Bergerie*, the poet addressed Charles IX with a direct allusion to the return of the Age of Gold (perhaps inspired by the peace of Amboise, March 1563) in a *Sonet au Roy*:

> Apres l'ardeur de la guerre cruelle
> Je vois fleurir le beau Siecle doré,
> Où vous serez des vostres adoré
> Pour la vertu qui vous est naturelle...[2]

In the libretto of a carnival entertainment given in the garden of the duc d'Orléans (the future Henry III) at Fontainebleau, one of the two 'sereines' who appeared in it was made to speak thus of the late king Henry II:

> Or tout ainsi comme il estoit parfait,
> Tel comme luy son peuple s'estoit fait,
> Vertu regnoit par toute sa contrée,

---

[1] *Ibid.* p. 109, lines 662–70.   [2] *Ibid.* p. 240, lines 1–4.

Qui d'un chacun le rendoit honoré,
Et bref c'estoit le bel aage doré,
Où fleurissoit Saturne avecq' Astrée.[1]

After five years made hideous by civil strife, the reign of
Henry II might be acquiring in retrospect some aura of the
'good old days': as for calling it the Age of Gold, only a
mermaid could commit such a giddy hyperbole. Almost
equally far-fetched is the quatrain, to be found among the
stanzas written in June 1565 for the meeting at Bayonne
between the Queen Mother and her daughter the Queen of
Spain:

O siecle heureux & digne qu'on appelle
Le siecle d'or, si onque en fut aucun,
Où l'Espaignol d'une amitié fidelle
Ayme la France, & les deux ne sont qu'un...[2]

If undying friendship between France and Spain was a pious
hope, the blossoming of a Golden Age in England must have
seemed to Ronsard, when he promised it to Queen Elizabeth I,
a polite fancy. Called upon by the Queen Mother, after the
Treaty of Troyes (1564) to honour her new ally, the poet not
only dedicated to the Queen of England the entire volume of
the *Elégies, Mascarades et Bergerie* (sending her the presentation
copy through the good offices of Paul de Foix, the French
Ambassador in London),[3] but also placed at the head of it an
Elégie à la majesté de la royne d'Angleterre, in which the following
prophecy was attributed to Merlin, concerning the effects of
unity between France and England (symbolised by their
fleur-de-lys and leopards):

Et l'age d'or voirra de toutes pars
Fleurir le liz entre les Leopars...

and further concerning the reign of Elizabeth:

[1] Lau XIII, p. 233, lines 25–9. [2] *Ibid.* p. 227, lines 19–24.
[3] Paul de Foix's covering letter to Sir Robert Cecil is extant in the Public
Record Office (SP 70/79, f. 200), but I have been unable to trace the book
itself; it is not in the royal collection in the British Museum (and not in the
library of Lord Salisbury at Hatfield House, as Miss Clare Talbot has
kindly checked for me).

> Elle rendra son pais honoré
> Par la vertu du beau siecle doré
> Qui florira souz sa riche couronne.[1]

Poems so blatantly written to order have naturally been dismissed with a sneer by the critics. The fact is, however, that poets sometimes even on such occasions speak truer than they know (as Paul de Foix said in the elegant Latin epistle he wrote to accompany the sending of the volume to Sir Robert Cecil, the Queen's principal secretary), and also that in these 'command performances' they may the more readily use whatever themes are uppermost in their minds. Thus Ronsard when addressing himself, however perfunctorily, to imagining the remote past of the British Isles before they were inhabited, set in motion his feelings for inviolate nature as he had revealed them in *Les Isles Fortunées*, though the picture is no longer, of course, a tropical paradise:

> Isle qui fus solitaire & deserte,
> D'aspres buissons & d'espines couverte,
> Haute maison des Sangliers escumeux,
> Et des grands Cerfs au large front rameux,
> Qui n'eus jamais la poitrine ferüe
> Du soc aigu de la bonne charüe...[2]

lines which contain the first germ of the invocation to the doomed forest in the *Elégie contre les bûcherons de Gâtine* twenty years later.[3]

That Ronsard's private opinion of his own age had not changed is plain from the utterances to friends and patrons with whom he could be frank.

To Paul de Foix he wrote personally:

> Hà quantes fois ay-je desiré d'estre
> Dedans un bois un gros chesne champestre,

---

[1] Lau. XIII, pp. 58–9, lines 439–40 and 447–9.
[2] *Ibid.* pp. 48–9, lines 221–6.
[3]   'Forest, haute maison des oiseaux bocagers,
           Plus le cerf solitaire et les chevreuls legers
           Ne paistront sous ton ombre,' etc.

Elégie XXIV, 'Quiconque aura premier la main embesongnée' (Lau. XVIII, 1, p. 145). Cf. below, p. 191.

Ou un escueil pendu de sur la mer,
Pour n'ouyr point ce vieil siecle nommer
Siecle de fer, qui la vertu consomme.[1]

And to Cardinal Charles of Lorraine (in *Le Procès*, a poem probably written as early as 1561, but first published in 1565) he complained of the treatment endured by himself and other poets as symptomatic of an age of iron:

Du Bellay qui avoit monté dessus Parnase,
Qui avoit espuisé toute l'eau de Pegase,
Qui avoit dans mon antre avecques moy dansé,
Ne fut, siecle de fer! d'un seul bien advancé.[2]

In reality, Ronsard's fortunes were about to take a turn for the better. Through the good offices of the Queen Mother and of the Duchess of Savoy, he obtained now his first important benefice, the abbey of Bellezone near Rouen. By March 1565 he had succeeded in exchanging this for one where he could usefully exercise his right to reside: the priory of Saint-Cosme-lez-Tours on the Loire. During 1566 he acquired also the little priory of Croixval, in the valley of the Cendrine, on the edge of the forest of Gâtine, and Saint-Gilles on the outskirts of the neighbouring town of Montoire, of which two members of his family had been priors in the previous century. He was now provided with a reasonable living, a position of dignity in his own province, and a choice of pleasant country residences within reach of his old home. Croixval, of which he became particularly fond, is indeed within walking distance of his birthplace, the manor of La Possonnière, at Couture (L.-et-Ch.).

And in the next collected edition of his works, in 1567,[3] there were no new allusions to the Age of Gold. There is, however, in it a noticeable attempt to bring together the poems he had written on this theme. Thus in volume III, entitled *Les Poemes*, under the heading *Premier Livre*, he grouped fifteen poems published in earlier collections, some as early as 1553,

---

[1] Lau. XIII, p. 154, lines 77–81.   [2] *Ibid.* p. 26, lines 201–4.
[3] 6 vols. 4° (4 April 1567).

others more recent: among them were *Le Procès* in which he had condemned his time as a 'siecle de fer' for its failure to appreciate Du Bellay;[1] 'Royne, qui de vertus passes Artemesie';[2] 'Au vieil temps de l'anfant de Rhée';[3] the *Complainte contre Fortune*,[4] and *Les Isles Fortunées*;[5] the two latter poems are placed one after the other, to conclude the *Premier Livre*[6] (apart from a group of translations of Greek epigrams) and they remained thus linked in subsequent editions.

LAST TRACES OF THE THEME (1567–84)

After 1565, there are in Ronsard's poetry only the most fleeting allusions to the Age of Gold and the related themes of Astraea, the rule of Saturn, etc. And even these lack altogether the distinctive preference for a primitive and woodland setting for it which has been up to now so prominent in his work.

For Charles IX's Entry into Paris on the occasion of his marriage (1571)[7] he was commissioned by the City of Paris— which knew him to be the young king's favourite poet—to provide a scenario and French mottos for the decorations along the traditional route of the procession. As we have seen, the theme of the Four Ages or the return of the Golden Age was already an established feature of these festive Entries, and Ronsard did not fail to comply with this convention. It was, however, in a relatively obscure position that the Age of Gold was displayed. In the temporary triumphal arch erected at the Porte aux Peintres, on the south side (not, that is, the side on which the king himself would see them as he rode in from Saint-Denis), a painting representing the Age of Gold filled the niche on one side, while Aglaia (Public Rejoicing) figured on the other. The printed account of the iconography may well preserve Ronsard's instructions to the painters; it describes a

---

[1] See above, p. 44.
[2] See above, p. 36.
[3] See above, p. 13.
[4] See above, pp. 27–8.
[5] See above, pp. 14–15.
[6] Lau. XIV, pp. 104–5.
[7] Simon Bouquet, *Bref et sommaire recueil...*, ff. 24ᵇ and 25ᵃ. See Frances Yates, 'Poètes et artistes dans les entrées de Charles IX et de sa reine à Paris en 1571', *Fêtes de la Renaissance*, I, ed. J. Jacquot (Paris, 1956), pp. 61–82.

representation of the 'aage doré renaissant en ce Roiaume' which

sembloit descendre du Ciel au travers de plusieurs nues, dont elle estoit demi couverte, ayant son vestement tout semé d'estoilles, & les bras plus hault eslevez que sa teste pour soustenir trois Serpens dorez entrelassez l'un dans l'autre, & se mordans par la queüe: signifians les trois aages. A costé d'elle estoit une faulx & plusieurs ronses fauchées, signifiant les noises & dissentions estre couppées par le benefice de la paix. Et estoit escript au dessus d'elle, 'Aurea secla ferens terras Astraea reviso'.

For the Entry of the queen three weeks later, the standing decorations along the route, which had been left *in situ*, were touched up; a ten foot high statue (painted and gilded wood or stucco) of Hymen, at the Fontaine des Innocents, was thus transformed into a golden Saturn, holding in one hand a silver ship and in the other a sickle. This symbolised the benefits to be expected from the Franco-Austrian alliance sealed by the king's marriage, 'lequel ramenant l'aage doré en ce royaume, fera que d'ores en avant le marchant pourra trafiquer & negotier librement partout; & le laboureur recueillir & serrer ses fruits avec seurté, comme il estoit signifié par le navire & faucille'.[1]

There is nothing here which any other sixteenth-century poet might not have equally well invented. During the years that had passed, since Ronsard hymned the entry of Henry II into Paris in 1549, he had evoked a very different Age of Gold to this, but there is nothing to show it.

In August 1573 the king's brother Henry of Anjou, the future Henry III, was offered the crown of Poland, then an elective monarchy. The Polish ambassadors entrusted with the mission of this offer were received in state at the French court, and the Queen Mother produced in their honour an entertainment in the garden of the Tuileries, her own residence adjoining the Louvre. The libretto, mainly composed by Dorat, in Latin (then more familiar to the Poles than French) included a ballet of the Provinces of France, performed by her ladies-in-waiting, among them Hélène de Surgères, Ronsard's 'dernière aventure'.

[1] Bouquet, *op. cit.* Part II, f. 9[b].

The masque introducing this ballet included a French speech in verse, written by Ronsard to be spoken by the personification of France ('La nymphe de France parle'), 'Je suis des Dieux la fille aisnée...' France boasts of having given birth to Clovis, Charlemagne and the present King Charles,

> qui redore
> Ce siecle, qui de luy dépend.[1]

On Charles IX's death (31 May 1574) Henry became king and did not have long to wait to receive a similar compliment; an *Elégie* prepared by Ronsard in December that year, as *étrennes* for the New Year, saluted him as a sun whose rays illuminated Europe:

> Que l'estranger admire et le sujet honore
> Et dont la majesté nostre siecle redore.[2]

This rising sun was in vain celebrated by Ronsard; the new king did not favour him as his elder brother had done. In the 1578 collected edition, Ronsard published only one new poem alluding to the myth of the Four Ages, and this allusion was in a sardonic form: *Les élémens ennemis de l'Hydre*—probably dating from 1569—inveighed against the Huguenot cause as the Hydra from which the earth itself revolted in an unnatural season of flood, famine and fever:

> Et maudissoit nostre siecle rouillé,
> Siecle de fer, de meurtre tout souillé,
> Tout détraqué de mœurs & de bien vivre,
> Un siecle, non, ny de fer ny de cuivre,
> Mais de bourbier...[3]

In this edition of 1578 he published the sequel to the *Amours de Marie*, and the two books of the *Sonnets pour Hélène*. These, like all his love-poetry until then, remained untouched by any connection with the Age of Gold theme. Only in the *Elégie à Marie*, originally printed in 1560, did he introduce a fleeting allusion to it: where the text had read

> Leur siecle estoit vraiment un siecle bien heureus,
> Où toujours se voyoit contre-aimé l'amoureus,

[1] Lau. XVII, 3, p. 415, lines 13–18.   [2] Lau. XVII, 1, p. 85, lines 5–6.
[3] Lau. XVII, 3, pp. 408–9, lines 15–19.

he wrote instead:

> Siecle vraiment heureux, siecle d'or estimé,
> Où toujours l'amoureux se voyoit contre-aimé.[1]

It is remarkable that the *Amours*, which contain much of his finest poetry, and which he consistently placed in volume I of all collected editions of his works, make no other concessions to the association of the Age of Gold with love. Ronsard even contrived to compose sixteen poems to a lady under the name of Astraea,[2] with lavish punning on Astraea and *Astre*, and allusions to the constellation Virgo, without resorting for so much as a single conceit to mention of Astraea as the presiding genius of the Age of Gold.

Six years later, in the last collected edition of his works to be published in his lifetime (1584), among the *Elégies*, he came out with his first, and only, declaration in favour of love, and free love at that, as characteristic of the Age of Gold. Deploring the day when some much-courted lady (? Anne d'Acquaviva) was persuaded to lapse into matrimony, the ageing poet hesitated neither to wish her ill nor to condemn the married state as contrary to nature and unknown in Saturn's happy reign:

> Que j'aime la saison, où le mari de Rhée
> Gouvernoit sous sa faux la terre bien-heurée:
> Lors Hymen n'estoit Dieu, et encores le doy
> Ne cognoissoit l'anneau, le Prestre ny la Loy.[3]

Ronsard had several times expressed the view that marriage was incompatible with love, particularly in the bold and passionate sonnets addressed in 1559 to the lady he called Sinope, who seems to have been spirited enough to ask him his intentions.[4] Amorous by disposition, and unwilling to give up the clerical status which made him eligible to hold benefices on

---

[1] Lau. X, p. 243, lines 105–6 and variants.
[2] *Sonets et madrigals pour Astrée*, Lau. XVII, pp. 179–90.
[3] *Discours*, 'Doncques, voici le jour', Lau. XVIII, I, p. 133, lines 97–100.
[4] Lau. X, pp. 87–101, especially sonnets VIII and IX (pp. 93–5). Published in the *Second Livre des Meslanges* (1559), they were incorporated in the Collected Works of 1560 but with excisions (sonnet IX was one of those deleted) and alterations which toned down the goliardic manner and removed the name of Sinope.

condition of remaining a bachelor,[1] he had a vested interest in maintaining this opinion: it was moreover a commonplace of French medieval literary tradition, with which, through the *Roman de la Rose*[2] and probably through other sources, he must have been quite familiar. This frank belief in free love had, however, never previously been associated with the Age of Gold in his poetry, as it was (if only momentarily) in this poem of 1584.

In contrast to this, the final reference to the Age of Gold to be found in his poetry associates it with an idealised picture of rustic piety. The fragment called *Les Hymnes*, published posthumously (1587), perhaps intended as part of a preface to his *Hymnes*, expressed his hankering for the country rites and festivals beloved of pagan antiquity, to be revived (if he had his way) in the form of innocent and gracious revels at the Christian festivals:

> Ah, les Chrestiens devroient les Gentils imiter
> A couvrir de beaux liz et de roses leurs testes,
> Et chommer tous les ans, à certains jours de festes,
> La mémoire et les faicts de nos Saints immortels...
> L'âge d'or reviendroit...[3]

In this posthumous edition of his works, the passage on the Age of Gold in the *Exhortation pour la Paix*, beginning 'Qu'heureuse fut la gent qui vivoit sous Saturne', was deleted.[4] That the passage on the Age of Gold was sacrificed, and not the passage on the benefits of Peace, is worthy of note: is it really significant? It might at least be natural, after the protracted horrors of the religious wars. Finally, when Ronsard wrote the so-called *Caprice* on the state of France after the death of the duc d'Anjou in June 1584, it was to confide to his friend Simon Nicolas his belief that the conversion of Henry of Navarre, now heir presumptive, to catholicism could save the country: were Henry to reign then, 'ceste saison dorée/Qui fut jadis par le monde honorée/Refleurira...'[5]

---

[1] Lau. X, p. 94, n. 1, and p. 95, n. 1.   [2] See below, p. 81.
[3] Lau. XVIII, 1, pp. 263–4, lines 8–11 and 21. Also in Lau. VIII, p. xx.
[4] See above, pp. 25–6.
[5] Lau. XVIII, 2, p. 322, lines 153–5.

CONCLUSION

Ronsard had shown a pronounced interest in the Age of Gold theme for about twelve years, chiefly in the middle period of his career. Taking all his poems into consideration, the most pedestrian as well as the most inspired, it is possible to muster over thirty in which the theme is mentioned.

The most eloquent of the passages he wrote upon this theme—no one poem is wholly devoted to it—are elegiac in tone. The Age of Gold inspires him most when thought of as an ideal state of human happiness existing only at the very dawn of history, a state which could never return.

A prince or patron might be credited with inaugurating a new Age of Gold: a friend might be extolled as an exception to the reigning Age of Iron.

These two uses of the theme exist in his poetry concurrently. They disappear together. If they are logically incompatible with each other, they seem to reflect an underlying interest in the theme which was characteristic of his mental world during this phase of his career.

It was a phase when, for the first time, he was conscious of some recession in his inventive powers, in so far as lyric poetry and love poetry were concerned; a phase too when his ambitions for material success and recognition were clearly not being realised and might never be.[1] Much of his poetry is accordingly devoted to reflective or satirical or eulogistic purposes, or, as Laumonier described it, 'de la littérature pratique'. With this went the adoption of riming couplets for most of his poetry, a form better adapted to these purposes than elaborate lyric metres. There is in all this, however, more than mere frustration. Ronsard was discovering, in this process, a new kind of inspiration—an elegiac inspiration—and with it a new kind of music, for the 12-syllable riming couplet (hitherto regarded as prosaic) was a challenge to his skill and taste which he met and mastered, developing its potentialities as no poet had ever done before.

[1] Cf. Laumonier, *Ronsard poète lyrique* (2nd ed. 1923), pp. 176–86.

Conclusion

The myth of the Age of Gold offered him a traditional way of expressing dissatisfaction with the present, and longing for a better state in the future or the past. His fondness for it can be explained partly as a sublimation of the disappointments attending this period of his life, merging them in a general reflection on the fortunes of the human race.[1]

Is his use of the theme, however, really traditional? Did other poets and artists of the time imagine it as he did? Did other literary sources, outside the Age of Gold theme altogether, affect his image of it? Did it reflect something fundamental in the world of his sentiments and his imagination?

[1] Cf. the discussion on the *Elegie* in Schiller's *Über naive und sentimentalische Dichtung*: 'Die Trauer über verlorne Freuden, über das aus der Welt verschwundene goldene Alter, über das entflohene Glück der Jugend, der Liebe usw. kann nur alsdann der Stoff zu einer elegischen Dichtung werden, wenn jene Zustände sinnlichen Friedens zugleich als Gegenstände moralischer Harmonie sich vorstellen lassen...Der Inhalt der dichterischen Klage kann also niemals ein äussrer, jederzeit nur ein innerer idealischer Gegenstand sein: selbst wenn sie einen Verlust in der Wirklichkeit betrauert, muss sie ihn erst zu einem idealischen umschaffen.'

2

‡ ‡

Classical, medieval and renaissance concepts of the Age of Gold

'COMMON-PLACE' AND CREATIVE ART

Ronsard was pre-eminently a learned poet.[1] His familiarity with Greek and Latin language and literature was respected, at a period when the subject attracted the finest minds and conferred the greatest rewards, and when it was particularly flourishing in France. He numbered professional classical scholars, like Lambinus, the editor of Lucretius, among his personal friends. It was the avowed policy of the group of poets to which he belonged, to bring into being a classical French literature which should stand comparison with the achievements of the Greeks and Romans.

It is natural to seek in classical literature, therefore, the sources of the passages he wrote about the Age of Gold, itself a part of classical mythology.

And it is natural—or at least tempting—to dismiss these passages, having located their sources, as expressions of a commonplace. This indeed was the attitude adopted by Paul Laumonier, in the commentary on them in his critical edition of Ronsard's poetry. Thus, commenting on the first serious treatment of the theme, in *Les Armes*, he remarked:

Ce lieu commun, qui part d'Hésiode pour aboutir aux déclamations de J.-J. Rousseau, est un thème favori de Ronsard.[2]

on the passage in the *Hymne de la Justice*:

Cette peinture de l'âge primitif où les hommes, naturellement justes, n'obéissaient qu'aux lois de leur conscience, revient souvent

[1] On this subject, see in particular Pierre de Nolhac, *Ronsard et l'humanisme*.
[2] Lau. VI, p. 205, n. 1.

chez Ronsard d'après Hésiode (*Trav. et Jours*) et Ovide (*Mét.* I,
début). J.-J. Rousseau n'a fait que systématiser cette conception.[1]

on the passage in the *Complainte contre Fortune*:

C'est maintenant pour eux l'âge d'or dont parle Hésiode (*Trav. et
Jours*). On voit que le proçès de la civilisation en faveur des hommes
primitifs ne date pas de J.-J. Rousseau.[2]

and on Navarrin's speech in the *Bergerie*:

L'éloge de l'âge d'or était un lieu commun, qui remonte à Hésiode
(*Théog.*) Ronsard l'a plus d'une fois traité, d'après Virgile, *Buc.* IV;
Georg. I, 125 sqq., et les élégiaques latins, Tibulle (I, 3), Properce
(III, 13), Ovide (*Met.* I, 89 sqq.); mais ici il a imité directement
Sannazar...[3]

The identification of commonplaces, or *topoi*, and the
labelling of them, is a matter of erudition and patience. It is a
useful tool in the study of literary history. It can become mis-
leading if it involves lumping together all passages devoted to
the same theme and showing some of the same features, as if
these passages necessarily showed the same image of it. Sixteenth-
century French poets accepted commonplaces and used them as
part of their stock in trade. The originality of a particular poet,
or poem, may lie precisely in the selection or treatment of them.
It was often on these themes, to us hackneyed and stale (at first
sight), that their creative genius worked, as is now more often
realised.[4] No one was, indeed, more aware of this than
Laumonier when his interest was aroused, and in dealing with
Ronsard's lyrical poetry (which was his speciality) his delicate
analysis of a poem in relation to its sources often served to
show the distinction of Ronsard's treatment.[5]

It is of course essential to know what elements of Ronsard's
picture are demonstrably derived from the poets of antiquity

[1] Lau. VIII, p. 51, n. 2.   [2] Lau. X, p. 34, n. 2.
[3] Lau. XIII, p. 101, n. 3.
[4] See Henri Weber, *La création poétique au XVIᵉ siècle en France.*
[5] *Ronsard poète lyrique, passim.* Studies of Ronsard's indebtedness to particular
classical authors, e.g. Storer, *Virgil and Ronsard*, even if apt to content
themselves with listing and labelling Ronsard's 'borrowings', rather than
to examine critically what part they play in his creative process, all helped
to clear the ground.

and from their humanist disciples. It is also essential, however, to take into account features in his sources which he *might* have imitated but which he in fact altered or ignored, and features of his own picture which are *not* accounted for by his predecessors' treatment of the theme. When the reader is referred, at every appearance of the theme over the first ten volumes of Laumonier's edition, to a selection of passages all falling within the limits of Hesiod, *Works and Days*, lines 47–247; Virgil, *Eclogue* IV and *Georgics* I, lines 125–46 and II, 474–84; Ovid, *Metamorphoses*, I, lines 89–150; and Tibullus, I, iii, lines 35–84, etc., an impression is eventually created that Ronsard can have had nothing original on this subject to say. If we look afresh at these authors, and at what they really said about the Age of Gold, the result is somewhat different.

THE GREEK POETS AND PLATO

Hesiod was ranked with Homer by Ronsard among the denizens of Parnassus,[1] and often recognised by him as the ultimate authority for the legend of the Four Ages.[2] The *Works and Days*, written in the ninth century B.C., is indeed the oldest record of the myth, and it was readily available in Ronsard's time in the original Greek, and in Latin and French translations.[3] The reader who turns to it, expecting to find there the prototype of Ronsard's forest-dwellers, may, however, be perplexed when confronted with this account:

First of all, the deathless gods who dwell on Olympus made a Golden Race of mortal men, who lived in the time of Cronus when he was reigning in heaven. And they lived like gods, without sorrow of heart, remote and free from toil and grief: miserable age rested not on them, but with legs and arms never failing they made merry with feasting, beyond the reach of all evils. When they died it was as though they were overcome with sleep, and they had all good

---

[1] *Hymne de la Mort* (1555), Lau. VIII, p. 163, line 13.
[2] See above, p. 18.
[3] I. Silver, *Ronsard and the hellenic Renaissance in France: 1, Ronsard and the Greek epic* (St Louis, 1961), pp. 103–11, and, for the relationship of Ronsard to Hesiod in general, pp. 306–45.

things; for the fruitful earth unforced bare them fruit abundantly and without stint. They dwelt in ease and peace upon their lands with many good things, rich in flocks and loved by the blessed gods.[1]

These splendid creatures are, be it noted, never said to be naturally virtuous. Nor are they in any way identified with a primitive or savage state of man. They are not the ancestors of the present race of men at all.

There followed a Silver Race and a Bronze Race, then a Race of Heroes, and finally the Iron Age, in which the poet lived: 'Therefore, would that I were not among the men of the fifth generation, but either had died before or been born afterwards. For truly now is a race of Iron.'

And with predictions of doom worthy of an Old Testament prophet he concludes: 'Then Aidos and Nemesis, with their sweet forms wrapped in white robes, will go from the wide-pathed earth and forsake mankind, to join the company of the deathless gods, and bitter sorrows will be left for mortal men and there will be no help against evil.'[2]

The nearest state left to the happiness of the Golden Race, according to Hesiod, is that of the men who do true justice. Of their reward, he says,

Light-heartedly they tend the fields which are all their care. The earth bears them victual in plenty, and on the mountains the oak bears acorns upon the top and bees in the midst. Their woolly sheep are laden with fleeces; their women bear children like their parents. They flourish continually with good things, and do not travel on ships, for the grain-giving earth bears them fruit.[3]

The true Age of Gold survived, however, only in the Isles of the Blessed, a haven reserved for the souls of heroes, where the earth of its own accord still bore fruit thrice each year.[4]

If we consider together Hesiod's description of the Golden Race, of the men who do true justice, and of the Blessed Isles, we certainly find a good many features which can be paralleled in one or more of Ronsard's writings on the Age of Gold: the

[1] Hesiod, *Works and Days, Theogony, The Homeric Hymns and Homerica*, trans. H. G. Evelyn-White (1954), lines 109–20.
[2] *Ibid.* lines 174–201.   [3] *Ibid.* lines 230–7.   [4] *Ibid.* lines 166–73.

fecundity of the earth, the bitter reflections on the contrast with the Age of Iron, the flight of Justice, the approving reference to the absence of sea-faring, etc. These are all, however, to be found in Ovid. By contrast, Hesiod's distinctive emphasis on health, wealth, longevity, and painless death, as the enviable lot of the Golden Race, is only echoed once in Ronsard, and that is in the *Bergerie* of 1565, where it comes through the intermediary of Sannazaro:

> Les vieillars sans douleur sortoient de ceste vie
> Comme en songe, & leurs ans doucement finissoient,
> Ou d'une herbe enchantée ils se rajeunissoient...[1]

Deeply concerned as Ronsard was with the passing of youth and strength, and with the prospect of ill health and old age and death, he only once, in this partial and indirect way, alluded to immunity from them as part of the Age of Gold.

Nor is Hesiod's Golden Race a society of forest-dwellers and wandering gatherers. They were free from toil and grief, but they lived none the less upon their lands and were rich in flocks. The men who do true justice tend fields and herds; if Nature provides acorns and honey, this does not imply that there was no other food.

In this connection, account must be taken also of the *Phaenomena* of Aratus, a poem telling the stories traditionally associated with the signs of the Zodiac and with the stars and planets. Aratus, who flourished in the third century B.C., is chiefly remembered now by non-classical scholars as the poet quoted by St Paul in his sermon at Athens.[2] But his reputation was considerable in antiquity, and in the revival of Greek learning: he was carefully read and annotated by Milton, in his own copy (bought in 1631) of the edition published by Guillaume Morel at Paris in 1559, on which the English poet transcribed the judgement of Ovid, 'cum sole et luna semper Aratus erit'.[3]

---

[1] Lau. XIII, p. 102, lines 532–4. See above, p. 39.   [2] Acts xvii, 28.
[3] BM C.60.1.7. Milton's annotations are printed in his *Works* by John Mitford, *Works of John Milton* (1851), I, clxxxi–clxxxii, and by the Columbia editors (Columbia U.P., New York, 1938), XVIII, 325 ff., and discussed by

ΑΡΑΤΟΥ

τὸ λύκαμον,παρ᾽ αἱ πόλῳ πινὶ ϗαφεὶς· ὃν λέγεται κινδωιϑὺ ὄντα σιὼ μῃτεὶ αἱαιρεϑιῶαι, κͅ᾽ τὸν ὃν λυκαίῳ νόμοϛ,ὁ ζιῶϛ ἐλεήσαϛ αὐτὸν,κατετέͅεͅσι. τῦτον ϑ λέγεται ϋϑ δὴ κλο-
᾽᾽ φύλακα,ϗ,βοώτιω,ϗμ ὠειωτα·φησὶ γᵈ ϗ ὁ ποιητὴϛ,Καὶ ὁ ψ δύοντα βοώτιω.λέγιταμ
ϗ τρυγητὴϛ.   Καὶ μάλα πᾶϛ)Ο νοιϛ,σρόὁρα γᵈ ἔχͅ τοιϛ πᾳντας λαμͅπρͅοͅτͅᾳτͅοͅιϛ ἕνα δὲ ἐχͅ ὅν μάσῃ ζὼνῃ,ὅϛ τιϛ διὰ τἰω ὑᾳρͅβͅολͅιὼ τῆϛ λαμπρͅοͅτͅῃτͅοͅϛ,ἰδίωϛ ϗ αὐτὸϛ λέγͅᾳ-τᾳμ ϗρ κλοῦροϛ,ὁμοίωϛ τῷ παῆ ἢ ἀρκτͅἰῳρͅῳͅ λαμπͅῃδͅὁͅνͅα γᵈ ἔχͅ ἰ ἢ τυχοῦσαμ.

Ἀμφοτέρͅοͅιͅσͅι δὲ ποσὶν ⟨ⲧⲟⲟⲟⲥⲕⲉⲯⲁⲓⲟ βοώτⲫⲩ ⟩

Γαρϑ́ͅνͅοͅνͅ,ἥ ρ᾽ ὃν χͅεͅρͅσͅὶ φͅέͅρͅͅͅ ςͅτͅᾴχͅυͅν αἰͅϡͅμ́ͅͅεͅνͅτͅα·

Εἴτ᾽ οὖν ἀςͅρͅᾳίͅοͅυͅ κͅεͅίͅῃ ϡͅυͅοͅϛͅ,ὃͅνͅ ρͅᾴτͅέͅ φͅᾳσͅιͅνͅ

Ἀςͅρͅῳνͅ δͅρͅχͅᾳίͅῳνͅ πͅᾳτͅέͅρͅ᾽ ἔͅμͅμͅεͅνͅᾳιͅ·εͅἴͅτͅέͅ τͅευͅ ᾄϡͅνͅ,

Εὔͅκͅῃϡͅοͅϛͅ φͅοͅρͅέͅοͅιͅτͅοͅ·λͅόͅϟͅοͅϛͅ γͅέͅ μͅιͅὼ ὀͅνͅτͅέͅχͅͅ ᾄϡͅοͅϛͅ ϟͅεͅνͅ

ᾈνͅθͅρͅῴͅπͅοͅιͅϛͅ,ᾡϛͅ δͅῂϡͅεͅνͅ ὀͅπͅιͅϟͅϑͅθͅνͅ πͅᾴͅͅρͅοͅϛͅ ϟͅεͅνͅ,

ᾝρͅχͅεͅτͅοͅ δ᾽ ᾀνͅθͅρͅῴͅπͅῳνͅ κͅᾳτͅεͅνͅᾳνͅτͅίͅῃ·οͅὐͅδͅέͅ πͅοͅτͅ᾽ ᾳἰͅνͅδͅρͅῳ̃ͅνͅ,

Οͅὐͅδͅέͅ πͅοͅτͅ᾽ δͅρͅχͅᾳίͅῳνͅ ᾐνͅίͅνᾳτͅοͅ φͅῦͅλͅα γͅυͅνᾳιͅκͅῳ̃ͅνͅ,

ᾈλͅλͅ᾽ ᾀνᾳμͅὶͅξͅ ἐͅκͅᾳϑͅῃτͅοͅ,ϗͅᾳὶͅ ᾀϑͅᾳίͅᾳτͅῃ πͅεͅρͅ ἐͅο̃ͅͅσͅᾳ·

Κͅᾳίͅ ἑͅ δͅίͅκͅῃνͅ κͅᾳλͅέͅεͅσͅκͅοͅνͅ· ᾀϟͅϟͅοͅρͅμͅόͅϟͅῃ δͅὲͅ ϟͅέͅρͅοͅνͅϟͅᾳϛͅ,

ᾘέͅ πͅοͅυͅ εͅἰͅνͅ ᾀϟͅρͅρͅῇͅ,ᾒ δͅρͅυͅχͅόͅρͅͅͅῳͅ ὀͅνͅ ᾀϟͅϟͅόͅϟͅͅͅͅ

Δͅῃμͅοͅτͅέͅρͅᾳϛͅ ᾔδͅͅͅ δͅεͅνͅ ὑͅπͅιͅᾳϟͅϟͅρͅόͅχͅοͅυͅσͅᾳ ϟͅέͅμͅιͅͅͅϟͅᾳϛͅ.

Οͅὔͅπͅω λͅͅͅϟͅᾳλͅέͅϟͅϛͅ ὅͅτͅεͅ νͅεͅίͅκͅεͅοͅϛͅ ᾐπͅίͅϟͅᾳνͅτͅοͅ,

Οͅὐͅδͅὲͅ δͅιͅᾳκͅρͅίͅσͅιͅοͅϛͅ· πͅεͅͅͅρͅιͅμͅεͅμͅφͅέͅοͅϛͅ,οͅͅͅοͅδͅὲͅ κͅυͅδͅοͅιͅμͅοͅυͅ·   *πͅλͅυͅμͅεͅμͅφͅέͅοͅϛ*

ᾼὔͅτͅῳϛͅ δͅ᾽ ἔͅζͅῳοͅνͅ.χͅᾳλͅεͅπͅῂ δͅ᾽ ᾀπͅέͅκͅεͅιͅτͅοͅ ϑͅᾴλͅᾳͅͅϟͅᾳ,

Κͅᾳὶͅ βͅίͅοͅνͅ οͅὔͅπͅω νͅῇεͅϛͅ ᾀπͅόͅϟͅϟͅρͅϟͅθͅεͅνͅ ᾐϟͅίͅνͅεͅσͅκͅοͅνͅ,

ᾈλͅλͅᾲ βͅόͅεͅϛͅ ᾀϟͅρͅͅͅϟͅᾳ·κͅᾳὶͅ ᾳὐͅτͅῂ πͅόͅτͅνͅιͅᾳ ϟͅᾳͅͅῳνͅ

Μͅυͅϟͅίͅᾳ πͅᾴνͅτͅᾳ πͅϟͅρͅ᾽ ͅῇχͅεͅ δͅίͅκͅῃ δͅͅͅϟͅεͅιͅρͅᾳ δͅιͅκͅϟͅῳνͅ.

Τͅόͅφͅρͅ᾽ ̃ͅͅͅͅῳ,ὅͅφͅρͅ᾽ ͅἔͅϟͅιͅ γͅᾳῖͅᾳ ϡͅυͅοͅϛͅ χͅρͅύͅσͅϟͅοͅνͅ ͅἔͅφͅεͅρͅϟͅεͅνͅ

ᾈρͅγͅυͅρͅέͅͅͅͅͅͅῳ δͅ᾽ ͅͅͅͅͅͅϟͅλͅίͅγͅῃ τͅεͅ,κͅϟͅᾳͅͅͅͅ ͅͅͅͅϟͅκͅέͅτͅιͅ πͅᾴμͅπͅͅͅͅͅͅϟͅνᾳͅ ͅϟͅτͅοͅίͅμͅῃ,

ῼ μͅίͅͅͅͅͅͅλͅϟͅ,πͅοͅͅͅͅͅϟͅοͅσͅᾳ πͅᾳλͅᾳιͅϟͅͅͅνͅ ͅᾔϟͅϟͅᾳ λͅᾳϟͅῳνͅ.

ᾈλͅλͅ᾽ ͅἔͅμͅπͅῃϛͅ ͅἔͅϟͅιͅ κͅεͅῖͅνͅοͅ κͅᾳτͅ᾽ ͅδͅρͅγͅύͅρͅͅͅͅϟͅοͅνͅ ϡͅυͅοͅϛͅ ͅϟͅεͅνͅ.

ᾝρͅχͅεͅτͅοͅ δ᾽ ͅͅͅὀͅϟͅξͅ ͅͅͅϟͅρͅέͅͅͅῳνͅ ͅͅͅϟͅπͅιͅδͅͅͅίͅεͅϟͅοͅϛͅ ͅῃχͅͅͅέͅνͅτͅͅͅͅῳνͅ

Μͅͅͅͅοͅͅͅͅϟͅᾳͅͅͅξͅͅͅͅ ͅͅͅδͅῄ τͅͅͅεͅ ͅͅͅͅϟͅπͅεͅμͅίͅϟͅϟͅεͅτͅοͅ μͅεͅιͅλͅιͅχͅίͅοͅιͅσͅιͅνͅ·

Figure 5. Aratus on the Legend of Astraea, copy
annotated by Milton and others
Phænomena, Paris, 1559, 4°

In the *Phænomena*, Ronsard could read the story of the goddess of Justice, Astraea, identified by Aratus with the constellation Virgo. Her flight from the earth, foreshadowed by

H. F. Fletcher, *The intellectual development of John Milton* (Illinois U.P., Urbana, 1956), II, 285–6.

57

Hesiod, is here described, after successive stages of withdrawal, before which—in the Age of Gold—she dwelt with men:

Nor yet in that age had men knowledge of hateful strife or carping contention, or din of battle, but a simple life they lived. Far from them was the cruel sea, and not yet from afar did ships bring their livelihood, but the oxen and the plough and Justice herself, queen of the peoples, giver of things just, abundantly supplied their every need. Even so long as the earth still nurtured the Golden Race, she had her dwelling on earth.[1]

In the Silver Age, Justice no longer was the daily companion of men, but her voice was still heard speaking from the hills at dusk, remote and severe. The Race of Bronze, 'First to forge the sword of the highwayman and first to eat of the flesh of the ploughing ox', finally disgusted her with human society and drove her to rejoin her peers in heaven. Aratus represents the four ages as successive stages of humanity as we know it and makes of them an allegory of gradual moral degeneration.

The pattern of the story—the presence of Justice on earth in the Age of Gold, and her withdrawal stage by stage as the later Ages succeeded it—was used by Ronsard in the *Hymne de la Justice*. But he took the description of Aratus, in which Justice presides over a simple agricultural society, and deliberately changed it.

Of his familiarity with the original text, there is some evidence. He paraphrased *Phaenomena*, lines 768–73, in the *Elégie à J. de la Péruse*, in 1553;[2] he referred in a jocular mood to his study of the text in a goliardic ode of 1554 beginning,

> J'ay l'esprit tout ennuié
> D'avoir trop estudié
> Les Phenomenes d'Arate:
> Il est tans que je m'ébate...[3]

he spoke of him and Nicander in the same breath as Homer and Hesiod, in the *Hymne de la Mort* already quoted, and he later

---

[1] *Phœnomena*, lines 96 ff. (*Callimachus, Lycophron, Aratus*, trans. of Aratus by G. R. Mair).
[2] Lau. v, pp. 259–60.   [3] Lau. vi, p. 105, lines 1–4.

congratulated his friend Rémy Belleau for having translated
into French
> le grand poète Arate
> Les signes vrais des animaux certains...[1]

that is to say the *Phaenomena* with its explanations of the signs
of the zodiac. He also quoted Aratus, either in the original or
in his own words, on several occasions.[2]

Thus Ronsard must have altered the 'early civilised' Age of
Gold in Aratus to a 'primitive' one knowing quite well what
he was doing.

It is true that the tradition even in antiquity had begun to
show some variation in this respect. The idea that Nature provided of its own accord for every human need (clearly further
removed from any realisable ideal on earth, and not even an
ideal state to men who prefer activity to idleness) gained
ground, and followers of Aratus, like Germanicus, anticipated
the alteration made by Ronsard.[3] It was perhaps held in check
by the incurable Greek sense of the ridiculous, for parodies, on a
Golden Age in which everything required for human life grew
on trees, figured irreverently in Greek comedy,[4] and in the
Saturnalia of Lucian.

A new development, to be found in Empedocles, and given
expression by the Alexandrian poets, was the tendency to
associate the Age of Gold with the reign of Love;[5] in the
Alexandrian poets too the Age of Gold may be drawn into the
pastoral convention, or into an idealised scene of actual
country life.[6] Indeed one authority on the pastoral convention
comes to the conclusion that the Age of Gold theme constitutes
the real driving force behind the pastoral convention itself, and

[1] Lau. xv, 1, p. 47, lines 180–1.
[2] I. Silver, *Ronsard and the hellenic Renaissance in France: 1, Ronsard and the Greek Epic*, pp. 71–2, and n. 37.
[3] E. Graf, 'Ad aureae aetatis fabulam symbola' in *Leipziger Studien zur classischen Philologie*, VIII (1885), 47–50 and 12.
[4] A. O. Lovejoy and G. Boas, *Primitivism and related ideas in antiquity* (1935), pp. 38–41.
[5] E. Graf, *op. cit.* pp. 15–18 and 52–4.
[6] *Ibid.* p. 55. For Ronsard's familiarity with this poetry, see P. de Nolhac, *Ronsard et l'humanisme*, pp. 101 ff.

regards both as inseparable from the concept of free love.[1] This is something of an overstatement, and based on the famous 'Age of Gold' chorus in Tasso's *Aminta* which, at the time when Ronsard was concerned with the theme, had not been written. It shows, however, that the elements of such an association between the themes of pastoral life, free love and Golden Age were present in late antiquity and were readily so associated by certain Italian renaissance poets. Ronsard, equally familiar with these sources, and equally practised in the pastoral and erotic style of poetry, kept both these themes almost entirely separate from the Age of Gold.

A very different picture of the Age of Gold could be derived from ancient Greek literature by readers who did not confine themselves to the poets, but also studied Plato.

This is a possible source of inspiration which it would be unrealistic to ignore. References to Plato in Ronsard's poetry are indeed fairly numerous, though they are often introduced to exploit the effect—easily obtained—of disagreeing or affecting to disagree with an established idol.[2] Certainly Ronsard was not a profound student of philosophy, least of all at the period when he was meditating on the Age of Gold. But he could hardly escape knowing the most celebrated of the dialogues. Among these, the *Politicus* or *Statesman* contains a highly poetic passage on the Age of Gold.

In speaking of the Age of Gold, or the Reign of Cronus,

[1] H. Petriconi, 'Über die Idee des goldenen Zeitalters als Ursprung der Schäferdichtungen Sannazaros und Tassos', *Die neueren Sprachen*, XXXVIII (1930), 265–83. But see E. Lipsker, *Der Mythos vom goldenen Zeitalter in den Schäferdichtungen Italiens, Spaniens und Frankreichs*, Berlin, 1933.
[2] E.g. the ode to Maistre Denis Lambin, 'Que les formes de toutes choses/ Soient, comme dit Platon, encloses/En nostre ame...', III, vii, in *Les Quatre premiers livres des Odes* (1550), Lau. II, pp. 15–16, and the conceit in sonnet LX of the *Amours* of 1552, 'Pardonne moy, Platon, si je ne cuide...', Lau. IV, p. 62. There is a reference to Book III of the *Republic* in the *Remonstrance au peuple de France* (1563), 'Si Platon prevoyoit par les molles musiques/Le futur changement des grandes republicques...', Lau. XI, p. 84, lines 391 ff.; the theoretical character of the *Republic* is criticised in the *Discours à François de Montmorency* (1567)—'Je m'esbahis des parolles subtiles/Du grand Platon qui veut regir les villes/Par un papier & non par action...', in the context of a compliment to a man of action, a Marshal of France and Governor of Paris, Lau. XIV, p. 186, lines 135 ff.

Plato, like Hesiod, refers to an earlier race of men, now extinct, not to the forebears of the present human race, nor indeed to the present cycle of the world at all. The human beings of that era came under the direct rule of God, and all the other creatures under their respective demigods, and there was no violence or devouring of each other:

> In those days God himself was their shepherd and ruled over them, just as man, who is by comparison a divine being, still rules over the lower animals. Under him there were no forms of government or separate possession of women and children, for all men rose again from the earth, having no memory of the past. And although they had nothing of this sort, the earth gave them fruits in abundance, which grew on trees and shrubs unbidden, and were not planted by the hand of man. And they dwelt naked, and mostly in the open air, for the temperature of their seasons was mild; and they had no beds, but lay on soft couches of grass, which grew plentifully out of the earth...

The children of Cronus furthermore had 'the power of holding intercourse not only with men but with the brute creation'.[1]

Ronsard did not adopt the ideas, accepted by the Pythagoreans and expressed here by Plato, that the Age of Gold was directly ruled by God and characterised by peace between man and beast.[2] The absence of families, dwellings and clothes, the freedom from memories of the past and fears for the future, the perfect reliance upon Nature—these are, however, ideas in keeping with his dreamworld of primitive content and they may have helped to shape it. The lack of private property was a feature to be found also in passages of Plato less strikingly poetic, as an ideal against which political systems should be measured.

The first and highest form of the state is defined in the *Laws* as 'that in which there prevails most widely the ancient saying, that "friends have all things in common"',[3] and knowledge of

---

[1] *Statesman* (271–2), *Dialogues of Plato*, trans. B. Jowett (4th ed. revised, 1953), III, 483–4.
[2] Except in the *Bergerie* in a passage closely imitated from Sannazaro's *Arcadia*. See above, p. 39.
[3] *Laws* (739), *Dialogues of Plato*, IV, 308.

this teaching was popularised by Erasmus, who placed the saying in question in the place of honour at the beginning of the *Adagia* with a commentary including the reference to the *Laws* ('The same Plato says that a State will be happy and blessed in which these words are never heard: *mine* and *not mine*').[1]

There is also a passage in Book v of the *Republic*, prescribing for the Guardians (the élite of professional administrators) renunciation of all private property except the bare necessities of life, so that they cannot be tempted to disrupt the unity of the state by differing about meum and tuum (τό τε ἐμὸν καὶ τὸ οὐκ ἐμόν).[2]

This communism was intended (as that of More's *Utopia* was to be) as a rational scheme in a civilised society, and seems therefore at first sight unlikely to have fired the imagination of a poet musing on primaeval Man. Perhaps for this reason, Laumonier referred to the *Republic* only in a single footnote:[3] this indeed is his only mention of Plato in his commentaries on the Age of Gold passages in Ronsard's poetry.

Ronsard's insistence on the absence of 'mien et tien', and the idea of common ownership for which it stood, is, however, sufficiently distinctive to suggest Platonic influence. Among the poets of antiquity who described the Age of Gold as such, the Greeks offered no prototype for such an association of ideas; the Romans moralised about the absence of boundary-stones and of rigidly demarcated divisions of the land, in the Age of Gold, both ruled out alike by man's contentedness and by Nature's liberality,[4] but the expression 'mine and thine' and the positive emphasis on common ownership are not to be found in this connection.

Though the passages in the *Laws* and the *Republic* are concerned with the ideal state, and not with the Age of Gold, they could hardly fail to remind any reader who knew the *Politicus*

---

[1] Cf. M. Mann Phillips, *The 'Adages' of Erasmus: a study with translations* (Cambridge, 1964), p. 12.
[2] *Republic* (462, 464), *Dialogues of Plato*, trans. B. Jowett, II, 320–1.
[3] 'Voir encore Platon, *Rép*. v.' Lau. VIII, p. 53, end of footnote 2.
[4] See below, pp. 65, 68.

of the passage on the Age of Gold in that dialogue, and re-inforce the effect of what was there said about the absence of private property.

The feelings evoked in Ronsard by the concept of the Age of Gold may well have been heightened by his reading of ancient Greek authors. Whether or not he fully understood the antiquity of Hesiod as compared with Aratus, both took the myth far back into ancient literature, and conferred upon it the aura of immeasurable age and sanctity, as well as the fascination which he was ready to find in everything Greek, a fascination the more potent because he had studied it of his own choice when already a grown-up man.

He did not, however, picture the Age of Gold as they did. His Age of Gold people are not the Golden Race of Hesiod, nor the god-fearing subjects of Astraea in the *Phaenomena*, nor the shepherds and lovers of the Alexandrians, nor the children of Cronus evoked in the *Politicus*.

The explanation that he was merely following a literary commonplace is not adequate if we seek its origins in Greek antiquity. Is it valid if we turn to Latin?

ROMAN POETS

Virgil's poetry was familiar to Ronsard long before he read Greek. He continued all his life to love it, and imitated it assiduously.

Il ne faut s'esmerveiller si j'estime Virgile plus excellent et plus rond, plus serré et plus parfaict que tous les autres, soit que dès ma jeunesse mon Regent me le lisoit à l'escole, soit que depuis je me sois fait une Idée de ses conceptions en mon esprit (portant toujours son livre en la main) ou soit que, l'ayant appris par cœur dés mon enfance, je ne le puisse oublier.[1]

He had before him here, as in so much classical literature, a choice between at least two conceptions of the Age of Gold. The blessings brought to mankind of flocks, farming and laws might

[1] *Préface sur la Franciade*, addressed *Au lecteur apprentif*, edited and published posthumously by Binet. Lau. XVI, 2, p. 339. On Ronsard's familiarity with Virgil, see the thesis of W. L. Storer, *Virgil and Ronsard* (Paris, 1923).

be regarded as ushering in this era of legendary happiness. Or even this degree of interference with man's 'natural' life might be deplored, and his most ideal state be identified with a frankly primitive condition. It is not enough to explain Ronsard's preference for the latter picture by finding sources in Virgil: Virgil offered him both.

In the Fourth Eclogue, with its prediction of the return of the Age of Gold and the reign of Saturn with Astraea, 'iam redit et virgo, redeunt Saturnia regna...'[1] we have the principal source of Guisin's speech in the *Bergerie* of 1563, as of all renaissance poems predicting the return of prosperity under a wise ruler. It also provided details for the idyllic life to be expected by Ronsard and his friends in *Les Isles Fortunées*. It is not here, however, that Ronsard found his favourite formula. In the visionary world that Virgil saw attending the career of the child whose birth he celebrated, Nature would indeed once more become friendly to Man; the cattle would come of their own accord to be milked; savage beasts and hurtful weeds would disappear; the earth would bring forth corn and wine unbidden, and the oaks distil honey. Lingering traces of human depravity might at first remain, among them the tilling of the ground and the walling of cities; eventually these practices would disappear. In the end all things required by men would grow of their own accord: the very wool would grow ready-dyed on the backs of the sheep. The miraculous fecundity of Nature, and the abolition of the need for human exertion, 'key' ideas of Ronsard's Age of Gold, are present. But they do not portend a humanity content to live on acorns and cold water in the woods.

Much closer to Ronsard's picture is the age before the reign of Jupiter (it is not actually called the Age of Gold) described in Book I of the *Georgics*. It was thus rendered into French by Jacques Peletier du Mans, Ronsard's first mentor in the art of French poetry ('ante Iovem nulli subigebant arva coloni...)':

Nul n'exerçoit avant le premier age
De Jupiter, ès Champs le labourage,

[1] *Ecloga* IV, lines 6 ff.

> Et si n'estoit loisible de donner
> Mercq à un Champ, ny mesme le bourner:
> Tous fruiz estoient en commun amassez,
> De soy la Terre apportoit biens assez
> Sans la semondre...

The fields had undergone no cultivation, nor was it lawful to mark them out with boundary stones, for they were an heritage held in common: Jupiter it was who withdrew these blessings from mankind, planning that men (for their own good) should learn virtue the hard way. Ronsard was certainly affected by this description. Nowhere, however, does he follow Virgil in attributing to fatherly providence Jupiter's decision to terminate the Age of Gold (in the immediately preceding lines):

> Il n'a pas pleu a ce Pere celeste
> L'Agriculture estre à tous manifeste,
> Et luy premier a esté reduisant
> Les Champs en art, de soucy aiguisant
> Les cueurs humains, & ceux du siecle sien
> Il n'a souffert languir sans faire rien.[1]

In Book II of the *Georgics*, we have the reference, which inspired Ronsard's *Avant-venue du printens*, to the era when Spring reigned all the year round on earth, the climate which made possible the first development of the human race.[2] Eternal Spring is not, however, easy to reconcile with living on acorns, and it is not here that Ronsard's characteristic picture has its source. In the closing passages of Book II, on the other hand, a tendency appears to equate the Age of Gold (if only by poetic licence) with real country life; that Justice lingered among country folk before finally abandoning mankind—

> extrema per illos
> Iustitia excedens terris vestigia fecit[3]

was accordingly an idea familiar to all readers of Virgil. Finally, in a passage necessarily just as familiar to Ronsard as the rest of

---

[1] *Georgics*, I, lines 121–8. J. Peletier du Mans, *Les Œuvres poétiques*, éd. M. Françon, first extract p. 198, second p. 181.
[2] See above, p. 10.　　　　　[3] *Georgics*, II, lines 473–4.

this book, Virgil identifies this rustic felicity with the life led by the Sabines and the Romans of old, and by those who lived under the golden rule of Saturn, ere men impiously slew their oxen for food, sounded the war-trumpet or forged the sword:

> Such was the life the frugal Sabines led;
> So Remus and his brother god were bred,
> From whom the austere Etrurian virtue rose;
> And this rude life our homely fathers chose.
> Old Rome from such a race derived her birth,
> (The seat of empire, and the conquered earth,)
> Which now on seven high hills triumphant reigns,
> And in that compass all the world contains.
> Ere Saturn's rebel son usurped the skies,
> When beasts were only slain for sacrifice,
> While peaceful Crete enjoyed her ancient lord,
> Ere sounding hammers forged the inhuman sword,
> Ere hollow drums were beat, before the breath
> Of brazen trumpets rung the peal of death,
> The good old god his hunger did assuage
> With roots and herbs, and gave the golden age.[1]

In the *Aeneid*, Virgil showed himself willing to regard also as a Golden Age the era when Saturn *after* his dethronement by Jupiter came to reign as a temporal king in Latium, where he was revered as the *founder* of agriculture.

> These woods were first the seat of sylvan powers,
> Of Nymphs and Fauns, and savage men, who took
> Their birth from trunks of trees and stubborn oak.
> Nor laws they knew, nor manners, nor the care
> Of labouring oxen, nor the shining share,

---

[1] *Georgics*, II, lines 532–40 (Dryden's translation). Ronsard probably had this passage in mind when he wrote the description of rustic content in the *Discours à Odet de Colligny* (*Second Livre des Meslanges*, 1559),

> Quant à moy j'ayme mieux ne manger que du pain
> Et boire d'un ruisseau puisé dedans la main, etc.

and concluded,

> Ainsi vesquit jadis Saturne le bon homme,
> Et le grand fondateur des murailles de Rome,
> Romule avec son frere...

Lau. X, pp. 14–15, lines 205–17. But Ronsard does not introduce the concept of the Age of Gold here.

Nor arts of gain, nor what they gained to spare.
Their exercise the chase; the running flood
Supplied their thirst, the trees supplied their food.
Then Saturn came, who fled the power of Jove,
Robbed of his realms, and banished from above.
The men, dispersed on hills, to towns he brought,
And laws ordained, and civil customs taught,
And Latium called the land where safe he lay
From his unduteous son, and his usurping sway.
With his mild empire, peace and plenty came;
And hence the golden times derived their name.[1]

The prophecy in *Aeneid* VI, beginning:

> hic vir, hic est tibi quem promitti saepius audis
> Augustus Caesar, divi genus, aurea condet
> saecula...[2]

concerning the return of the Age of Gold with the rule of
Augustus, likewise seems to evoke an era of justice under a
strong and wise sovereign rather than a society without fields,
flocks, laws or ambitions:

> But next behold the youth of form divine—
> Caesar himself, exalted in his line—
> Augustus, promised oft, and long foretold,
> Sent to the realm that Saturn ruled of old;
> Born to restore a better age of gold.
> Afric and India shall his power obey, etc.

The people of Saturn, the inhabitants of Latium, are indeed
virtuous of their own accord, as Aeneas is told by Latinus,
'Saturni gentem haud vinclo nec legibus aequam',[3] but they
are not in any way 'primitive' folk.

This is material for picturing the Age of Gold which Ronsard
had at his disposal, and rejected.

The full-scale account of the Four Ages in Ovid's *Metamorphoses*, Book I, beginning:

[1] *Aeneid*, VIII, lines 314–25 (Dryden's translation).
[2] *Ibid.* VI, lines 791 ff.   [3] *Ibid.* VII, line 203.

Aurea primata sata est aetas, quae vindice nullo
Sponte sua sine lege fidem rectumque colebat...

is, on the other hand, much closer to Ronsard than that of
Hesiod:

The Golden Age was first: when man, yet new,
No rule but uncorrupted reason knew;
And, with a native bent, did good pursue.
Unforced by punishment, unawed by fear,
His words were simple, and his soul sincere.
Needless was written law, where none opprest;
The law of man was written in his breast.
No suppliant crowds before the judge appeared;
No court erected yet, nor cause was heard.
But all was safe, for conscience was their guard.
The mountain trees in distant prospect please,
Ere yet the pine descended to the seas;
Ere sails were spread, new oceans to explore
And happy mortals, unconcerned for more,
Confined their wishes to their native shore.
No walls were yet, nor fence, nor moat, nor mound;
No drum was heard, nor trumpet's angry sound;
No swords were forged, but, void of care and crime,
The soft creation slept away their time.
The teeming earth, yet guiltless of the plough,
And unprovoked, did fruitful stores allow;
Content with food, which nature freely bred,
On wildings and on strawberries they fed;
Cornels and bramble-berries gave the rest;
And falling acorns furnished out a feast.[1]

There followed the Age of Silver, the Age of Bronze, and the
Age of Iron, the latter characterised particularly by the actual
discovery of mining and metal-working, leading to the use of
weapons and of coins, both productive of discord among men.
Boundaries of land were now measured out whereas it had been
common property 'ceu lumina solis et aurae'. At this point
Astraea the virgin goddess forsook mankind and took her

---

[1] *Metamorphoses*, I, lines 89–106 (Dryden's translation).

flight to heaven.[1] Here we are told that Age of Gold men cherished of their own free will what was true and right; here too for the first time is an account of the Age of Gold and its successors which unequivocally treats the cultivation of the earth as an impiety; only with the Age of Silver and the

---

I ætus an
re

præcipites fossæ

pasunia famis ar
hor .i. euercus.

> A urea primo fata eſt ætas, quæ vindice nullo
> S ponte ſua ſine lege fidem, rectúmq3 colebat.
> P œna, metúſq3 aberant, nec vincla minacia collo
> Æ re ligabantur, nec ſupplex turba timebat
> I udicis ora ſui, ſed erant ſine iudice tuti.
> N ondum cæſa ſuis peregrinum vt viſeret orbem,
> M ontibus, in liquidas pinus deſcenderat vndas.
> N ulláq3 mortales, præter ſua littora, norant,
> N ondum præcipites cingebant oppida foſſæ,
> N on tuba directi, non æris cornua flexi,
> N on galeæ, non enſis erat, ſine militis vſu,
> M ollia ſecuræ peragebant ocia gentes.
> I pſa quoq3 immunis, raſtróq3 intacta, nec vllis
> S aucia vomeribus, per ſe dabat omnia tellus,
> C ontentíq3 cibis nullo cogente creatis,
> A rbuteos fœtus, montanáq3 fraga legebant,
> C ornáq3, & in duris hærentia mora rubetis,
> E t quæ deciderant patula Iouis arbore glandes.

Figure 6. Ovid on the Age of Gold, copy annotated by
a sixteenth-century reader
Metamorphoses, Paris, 1529, 8°

---

accession of Jupiter comes the earliest pastoral and agricultural work, not by the wise decree of the god, but as a result of human depravity, men being no longer content to live on Nature's bounty. Here we have an Age of Gold where mankind is praised for being idle and carefree, and where the poet dwells with pleasure on the picture of an earth unviolated by human

[1] *Ibid.* lines 149–50.

Classical, medieval and renaissance concepts

interference, and on a humanity happily plucking the fruit of hedgerow and forest.

Scarcely less striking is the passage in the *Amores*, III, viii, beginning, 'At cum regna senex coeli Saturnus haberet...'. Here, after lamenting the tendency of modern girls to prefer wealth to talent in their suitors, the poet sings regretfully of the age when gold was safely hidden in the earth:

But when ancient Saturn had his kingdom in the sky, the deep earth held lucre all in its dark embrace. Copper and silver and gold and heavy iron he had hid away in the lower realms, and there was no massy metal. Yet better were his gifts—increase without the curved share, and fruits and honeys brought to light from the hollow oak. And no one broke the glebe with the strong share, no measurer marked the limit of the soil, and they did not sweep the seas, stirring the waters with dipping oar...[1]

lines which harmonised with his description of the Age of Gold in Book I of the *Metamorphoses*.

In the last book of the *Metamorphoses*, expounding the Pythagorean philosophy, there is a reference to the Age of Gold in a very different connection (a reference not mentioned in the Laumonier commentary because Ronsard does not make any use of it, but which he certainly knew just as well as those he adopted). The speech given by Ovid to Pythagoras includes an allusion to the Age of Gold as innocent of the slaughter of animals for human food:

> At vetus illa aetas, cui fecimus aurea nomen,
> Fetibus arboreis et, quas humus educat, herbis
> Fortunata fuit...[2]

Further on, as Pythagoras describes the constant process of change and transmutation of all things on earth, he gives as an example the succession of the Ages of Gold and Iron and the gradual change of the earth's surface itself, so great that what is now dry land has once been sea:

[1] *Heroides and Amores*, with trans. Grant Showerman (1914), lines 35–43.
[2] *Metamorphoses*, XV, lines 96–8.

sic ad ferrum venistis ab auro,
Saecula: sic totiens versa est fortuna locorum...[1]

And with these lines we come to a passage which was evidently
in Ronsard's mind when he meditated on the transformation of
the forest into ploughland in the *Elégie contre les bûcherons de
Gâtine* of 1584.

By contrast with this solemn mood, in *Amatoria* the Age of
Gold is invoked only to score a verbal point. The present is an
Age of Gold only in the most ironic sense: an age ruled by
cash considerations: 'Aurea nunc vera sunt saecula.'

Propertius sighed for the days of rustic simplicity when girls
were satisfied with gifts of flowers and fruit picked by their
suitors, and when human piety was such that gods and
goddesses did not disdain to dwell among men; like Ovid, he
contrasted that period with the present, an 'Age of Gold' only
in the sense of being wholly ruled by money.[2]

Tibullus, fearing to die abroad and alone, thought with
longing of the era before men indulged in travel, trade or
warfare, and evoked (in this connection) an Age of Gold also
distinguished by absence of ploughing with oxen and of clearly
marked-out landed property, in the passage beginning 'Quam
bene Saturno vivebant rege':

How well lived folk in olden times when Saturn was the king,
before the earth was opened out for distant travel! Not as yet had
the pine-tree learned to scorn the blue sea wave or offered the
spreading sail to belly before the wind; nor, seeking gain in unknown lands, had the vagrant seaman loaded his bark with foreign
wares. That was a time when the sturdy bull had not bent his neck
to the yoke, nor the tamed horse champed the bit. No house had
doors; no stone was planted on the land to set fixed boundaries to
men's estates. The very oaks gave honey; and with milky udders

---

[1] *Ibid.* lines 260–1.
[2] Propertius, III, xiii (*De avaritia puellarum*), lines 25–58. Cf. R. E. Hallowell,
Ronsard and the conventional Roman elegy (Urbana, 1954), pp. 97–8, and, on
the 'borrowings' of Ronsard from Tibullus, pp. 109–10. See also his
appendix of parallel passages, pp. 121–8. The use of the Age of Gold theme
in nine of Ronsard's poems is considered in his work.

came the ewes unbidden to meet the carefree swain. Then were no marshalled hosts, no lust of blood, no battles; no swords had been forged by the cruel armourer's ruthless skill.[1]

This picture is by no means identical with Ronsard's. The houses had no doors, but there were houses; the ox and the horse had not been domesticated, nor the boundaries marked in the fields, but the people did not live on acorns and water; the oaks gave honey, but the people were not specifically forest-dwellers; the sheep brought their milk of their own accord (as in the Fourth Eclogue of Virgil) but this is an idealised pastoral amenity, not to be expected by a community of gatherers.

In one passage, Tibullus speaks in terms much more like Ronsard's of a former age, living on acorns and water: 'Glans alat, et prisco more bibantur aquas'. This, however, must be read in its context. The poet was deploring the fate that had caused his beloved one to be carried off by her husband to his place in the country. In a series of extravagant protestations of his love and desperation, he offered even to become a plough-man if only he could thereby continue to see her, and finally cursed the 'cruel field Ceres' which was the reason for her departure: 'Oh, let the corn go, so there are no lasses in the country; let acorns be our fare and water our drink in the olden way. Acorns were the food of the ancients, and they had love always wherever they were. What hurt to them if they had no furrows sown with seed?'[2] This utterance is not connected with the Age of Gold: indeed, the poet is assuming that a diet of acorns and water, though a man could live on it, was the most primitive form of subsistence, and one only desirable for the freedom which was then enjoyed to love as people pleased.

Much more often, Tibullus sings of the work of the farm, and the immemorial rituals of the countryside, with longing and affection: in I, i, he sings of his own little farm; in I, v, he imagines Delia living with him as the lady of the manor; in I, vii, he celebrates the benefits brought to men by Osiris, who

[1] Tibullus, I, iii, lines 35–48. In *Catullus, Tibullus, Pervigilium Veneris*, trans. J. P. Postgate, pp. 207–9.
[2] *Ibid.* II, iii, lines 67–70, pp. 265–7.

72

taught them how to grow corn and wine, and hence the arts of
song and dance; in II, i he hymns the festival of the Ambervalia:

I sing the country and the country's gods. They were the guides
when men first ceased to chase his hunger with the acorns from the
oak. They taught him first to put the planks together and cover his
humble dwelling with green leaves. They too, 'tis told, first trained
bulls to be his slaves, and placed the wheel beneath the wain. Then
savage habits passed away; then was the fruit-tree planted, and the
thriving garden drank the water from the rills,

and the making of wine, the spinning and weaving of wool, and
the evolution of song and dance, are recorded as part of this
beneficent early process of civilisation.[1]

Tibullus, while certainly one of Ronsard's favourite poets,
and much in his mind at the period when he wrote about the
Age of Gold, did not, therefore, determine the way in which the
Age of Gold is represented in his poetry. He could equally
readily have suggested an Age of Gold in an early pastoral or
even agricultural society, or an Age of Gold which was
primarily a paradise of free love, or of the arts.

Freedom from war, freedom from hunger, freedom from
ambition, freedom from oppression—these are basic desiderata
of the classical Age of Gold. But the classical authors, even those
drawn upon by Ronsard, do not present a uniform picture, and
none of them in fact dictate the pattern which he chose.

BOETHIUS AND JEAN DE MEUNG

Ronsard did not have to wait to hear of the Age of Gold, until
he could read Greek, or even Latin, nor even for that matter
until he could read at all. His family, while not in the least
academic, could certainly have told him as a child about the
festive Entries which so often made a feature of the Age of
Gold and its hoped-for return, and even about the more varied
pictures of it to be found in the poets. For the sixteenth century
did not have to rediscover the Age of Gold. In forms shaped by

---

[1] *Ibid.* II, i, lines 37 ff. (p. 255).

late antiquity and by the intervening centuries, it was well known
in popular vernacular works, some of which at least might
quite well have been among the books possessed by Ronsard's
father, himself a lover of poetry and even (if we are to believe
Claude Binet) himself the author of some poems remembered
with pleasure by Pierre in after-life.[1]

Very well known, both in the original and in translation,
was the *Consolation of Philosophy* of Boethius, a work which
need not be excluded from consideration of Ronsard's possible
classical sources. And no feature of the *Consolation* was
more popular than the poem on the Former Age, 'Felix
nimium prior aetas' (II, m. v).[2] In terms which both Stoic
wisdom and Christian meditation had helped to determine,
Philosophy in person urged Boethius, as he lay in prison and
expecting death at the hands of a tyrant, to understand that no
man is truly free whose happiness depends upon his wealth and
position. An imagined era is then recalled—and Philosophy at
this point goes over from prose to verse—when greed and
ambition had not yet confused man's judgement:

> Too much the former age was blest,
> When fields their pleaséd owners failéd not,
> Who, with no slothful lust opprest,
> Broke their long fasts with acorns eas'ly got.
>
> No wine with honey mixéd was,
> Nor did they silk in purple colours steep;
> They slept upon the wholesome grass,
> And their cool drink did fetch from rivers deep.
>
> The pines did hide them with their shade,
> No merchants through the dangerous billows went,
> Nor with desire of gainful trade
> Their traffic into foreign countries sent.
>
> Then no shrill trumpets did amate
> The mind of soldiers...

[1] *Discours de la vie de Pierre de Ronsard* (1586), ed. P. Laumonier (1910), p. 3.
[2] See H. R. Patch, *The tradition of Boethius* (1935), pp. 122 ff. The exclamation of Jean Raulin, 'O felix nimium prior illa aetas', quoted above, p. 6, note 2, is of course an allusion to the opening line of this poem.

Boethius and Jean de Meung

O that the ancient manners would
In these our latter hapless times return!
Now the desire of having gold
Doth like the flaming fires of Aetna burn.

Ah, who was he that first did show
The heaps of treasure which the earth did hide,
And jewels which lay close below,
By which he costly dangers did provide?[1]

It is easy to recognise in this poem a familiar group of ideas associated with the Age of Gold: the fertility of the soil, the contentedness of the people, the absence of sea-faring, and the absence (particularly saluted by Ovid) of mining, the source of metals and hence of weapons and of money. It is also easy to recognise whole phrases echoing (and no doubt deliberately) phrases used by Virgil and Ovid in passages on the Age of Gold or on related themes like the happy countryman.[2] Yet, in a few terse lines, with the earnestness of a hard-won personal conviction and the finality of a proverb, Boethius formulated a distinctive picture of the Former Age which exerted considerable influence on subsequent writers. As against a hedonistic (or 'soft' primitivist) treatment of the Age of Gold, flowing with milk and honey and even wine, as found in Virgil and Ovid, he imagined as the ultimate happiness a life lived very close to real nature: willingness to breakfast on acorns (though 'contenta fidelibus arvis' seems to assume some agricultural produce too), and to enjoy sleep in the open air on the grass, water from a sparkling brook to quench thirst, and a lofty tree as shelter. A frugal (or 'hard' primitivist) ideal of the Age of Gold is at first sight a contradiction in terms,[3] but Boethius, if he has not reconciled them, at least succeeded in investing with idyllic beauty a conception of the Former Age opposed to self-indulgence.

[1] Boethius, *The theological tractates, The consolation of philosophy*. The English translation is that of 'I.T.' (1609), revised by H. F. Stewart, pp. 205–7.

[2] E.g. 'Nec lucida vellera Serum / Tyrio miscere veneno'. Cf. 'vellera ut foliis depectant tenuia Seres'. *Georgics*, II, line 121, cf. line 465. 'Fervens amor ardet habendi'. Cf. 'et belli rabies et amor successit habendi', *Aeneid*, VIII, lines 315–27, etc.

[3] Cf. Lovejoy and Boas, *Primitivism and related ideas in antiquity*, p. 11.

75

The direct influence of Boethius continued to be felt in the sixteenth century, and in humanist as well as scholastic circles. To the time-honoured commentary of St Thomas Aquinas, there was added that of the Paris scholar-printer, Josse Badius Ascensius; editions, both of the text alone, and of the text with both commentaries, continued to be published both in northern Europe and in Italy. The commentary of St Thomas Aquinas already glossed the poem on the Former Age with an account

C Metrum Quintum Secundi Libri.

Felix nimiū prior ętas,
Cōtenta fidelibus aruis,
Nec inerti perdita luxu,
Facili quę fera folebat
Ieiunia foluere glande.
Nec bacchica munera norat
Liquido confundere melle.
Nec lucida vellera ferum
Tyrio mifcere veneno.
Somnos dabat berba falubres.
Potuz quoqz lubricus amnis.
Ambras altiffima pinus.
Nondum maris alta fecabat.
Nec mercibus vndiqz lectis

Noua littora viderat hofpes.
Tunc claffica fęua tacebant.
O dijs neqz fufus acerbis
Cruor borrida tinxerat arma,
Quid enim furor bofticus vlla
Vellet prior arma mouere,
Cum vulnera fęua videret.
Nec pręmia fanguinis vlla?
Vtinam modo noftra redirent
In mores tempora prifcos,
Sed fęnior ignibus ętnę
Feruens amor ardet babendi.
Heu quis primus fuit ille
Auri qui pondera tecti
Gemmafqz latere volentes
Pręciofa pericula fodit?

Figure 7. 'Felix nimium prior aetas'
Boethius, *De consolatione philosophiae*, Venice, 1524, fol.

of the Four Ages as related by the poets—chiefly, in fact, following Ovid: it must have gone far to familiarise the learned public with the idea that the Age of Gold was contented and frugal, living on acorns and water, while the Age of Silver saw the invention of agriculture, the inhabiting of fixed dwellings, and the planting of vines.[1] Badius supplied the relevant passages from the *Metamorphoses*, Book I, from Satire VI of Juvenal, and from the Elegy of Tibullus, and a reference to the Natural

[1] *De consolatione philosophiae et disciplina scholarium* (1524), f. 30[b].

History of Pliny. Jean du Choul, the Lyons humanist,
quotes Boethius, as well as Virgil, Lucretius, etc. as one of the
authorities for the acorn-eating habits of early man, in his
learned little essay on the Oak, published in 1555,[1] the same
year as the collections of poetry containing *Les Armes* and the
Hymne de la Justice.

Among the vernacular texts best known to the generation
of Ronsard's grand-parents, and even later, was the adaptation
in French verse of the *Consolatio philosophiae* made by Renaud de
Louhans, preserved in numerous manuscripts and very popular
throughout the fourteenth and fifteenth centuries in France.[2]
Renaud expanded the thirty lines of Boethius' poem on the
Former Age[3] with the aid of Ovid's passage on the Four Ages
at the beginning of the *Metamorphoses* and some little touches of
his own, to nearly a hundred lines, clearly enjoying his own
description as well as preaching frugality and contentedness.
His treatment of the subject led him into some curious antici-
pations of the wording used by Ronsard in, for instance, the
passage on the Age of Gold in *Les Armes*:

> L'un ne portoit a l'autre envie,
> Car innocent estoit leur vie...
>
> Tuit [*tous*] vivoient selon Nature
> En innocence et en droiture...[4]
>
> En commun avoient le bien:
> Nul ne disoit: 'C'est tien, c'est mien.'[5]   RENAUD DE LOUHANS
>
> Et lors on n'oyoit point ce mot de tien ne mien,
> Tous vivoient en commun, car tous n'avoient qu'un bien.[6]
> De ce que l'un vouloit l'autre en avoit envie
> Et tous d'acord passoient heureusement la vie:
>
> RONSARD

---

[1] *De varia quercus historia* (1555), pp. 13–14.
[2] A. Thomas, 'Traductions françaises de la *Consolatio philosophiae* de Boèce',
completed by Mario Roques on the version of Renaud de Louhans, in the
Histoire littéraire de la France, XXXVII (1938), 419–88.
[3] See above, p. 74, and Fig. 7.
[4] A. Thomas and M. Roques, *op. cit.* p. 486.
[5] *Ibid.* p. 487.   [6] Lau. VI, p. 205, lines 17–20.

The woodland setting and the outdoor life were also to be found in Renaud's description. Developing the lines of Boethius, 'Somnos dabat herba salubres', etc., he wrote that the people of the Former Age took their rest, fully dressed, upon the grass (in spite of which dangerous habit they were as healthy as any doctors...) and drank nothing but spring water, and had no other mansions but the shelter of the oaks and pines.[1]

For those who preferred a closer translation of Boethius, various French versions had been produced since the thirteenth century, some wholly in prose, others offering verse renderings of the metrical passages like the poem on the Former Age.[2] Among the prose versions, a famous one was that of Jean de Meung, author of the second part of the *Roman de la Rose*; this version, dedicated to Philip V, was still being copied for wealthy patrons at the end of the fifteenth century.

In the *Roman de la Rose* itself, Jean de Meung dealt with the Age of Gold in several episodes of his romance.

The Lover, in his dialogue with Reason, asks whether Justice or Love is to be preferred. Reason replies, that Justice could never be superior to Love, even were Justice to return to earth in the uncorrupt form she bore in the reign of Saturn, for Love can make Justice redundant. If men loved one another, they would never wrong one another. And if wrongdoing were to cease, what good purpose would be served by Justice? Everyone would live peaceably and quietly, without kings or princes, bailiffs or magistrates, that there would be no lawsuits. In reality—Reason hastens to add—Justice on earth is a delusion,

[1]
Tuit vestu sur l'erbe gisoient
Et si estoient aussi sains
Comme sont les phisiciains.
Ilz buvoient a grant alainne
L'aigue qui vient de la fontainne,
Car ne cognoissoient les vins.
Soubz les chesnes et soubz les pins
Estoit leur habitacion—
N'avoient autre mansion.
(A. Thomas and M. Roques, *op. cit.* p. 486.)

[2] For a complete survey, see *ibid.* pp. 425–88, and L. W. Stone, 'Old French translations of the *De Consolatione Philosophiae* of Boethius', *Medium Ævum*, VI (1937), 21–30.

Boethius and Jean de Meung

and she denounces the abuses of it for several hundred lines.[1] Later in the poem, Ami explains to the Lover that cupidity and constraint (both the bane of Love at the present day) were unknown to our first fathers and mothers, in 'li siecles mout precieus':

By way of bread, meat and fish they gathered acorns in the woods, and sought in the groves (across hills, plains and valleys) apples, pears, nuts, chestnuts, buds, mulberries and sloes, raspberries and strawberries, hips and haws, peas and beans and such-like trifles, with fruits, herbs or roots. They rubbed ears of corn, and they picked grapes in the fields without putting them into presses or vats. Honey ran from the oaks on which they fed in plenty, and they drank plain water nor sought wine, spiced or mulled, nor drank strong drink at all. The earth was then not tilled, but was as God had decked it out, and of its own accord it bore what every man required to live on. They did not fish for salmon or pike. They were clad in hairy skins, and made clothes of wool exactly as it came off the animals, without dyeing it with seed or herb. Their homesteads and hamlets were roofed with broom, foliage and branches, and they dug trenches in the ground. When they feared the foul weather of some approaching storm, they took refuge in rocks or in the mighty trunks of hollow oaks, and when at night they wished to sleep, instead of feather-beds they carried into their huts piles and sheaves of grass, leaves and moss...On such couches as these I tell you of, lovers embraced and kissed without a thought of violence or greed; green trees in the groves spread their boughs like tents and curtains to shade them from the sun. There they led their dances, their sports, their gentle pastimes—quiet, simple people they were, with no cares except the care to live merrily and in honest companionship. No king or prince had yet laid criminal hands on others' goods. All men were used to being alike, and they desired nothing owned in private.[2]

[1] *Le Roman de la Rose*, ed. E. Langlois (Paris, 1914–24), vol. II, lines 5474–561. E. Langlois, *Origines et sources du roman de la Rose* (1890), pp. 125–7, and E. Faral, 'Le Roman de la Rose et la pensée française au XIIIe siècle', *Revue des Deux Mondes*, V (1926), 439–57. Both these authors attempt to explain Jean de Meung's representation of early human society and of the origins of the State by reference to his sources.

[2] *Le Roman de la Rose*, vol. III, lines 8364–402 and lines 8431–48. There are plainly reminiscences of this passage, as well as of the 'Felix nimium prior aetas' in Boethius' *Consolation of philosophy* which both poets knew, in Chaucer's *The former Age*.

In an episode forming a sequel to this, the poet adds that people did not then practise sea-faring, finding everything they thought worth seeking in their own land.[1] He then relates how all this happy state was destroyed by the onset of Barratry (chicanery) assisted by Sin and Misfortune, Pride, Greed, Avarice and Envy, and all the other Vices, who in turn brought Poverty (from Hell, where she had hitherto dwelt) into the world, and overran it with wars and quarrels. The bowels of the earth were ransacked for metals and precious stones, and men became jealous of their private property: to protect this from their neighbours, they eventually appointed a king, chosen from among their number for his physical strength, and, when his personal exertions proved insufficient, paid him taxes to employ underlings to assist him. The wealthier cavemen thus contrived to appropriate for good what had once been, 'like the sun and air', common to all mankind.[2]

The idea that all things were by nature the common property of all men was one which appealed to Ronsard greatly at the period when he wrote with special pleasure about the Age of Gold. This idea he could have found also, if in a less strikingly radical form, in the final sermon of Genius, high priest of Nature. Here the story of the Four Ages is recalled, complete with references to Virgil and Ovid, the former of whom the poet knew to have derived his knowledge from the Greeks ('es livres grezeis'). Before the accession of Jupiter, no man had held a plough or fixed a boundary stone: together men sought those good things which grew unbidden. Jupiter it was who changed all this. 'Mout ot en lui mol jousticier', says the poet severely, refusing to accept these changes as intended for the good of man:

He put an end to the Ages of Gold and made the Ages of Silver; then came the Ages of Bronze, for men went on degenerating, so much did they desire evil. Then the Ages of Bronze turned into Iron, so far have they strayed from their state. Of this right glad are the gods of the ever-dark and dire mansions who envy men as long as they see them alive.[3]

[1] *Le Roman de la Rose*, vol. III, lines 9517–95.
[2] *Ibid.* lines 9526–664.　　　　　[3] *Ibid.* vol. v, lines 20115–208.

1. *Les Armes* (1556): bas-reliefs of trophies on Guillaume du Bellay's tomb (1557) in Le Mans Cathedral.

2. The Age of Gold in the *Roman de la Rose* (French, c. 1400).

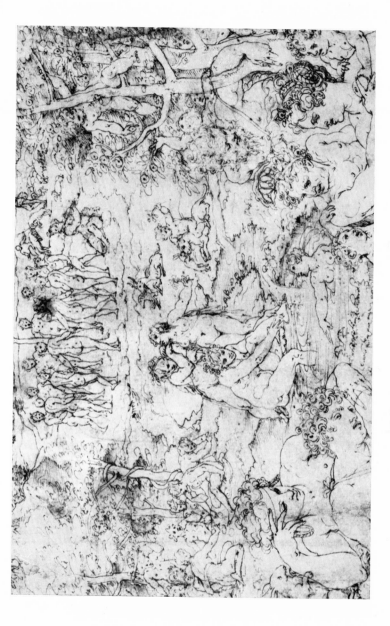

3. Vasari, *L'età dell'oro* (*c.* 1567), detail.

4. Manoir de La Possonière, Couture (L.-et-Ch.).

This hint that evil powers hostile to Man brought to an end
the Age of Gold with its untilled and undivided fields may have
lent the more emphasis to that picture of man's lost felicity.[1]
And this was in all probability some of the first poetry which
Ronsard ever read. His earliest published poem, *Des beautez
qu'il voudroit en s'amie* (1547) spoke of:

> la Rose par Meun décritte
> Et contre les femmes despite,
> Avecques qui jeune j'auroy' hanté,

and the last line of this was amended in 1550 to read: 'Par qui
je fus des enfance enchanté'.[2]

There are no *verbal* resemblances between Ronsard and Jean
de Meung, as there are between Ronsard and Renaud de
Louhans; nor does Ronsard's primitivist picture of the Age of
Gold with its woodland setting and wandering, homeless habit,
seem to owe much to Jean de Meung. And where the *Roman de
la Rose* is most arresting in its ideas, in (for instance) its challenge
to the predominant belief that there were moral foundations
for the authority of the state and for the institution of marriage,
Ronsard does not follow it.

But the very prominence given to the theme in the *Roman de
la Rose* was well calculated to impress a boy who was fond of
poetry. In particular, the passage on 'li siecles mout precieus'
(lines 8364 and following) represent as romantically happy a
life which, if not spartan, was simple, communal, and even

---

[1] Cf. the description earlier in the poem of the Flock of the Good Shepherd,
and its Eternal Spring: 'Si bel ne vit ne si pur nus / Neis quant regnait
Saturnus / Qui tenait les dorez aages / Cui Jupiter fist tant d'outrages'
(*ibid.* lines 20031–4).

[2] Lau. I, p. 6, lines 38–40. Cf. Binet, 'Ronsard ayant toujours en main quelque
poete françois qu'il lisoit avec jugement et principalement comme luy-
mesmes m'a maintes-fois raconté un Jean le Maire de Belges, un *Romant de la
Rose* et les œuvres de Coquillart et de Clement Marot' (p. 10). Ronsard's
debt to the *Roman de la Rose* has been studied chiefly for his treatment of
courtly love, and his use of allegory in, for instance, H. Guy, 'Les sources
françaises de Ronsard', *RHLF*, IX (1902), 237–46. Karl Bühler, *Ronsard und
seine Stellung zur mittelalterlichen französischen Literatur* (Heidelberg dissertation, 1918), takes the investigation no further in this respect, though he lists
some instances of Old French forms like 'greignour' for which the *Roman
de la Rose* would have been Ronsard's most obvious source.

communist. Jean de Meung's picture is the more attractive because it presupposes nothing alien to nature, and is imagined in terms of real country life, however wonderfully exempt from its normal hardships and contentions. The diet of cold water and uncooked vegetarian food, in itself somewhat ascetic, takes on a delicious rather than austere character, recalling the expeditions to collect wild strawberries, blackberries and nuts (according to the season) by which village people in the old days always reckoned to supplement and vary their monotonous staple diet. Provision of rivers running with milk and honey and even wine was disdained by Jean de Meung and by Ronsard too, except in fleeting allusions to milk-rivers in *Les Isles Fortunées* (line 109) and in the Eclogue *Daphnis et Thyrsis* (line 163), and in the speech of Guisin in the *Bergerie*.

An 'acorns and water' conception of the Age of Gold thus existed in the world of Ronsard's childhood, based on the relatively primitive state identified with it in the first book of Ovid's *Metamorphoses*, and on some of the allusions in the first book of Virgil's *Georgics*, but affected by Stoic and Christian ideals of frugality and temperance, and by the interpretations given to it by thirteenth and fourteenth century French poets.

This tradition makes it more comprehensible that Ronsard should adopt so austere a picture of the Age of Gold, in a period which we associate rather with robust assertions that the Age of Gold was coming or had come, in the form of peace, prosperity and artistic splendour. There is, however, nothing here which might not have been equally well known to his fellow-poets. And other medieval sources offered a picture very different in emphasis.

Thus the *Ovide moralisé*, completed not long after Jean de Meung's portion of the *Roman de la Rose*, offered a frankly apolaustic Age of Gold. If its people depended on Nature's bounty, and had no private ownership, they did not eat only roots, berries and nuts, for corn and wine, milk and honey, also came conveniently to hand:

> Sans arer estoient de blé
> La terre et li champ tout comblé;

Adont coroient les rivieres
Par la terre, grans et plenieres
De lait, de miel et de piment:
Mout vivoient joiousement.[1]

This work (recast in prose in the fifteenth century) was still popular in the generation before Ronsard's, despite its bulk (70,000 lines).

Such visions were no doubt closer to popular conceptions of the Age of Gold, of the kind which might have occurred to onlookers watching the Entries.

A late but authentic piece of evidence for the latter is provided by the patois verses on the Entry of the prince d'Enghien into Dijon in 1636: when the Age of Gold returned, the poet assured his readers, their vines would never be frosted (and there would be three crops a year), and meat would be given away for nothing.[2]

It is fitting that so vigorous an assertion of the ideal of 'good cheer' should emanate from Burgundy. It is, however, a salutary reminder that, for the man in the street, whether in Dijon or elsewhere, the moralist's ascetic picture of the Age of Gold would be wholly out of touch with the common idea of a pleasurable life. That is, unless the picture was transformed by the magic of true poetry.

ITALIAN POETS AND ANTOINE HÉROËT

The Age of Gold as a symbol of plain living and high thinking had been celebrated by some of the greatest poets of Italy (though the blessings to be hoped for from some enlightened ruler were the favourite pretext for introduction of the theme).

Dante contrasted it with the excesses which had been the undoing of the gluttons: in a passage inspired by the poem of Boethius on the Former Age, he told how healthy hunger and thirst, in the First Age, had made acorns seem tasty and the

[1] *Ovide moralisé, poème du commencement du quatorzième siècle*, ed. C. de Boer, 5 vols (Amsterdam, 1915–36), I, lines 495–500.
[2] 'Dialogue de Silène, Nasillon et Groindor sur la venue de Mgr. le prince d'Anguien à Dijon', quoted by Marcel Bouchard, *De l'humanisme à l'encyclopédie: L'esprit public en Bourgogne sous l'ancien régime* (Paris, 1930), p. 108.

water of every brook as sweet as nectar.[1] That Virgil, and other ancient poets, when they wrote of the Age of Gold, might have been granted an imperfect vision of the Earthly Paradise is a proposition seriously put forward in the same book.[2] There is little reason to suppose that Ronsard knew first-hand the work of Dante. The very serious and indeed religious attitude towards the Age of Gold which he expressed was, however, by no means forgotten by later Italian poets, with whom Ronsard's acquaintance is more probable.

In Poliziano's *Stanze per la giostra* (Libro Primo), praise of rural sports and of rustic life leads to an evocation of the Age of Gold, by a train of thought already to be found in the conclusion of the *Georgics*, Book II. This Age of Gold is imagined in an era not only before warfare, but before seafaring and even before ploughing (at least with the help of oxen), when men dwelt under the mighty oaks, whose trunks bore honey and whose branches bore acorns. Thirst for gold had not yet entered the world: the human race lived free and happy, and the fields, unploughed, were fruitful. Fortune, envious of this happiness, destroyed its laws and banished piety, causing sensuality and 'that frenzy which the poor folk call Love' to enter human breasts.[3]

1   'Lo secol primo quant' oro fu bello:
               fe' saporose con fame le ghiande
               e nettare con sete ogni ruscello.'   (*Purg.* xxii, 148–50.)

2   'Quelli che anticamente poetaro
               l'età dell' oro e suo stato felice
               forse in Parnaso esto loco sognaro.

       Qui fu innocente l'umana radice,
          qui primavera è sempre, ed ogni frutto:
          nettare è questo di che ciascun dice.'   (*Purg.* xxviii, 139–44.)

    The theme of the Earthly Paradise, and its relationship to the Age of Gold theme, is fully treated in *The Earthly Paradise and the Renaissance Epic*, by A. Bartlett Giamatti (Princeton University Press, 1966).

3   In cotal guisa già l'antiche genti
          Si crede esser godute al secol d'oro:
          Nè fatte ancor le madri eron dolenti
          De' morti figli al marzial lavoro:
          Nè si credeva ancor la vita a' venti:
          Nè del giogo doleasi ancora il toro:
          Lor case eron fronzute querce e grande,
          Ch'avean nel tronco mèl, ne' rami giande. (20.)

Here, therefore, Ronsard could have found a hint of an Age of Gold where the oaks provided both food and shelter, though the primitive character of the resulting way of life is not stressed. He could also find a conception of the Age of Gold from which love, in the ordinary sense of the word at least, was specifically excluded.

Whether in fact he had already read the *Stanze per la giostra* when he was himself interested in the Age of Gold theme is an open question. It is certain that he had done so when he composed the second group of *Stances* in the *Amours d'Eurymédon et de Callirée* for Charles IX in honour of Anne d'Acquaviva:[1] the episode, in which Diana punishes the hunter Eurymédon for his slaughter of her deer by wounding him with Cupid's arrow and causing him to love the nymph Callirée and so forget his passion for the hunt, is modelled upon Poliziano's stanzas (8 and following) describing how Giuliano de' Medici fell in love. Although nowhere really *translated* from the Italian, there are here, and possibly in later stanzas too, resemblances too close to be accidental. At this period Ronsard was sometimes working under pressure to produce what was asked of him by his royal patrons, and he may have resorted to reading some of the Italian poets in search of inspiration, but not necessarily then for the first time.[2]

> Non era ancor la scelerata sete
> Del crudel oro entrata nel bel mondo;
> Viveansi in libertà le genti liete;
> E non solcato il campo era fecondo.
> Fortuna invidiosa a lor quiete
> Ruppe ogni legge, e pietà misse in fondo:
> Lussuria entrò ne' petti e quel furore
> Che la meschina gente chiama amore. (21.)

Angelo Poliziano, *Le Stanze. L'Orfeo e le rime*, ed. A. Momigliano, pp. 52–3.

[1] Lau. xvii, 2, pp. 144–65. Not published until 1578, probably because (as Laumonier supposes) the poet did not wish to offend the queen, Elizabeth of Austria, who, after Charles IX's death, remained in France until December 1575. Eurymédon—the king—is described in line 26 as 20, which would date the poem 1570, but this is only a rough guide to the period of its inception.

[2] E. Parturier, 'Quelques sources italiennes de Ronsard au XVᵉ siècle: Politien et Laurent de' Medicis', *Revue de la Renaissance*, vi (1905), 1–21; for the parallels with the *Stanze per la giostra*, see especially pp. 3–6. Parturier also saw parallels with them in earlier works of Ronsard, e.g. the reference to

A more elaborate and more powerful picture of the Age of Gold, perhaps among the most personal to be found in any poet, is to be found in the *Selva seconda* of Lorenzo de' Medici, stanzas 84 to 117. The torments of hope and jealousy endured by a lover here provoke thoughts of an ideal world where love, at least as commonly understood, can never enter—a conception perhaps not far removed from Poliziano's

> furore
> Che la meschina gente chiama amore

for all that can trouble the composure of body, soul or intellect, or hurt others, is unheard-of:

> D'amore accesi sanza passione,
> speranza o gelosia non li accompagna:
> un amor sempre, qual il ciel dispone
> e la natura, ch'è sanza magagna.[1]

With this may be compared the third song in Book 1 of Bembo's *Gli Asolani* (1504), sung by the fairest maid of honour of the Queen of Cyprus, claiming that, were Love *rightly* understood, human life would take the path of wisdom, and the Golden Age be renewed in all its blessedness.

Ideas like these may well have tended to discourage Ronsard from including in his Age of Gold such facile notions of idyllic love as those of the roman elegiac poets, of Jean de Meung or even of Sannazaro in the Song of Opico.

The *Selva seconda* admittedly elaborates two ideas about the Age of Gold which can scarcely be found in Ronsard at all. One is the eloquently described peace between man and the

Hercules enslaved by love in the *Elégie à Muret* (1553), but these are not regarded by Laumonier as certain instances of Poliziano's influence (Lau. v, p. 229, n. 2).
[1] Lorenzo de' Medici il Magnifico, *Opere*, ed. Attilio Simiono (Bari, 1914), I, 278 (103). Laumonier appears not to accept the suggestion of Parturier (*op. cit.* pp. 9–13) that Ronsard in *Le cyclope amoureux* (Lau. x, pp. 275–90) was drawing upon Lorenzo's *Corinto* as well as upon their common source, the eleventh idyll of Theocritus. It is, however, hard to suppose that Ronsard was ignorant of Lorenzo's works, and he certainly mentions him by name in the sonnet *A Lodovico Dajacetto florentin*. The *Selve d'amore* had been printed several times before Ronsard was born, and were of course included in the Aldine edition of Lorenzo's *Poesie volgari* published in Venice in 1554.

animals which then held sway, no beast or bird being ever slain
for sport or food, either by Man or by other creatures;[1] the
other is the intellectual humility, which made possible perfect
understanding of the truth in all matters within Man's
competence:

> non dubbio alcun, non fatica ha il pensiero;
> sanza confusion intende il vero...[2]

a blessed state destroyed by the desire of knowing too much,
symbolised by Prometheus and his theft of Fire. The opening
lines of the whole description introduce the Prometheus theme,
and with them comes a pair of stanzas similar in several respects
to some passages of Ronsard:

> Pria che venissi al figlio di Iapeto
> del tristo furto il dannoso pensiero,
> reggeva nel tempo aureo quieto
> Saturno il mondo sotto il giusto impero.
> Era il viver uman più lungo e lieto:
> era e pareva un medesimo il vero:
> frenato e contento era ogni disio,
> né conosceva il mondo 'tuo' o 'mio'.

> La terra liberal dava la vita
> comunemente in quel bel tempo a tutti.
> Non da vomero o marra ancor ferita,
> produceva frumenti e vari frutti;
> di odorifere erbette e fior vestita
> non mai dal sol, non mai dal gel distrutti:
> l'acque correnti dolci, chiare e liete
> spegneano allor la moderata sete.[3]

The Platonic expression 'mine and thine' is used here in
connection with the Age of Gold as Ronsard was to use it, in
emphasising absence of private property: the earth gave corn
and fruit without being ploughed or hoed, and clear streams
quenched men's thirst. On the other hand, there are obvious
differences.

[1] *Ibid.* pp. 274–7 (86–97).
[2] *Ibid.* pp. 279–81 (105–14).   [3] *Ibid.* p. 274 (84–5).

Lorenzo likes to think that human life was then longer and happier: this idea of longevity, which is to be found already in Hesiod's description of the Golden Race, was mentioned in none of Ronsard's passages on the Age of Gold except in the speech imitated from Sannazaro in the *Bergerie* of 1565. Lorenzo speaks of truth *being* and *seeming* the same; such an aspiration is quite foreign to Ronsard's picture of the Age of Gold. Lorenzo speaks of every desire being *restrained* as well as contented: Ronsard's idea is rather of a natural benevolence in which self-control is not called upon to play any part.

There are, in the later stanzas of the *Selva seconda*, signs of a sensibility to nature and to the world of the open air which break through the moralising. His picture of man, in the Age of Gold, sleeping out of doors and waking at dawn with the animals and flowers, is striking in this respect:

> Il dolce sonno per gli erbosi letti
> è quando sanza sole à il nostro cielo:
> quando i raggi del sol le nebbie purgono,
> cogli animal, co' fiori insieme surgono.[1]

We have here not necessarily a source of Ronsard's favourite Age of Gold picture, but at least an illuminating parallel.

Ronsard certainly read, on the other hand, the *Arcadia* of Sannazaro, and the passage in that work where Opico sings of the Age of Gold as an era of lost happiness, with great feeling and melancholy, anticipates the mood in which Ronsard approached the theme. Whether he read it at a stage when it could have influenced his way of picturing the Age of Gold, is more doubtful.

There is direct evidence of imitating the song of Opico in the *Bergerie* which he composed in 1563 (for which he used to some extent at least the French translation by Jean Martin).[2] The speech of Navarrin in the *Bergerie* includes features which were new in Ronsard's picture of the Age of Gold, which are attributable to Sannazaro's work, such as the platonic concep-

---

[1] *Opere*, I, 278 (102).
[2] Lau. XIII, pp. xv–xvii and 101–3. See Alice Hulubei, *L'Eglogue en France au XVIe siècle*, pp. 481 ff.

tion of it as an era directly in contact with the gods and innocent of conflict between man and man or between man and beast. On the other hand, he made significant alterations: for instance, where Opico tells how the old men in the Age of Gold either took their own lives or regained their youth by taking magic herbs, Ronsard tones down the first alternative as follows:

> Les vieillars sans douleur sortoient de ceste vie
> Comme en songe, & leurs ans doucement finissoient.[1]

Moreover, Ronsard breaks off his imitation of the song of Opico at the point where Sannazaro begins to speak of the Age of Gold as a paradise of lovers without jealousy: there is nothing to correspond to the lines beginning 'I lieti amanti e le fanciulle tenere...'[2] The absence of love from the *Bergerie* (conspicuous in this example) has been adduced as evidence that the work could not have been composed for performance before the French court: instead (it has been argued) it was a show piece specially commissioned by Catherine de' Medici for presentation to her new ally Queen Elizabeth I, whose 'puritan' court would not have tolerated the introduction of love interest.[3] (The English court was surely not so strait-laced as all that?) As we have found Ronsard consistently omitting love from all his pictures of the Age of Gold, and the Age of Gold theme is so prominent in the *Bergerie*, it seems more natural to suppose that he omitted love-interest because he thought it inappropriate in an Age of Gold context.

Among the Italian poets who, like himself, treated the Age of Gold as irrecoverable, there was thus a store of ideas from which he drew some and rejected others.

It will be remembered that Ronsard's first serious treatment of the Age of Gold, *Les Isles Fortunées*, was not concerned with the past (whether primitive or civilised) at all, but with the present, a living paradise to which he and his friends might in fancy find the way.[4] There is just a hint of this notion in the final

---

[1] Lau. XIII, p. 102, lines 532–3.
[2] *Opere di Iacopo Sannazaro*, ed. E. Carrara (Turin, 1952), p. 105, lines 103 ff.
[3] Hulubei, *L'Eglogue en France au XVIᵉ siècle*, p. 490.
[4] See above, pp. 14–17.

episode of the hermit's discourse in Bembo's *Gli Asolani*,
Book III, the myth of the Queen of the Fortunate Isles; the hint
had been taken by the French neo-platonic poet Antoine Héroët
in his poem called *La parfaicte Amie* (1542), and combined with
direct reminiscences of Plato to make the following passage:

> On dict que pleine est une isle de biens
> D'arbres, de fruicts, de plaisante verdure,
> Qu'en elle a faict son chef d'œuvre Nature,
> Et qu'immortelz les hommes y vivants
> Sont touts plaisirs et delices suyvants.
> Là ne se rend ny jamais n'a esté
> Froydeur d'yver ny la chaleur d'esté.
> La saison est ung gracieux printemps
> Ou touts les plus malheureux sont contents.
> De son bon gré terre produict le bien,
> On ne dict poinct entre eulx ny tien ny mien;
> Tout est commun, sans peine et jalousie,
> Raison domine et non pas fantasie...
> Cette isle là se nomme fortunée
> Et, comme on dict, par Royne est gouvernée (etc.).[1]

Héroët was not only one of the most respected of the older
poets still writing when Ronsard and his friends began to
publish, but was expressly exempted by Ronsard (along with
Maurice Scève and Mellin de Saint-Gelais) from his condemna-
tion of all existing French poetry as 'foible & languissante' in
his preface *Au Lecteur* to *Les quatre premiers livres des Odes* in
1550.[2] It is possible therefore that this passage may have
played some part in inspiring the poem *Les Isles Fortunées*
which Ronsard published in 1553, also written in decasyllabic
couplets. It may also have been in his mind when he wrote, in
Les Armes, the couplet,

> Et lors on n'oyoit point ce mot de tien ne mien
> Tous vivoient en commun, car tous n'avoient qu'un bien.[3]

[1] Héroët, *Œuvres poétiques*, ed. F. Gohin, p. 48, lines 1044–56 and 1061–2.
Cf. the opening lines of the same poet's *L'Androgyne*.
[2] Lau. I, p. 46.
[3] Lau. VI, p. 205, lines 17–18.

The more we enlarge the field of investigation into the background to Ronsard's Age of Gold, the more possible sources of ideas and inspiration we encounter. Poetic tradition, and even more, literary tradition in general, far from presenting him with a threadbare commonplace, offered a group of ideas and images which was turned this way and that by writer after writer according to his tastes, his convictions and his conception of the ultimate happiness.

Comparison with other poets and with artists open to the same influences as himself will show how far his picture of the Age of Gold was from being the inevitable one.

3

Other representations of the Age of Gold in Ronsard's time

RONSARD'S FRIENDS AND FELLOW-POETS

Did Ronsard's friends and contemporaries write as often of the Age of Gold and in the same terms as he? The poets who produced enough to provide grounds for comparison were naturally all familiar with the theme, but rarely used it outside the time-honoured field of eulogy of a ruler or patron; when they did so, they were as likely as not to place the Age of Gold at some early and simple stage of civilisation or give it a significance of their own.

To give here the results of a complete survey of all the poetry of the time—even that written in the vernacular—would be tedious. The essential is to see what the poets did who were the most likely to anticipate or keep pace with Ronsard's own imaginations—those who shared his social background, his education and his literary tastes, and who (at the time particularly of his greatest interest in the Age of Gold) had taken part in the same discussions and exchange of literary ideas and works as he had himself.[1]

Ronsard perhaps experimented seriously for the first time with poetry when it became clear that he could not hope for a military or diplomatic career, the after-effects of an illness having left him partially deaf before he was twenty. His earliest confidant seems to have been Jacques Peletier du Mans, who recorded in his *Art Poétique* (1555) that Ronsard had shown

[1] On the writings and careers of the poets discussed in this section, and on their relations with Ronsard and with each other, see H. Chamard, *Histoire de la Pléiade* (Paris, 1939–40): the first volume of this work begins with a detailed bibliography.

him some of his poems when he was still a very young man. The occasion of this consultation was probably in March 1543, when Loys de Ronsard took his young son with him to Le Mans to attend the funeral of Guillaume du Bellay in the cathedral, and (seeing an ecclesiastical career as the only remaining opening to him) had the tonsure conferred upon him by the bishop. Peletier, who was the bishop's secretary, may well have entered into conversation with Ronsard at that time.

Certainly when Peletier published his own poems for the first time, in 1547,[1] he gave a prominent place in them to Ronsard. Out of the sixteen poems which are not dedications or translations, one is an ode to Ronsard inviting him on an excursion into the country; one is an ode to him *by* Ronsard, 'Des beautez qu'il voudroit en s'amie' (his first work to appear in print); and another is Peletier's reply to the latter, 'Des beautez & accomplissemens d'un Amant'.

The first of Peletier's 'vers lyriques de l'invention de l'auteur' (as opposed to translations and dedications) is a group of odes to the four seasons. The *Description du Printems* antici-pates in many ways the early *Avant-Venue du Printens* of Ronsard, even down to recalling the statement in *Georgics*, II that there was no winter but continual moist warm weather in the years when the world first began; there is, however, no attempt to link this with the Eternal Spring of the Age of Gold as Ronsard was to do.[2] The ode inviting Ronsard to a day in the country also ignores a possible opening for a reference to the Age of Gold: Peletier evokes the fields and streams in a quatrain of quite Ronsardian wording:

> Nous verrons le ruisseau
> Es prez faisant son tour,
> Avec maint arbrisseau
> Planté tout alentour,

but hastens to reassure his guest that the pure water is not going to be their drink. Since the ravages of marauding troops have left the villages destitute, Peletier intends to bring supplies of

---

[1] *Les Œuvres poétiques de Jacques Peletier du Mans*, éd. M. Françon (1958).
[2] *Ibid.* pp. 227–31. Cf. above, p. 10.

chicken and ham, to which he adds a bottle of good wine. With
a rueful reflection on the times they lived in, when townspeople
took food and drink to the country instead of the other way
round, he throws in a hope for the future:

> Or le temps reviendra
> En despit de rigueur,
> Qu'aux champs on se tiendra
> En joye et en vigueur...

but, far from idealising this return of prosperity as an Age of
Gold, he concludes on a personal and practical note—when it
came about, he and Ronsard would stay in the country without
sadness, whereas at present it is folly to go for more than a day.[1]
Peletier's poem *Des grans chaleurs de l'année 1547* (printed
immediately before Ronsard's Ode *Des Beautez qu'il voudroit
en s'amie*) inevitably brings to mind *A Dieu, pour la famine*,
according to Laumonier probably inspired by the famine of
1546, which would place it within a year of *Des grans chaleurs*.
But Peletier evokes the spectacle of the parched countryside,
expostulates with the Sun-god for his violence, and concludes
with a prayer to Juno 'de l'Air haute princesse' to send rain,
while Ronsard was to end *A Dieu, pour la famine* by proposing
that the deity should either divert the plague to the heathen or
bring back the Age of Gold when Nature provided all things
needful for humanity.[2] Peletier's eulogies and dedications, such
as the sonnet to Marguerite of France and the *Epistre au Roy
François premier* on the translation of Homer, both placed at the
head of his collected verse, or the *Congratulation sur le nouveau
regne de Henry II*, are innocent of any resort to the Age of Gold
theme:[3] Ronsard alluded to it in his poem on the forthcoming
Entry of Henry II into Paris in 1549, and used it in several
subsequent addresses to royalty and even to private persons.[4]

Still more significant is the comparison with Ronsard's
friends and fellow-poets, whose social background and outlook
strongly resembled his own, and who had shared the same

[1] *Op. cit.* pp. 243–7.   [2] *Ibid.* pp. 256–8. Cf. above, p. 10.
[3] *Ibid.* pp. 104–12, 268–71, etc.
[4] See above, pp. 8–9, and chapter I *passim*.

education: the other members of the 'Pléiade'. On the accession of Henry II (1547), Joachim du Bellay saluted the reign of Francis I for having restored the Age of Gold, because the king by his encouragement of learning had slain the monster Ignorance:

> Comment te peut assez chanter la France,
> O grand Françoys, des neuf Seurs adoré?
> Tu as defaict ce vil monstre Ignorance,
> Tu as refaict le bel aage doré.[1]

Ronsard seems to be adopting almost the very words of Du Bellay when he pays tribute in 1550 to the zeal of Jacques Bouju in promoting the same good cause, being,

> L'un de ceus qui ont defait
> Le villain monstre Ignorance
> Et le siecle d'or refait.[2]

The second edition of Du Bellay's *L'Olive* (1550) was dedicated to Princess Marguerite, sister of Henry II, in a sonnet apostrophising her as,

> O Vierge donc, sous qui la Vierge Astrée
> A faict encor' en nostre siecle entrée![3]

Here again, Ronsard seems at this period to follow suit, though more cautiously, in addressing the princess two years later as:

> Vierge, dont la vertu redore
> Cest heureux siecle qui t'adore...[4]

Du Bellay continued to use this device, for purposes of compliment, about as frequently as Ronsard, perhaps with more emphasis on the Age of Gold as a golden age of literature and learning, as well as an age of peace and prosperity.

In the *Musagnœomachie* (1550) celebrating the men of letters who were the ornaments of the age, he mentioned Jean Dorat and was unable to resist the obvious pun,

[1] 'Salutation prosphonegmatique au roy tres-chrestien Henry II, 1547', *Œuvres poétiques*, ed. H. Chamard, III, 70.
[2] Lau. II, p. 88, see above, pp. 11-12.
[3] *Œuvres poétiques*, ed. H. Chamard, I, 10.
[4] Lau. III, p. 105, see above, p. 12.

> Dorat, qui dore
> Ses vers, que Parnase adore,
> Dont l'art bien elabouré
> De l'or de Saturne encore
> A ce siecle redoré.[1]

Offering a New Year compliment to Pope Julius III (1554), he uttered the prayer:

> Vive la Vierge au vieux siecle adorée
> De Jupiter Saturne soit vainqueur,
> Regne Pallas sur le Dieu belliqueur,
> Cède le fer à la saison dorée.[2]

while his *étrennes* to his cousin Cardinal John Du Bellay express the hope that the New Year might open its gates to the virgin goddess Astraea,

> et refaire encor'
> Ce beau siecle d'or,
> Qui doroit la terre,
> Avant que la guerre
> Eust par art d'enfer
> Emoulu le fer...[3]

He wrote a sonnet to Mary, Queen of Scots, optimistically hoping that she might bring about the end of the age-old enmity between England and Scotland, and that

> par vous la belle Vierge Astrée
> En ce siecle de fer reface encor' entrée,
> Et qu'on revoye encor' le beau Siecle doré.[4]

and a similar compliment is pressed into service in honour of Marguerite, the king's sister, in *Les Regrets*, in (for instance) the sonnet beginning:

> Quand ceste belle fleur premierement je vey,
> Qui nostre aage de fer de ses vertus redore...[5]

Once he alludes to the reign of Augustus, and praises the Emperor for having remade the Age of Gold (an allusion to the

[1] *Œuvres poétiques*, ed. H. Chamard, IV, 15.   [2] *Ibid.* II, 264.
[3] *Ibid.* V, 325.   [4] *Ibid.* VI, 36.   [5] *Ibid.* II, 198.

prophecy in *Aeneid*, VI), but goes on to recall as an added reason for regarding it as the Age of Gold that 'one might say, it was under his Empire that the King of Kings was born'.[1] This reference to the birth of Christ, as having conferred supreme worth upon the earthly rule which held sway at the time of the event, occurs fleetingly, and a little incongruously, in a poem congratulating Henry II on the capture of Calais. It is sufficient to reveal a train of thought on the subject which seemed natural to Du Bellay but was quite alien to anything that we know of Ronsard.

On the other hand, opportunities to introduce the theme in other connections are sometimes disregarded. Thus in *Divers jeux rustiques* (also in 1558) there is a long poem, in four-line stanzas, called *Chant de l'Amour et du Primtemps*: here the poet calls upon Bacchus, Priapus and Ceres, Pales, Vertumnus and Pomona, and every god of the forests, to weave for themselves a coronet, and adds:

> Tel fut le siecle doré,
> Tel sera le nostre encore
> Dessoubz le sceptre honoré
> De Henry, qui le redore:
>
> Despouillant de ses butins
> La monstrueuse ignorance,
> Pour accabler les mutins
> Dessoubz les bras de la France.[2]

The association of the spring with the myth of the Age of Gold might have led to some idyllic passage, but instead it brings the poet back immediately to the benefits of the king's reign, in terms very similar to those he had used in 1549 to salute his accession,[3] and back to the theme of love and spring.

In his earliest published collection of verse, the sonnet sequence entitled *L'Olive* (1549) Du Bellay uttered the customary curse on the inventor of mining and metal-working, particularly (in this instance) the mining and working of gold, and blamed the discovery on the disappearance of 'L'antique

---

[1] *Ibid.* VI, 20.   [2] *Ibid.* V, 40–1.   [3] See above, p. 95.

foy, et la justice aussi'.[1] The only considerable reference to this aspect of the Age of Gold occurs in one of his Latin poems, *De pace inter principes christianos ineunda*, published on his return from Italy (1558) and referring to the negotiations which were to result in the Treaty of Cateau-Cambrésis. The appeal for a speedy peace is heartfelt, but the Age of Gold is invoked only in the conventional Ovidian terms: there was no use of iron, no sound of trumpets, no locking of houses or dividing of fields, no money and no mining, and the earth gave riches of her own accord, without being ploughed.[2] This passage appears to be the only one in his poetry which offers any scope for comparison with Ronsard's treatment of the theme; and not only is it too late to have played any part in focusing Ronsard's attention on the subject—the key passages in *Les Armes* and the *Hymne de la Justice* had been in print since 1555—but it lacks the characteristic Ronsardian emphasis on the wandering and forest-dwelling habits of the Age of Gold. There may have been an influence of Ronsard on Du Bellay. More probably—Du Bellay having been in Italy from April 1553 in the household of his cousin Cardinal Jean du Bellay—Du Bellay's poem was arrived at independently, the Age of Gold being already a stock device for celebrating such occasions as the signing of a treaty.

Jean-Antoine de Baïf published in 1555 a charming sonnet on the Age of Gold, which is thus exactly contemporary with the passages on the Age of Gold in *Les Armes* and *L'Hymne de la Justice*. In contrast to Ronsard, however, his picture is of luxury and love, and takes its place among the *Amours de Francine*, his counterpart to Ronsard's sonnets to Cassandre:

> Que le siecle revinst de celle gent dorée
>   Quand les ruisseaux de vin par les prez se rouloyent,
>   Les sourgeons de doux lait hors des roches couloyent,
>   La terre portoit tout sans estre labourée;
> Quand l'amant & l'amie en franchise asseurée
>   Par les bocages frais sans soupson s'en aloyent:
>   Ou mussez sous l'ombrage, à l'heure qu'ils vouloyent,

---

[1] *Œuvres poétiques*, ed. H. Chamard, I, 113 (sonnet CI).
[2] *Poésies françaises et latines*, ed. E. Courbet, I, 440–1.

Ils flatoyent de plaisir leur ame enamourée:
Souvent, Dieux de ces bois, avecques ma Francine
Vous me verriez icy; O Nymphe Iobertine,
Souvent tu nous verrois nous laver de tes eaux.
Mais ô siècle de fer qui l'amour desassemble,
Ta mauvaise façon nous garde d'estre ensemble,
Et seul me fait languir parmy ces arbrisseaux.[1]

In a poem *Sur la Paix avec les Anglois*, dated 1549 but not
published until the collected edition of his poetry in 1573, he
wrote, referring to Henry II,

J'entend déjà la joieuse nouvelle
Du siecle d'or, qui sous luy renouvelle...

and proceeded to hymn the reign of Saturn:

Lors que n'estoit le sapin abatu,
Lors que le pin des flots marins batu
Au gré du vent ne souloit se ranger
Au nouveau sein du rivage étranger:
Encor n'estoient ceints de parfondes fosses
Les bourgs peuplez, ne de murailles grosses:
Encor n'estoyent ne sagettes ny arcs
Ne morrions ne trompettes ne dars:
Ains toutes gens vivoyent hors de tout soin
Sans point avoir du gendarme besoin
Et sans avoir nulle atteinte mauvaise
Comme dormans ils mouroyent à leur aise,

not neglecting to add: 'Maudit, par qui fut le fer deterré', etc.[2]
If Baïf indeed wrote these lines in 1549 they represent an
attempt at a descriptive passage on the Age of Gold earlier than
any composed by Ronsard, and may have helped to arouse
Ronsard's interest in the theme. It will, however, be noticed
that Baïf allows 'bourgs peuplez' in his Age of Gold, a concep-

[1] Baïf, *EUvres en rime*, ed. Ch. Marty-Laveaux, I, 107. Cf. the lines in the
earlier *Amours de Méline* (1552):
Siecle de fer! quand les dames cruelles,
Ne pour prier ne pour la loyauté
De leurs esclaves plus fidelles
N'adoucissent leur cruauté... (*Ibid.* p. 22).
[2] Baïf, *ibid.* II, 404–5.

tion far removed from Ronsard's wandering forest-dwellers; apart from the absence of sea-faring, his Age of Gold is simply an Age of Peace. A distinctive feature none the less may be detected in one detail: that the people of the Age of Gold died as if going to sleep. This point, derived from Hesiod, is never made by Ronsard (except in the *Bergerie*) though he knew the source as well as Baïf did.

In a lighter vein, Baïf assured Rémy Belleau, another poet of the Pléiade circle, of his friendship, playfully claiming that it could only come direct to them from Heaven since sincere friendship (once, in the Age of Gold, well known to men, like virtue and pity) had deserted the earth with Astraea.[1] Later, in one of the *Eclogues*, imitating Virgil, he told how Pan had sung of the creation of the world, finally describing how men, at first living wild, had abandoned the fruits of the forest for the presents of Ceres:

> Puis des hommes le genre, & leur âge dorée
> Qui sauvage vagoit par les bois égarée,
> Vivant des glans cueilliz: & comme des forests
> Ils quitterent les fruits pour les dons de Cerés...[2]

This was written when Ronsard's portrayal of the Age of Gold was already well known. Baïf did not, however, share Ronsard's belief that men were better off before they learnt to plough and sow. Indeed he treats it as axiomatic that no one would live on acorns if they could get flour:

> Puis l'eure ke Sérês
> Aus mortels a doné le froumant, ki rechêrche le vieu glan?[3]

Rémy Belleau, who made his début in Ronsard's *Bocage* of 1554 with a 'blason' (celebration, in octosyllabic couplets) of the Butterfly,[4] contributed more 'blasons' to the *Continuation des Amours* of Ronsard in 1555, one on the subject of the Cherry.[5]

---

[1] Baïf, *op. cit.* II, 401. [2] *Ibid.* III, 53.
[3] *Ibid.* V, 299. *Au roé*, first poem in *Etrenes de poezie fransoeze* (1574), written in quantitative verse and printed in Baïf's phonetic spelling.
[4] Lau. VI, pp. 97–101.
[5] Lau. VII, pp. 207–11. See also *L'Heure*, *ibid.* pp. 204–7, and *L'Escargot*, pp. 216–20.

When he reprinted the 'blason' of the Cherry in the first collection of his own verse, the *Petites Inventions* following his translations from Anacreon (1556), Belleau inserted into it an allusion to the Age of Gold. Describing how the gods competed with one another to improve the lot of man 'in that good and famous former age', he tells how Bacchus invented wine where mankind had hitherto shared the common drink 'qu'avions à la beste sauvage', how Ceres taught them how to till the earth where they had hitherto depended on 'ceste brutale pasture / De glans broyez', etc. The god of gardens, not to be outdone by his grander colleagues, promptly invented the cherry.[1] It is likely that Ronsard's poems *Les Armes* and the *Hymne de la Justice* were known to Belleau as soon as they were printed (if not before) and that they suggested to him the addition of this episode to the original text of *La Cerise*. The firmly anti-primitivist view he takes is the more noteworthy. In his most famous work, *La Bergerie* (1565), Belleau made no mention of the Age of Gold, though in this fantasy freely imitated from the *Arcadia* of Sannazaro and celebrating the castle and grounds of Joinville he had ample opportunity to do so. And in *Les Amours et nouveaux eschanges des pierres precieuses* (1576) he was to hymn a succession of precious and semi-precious stones, nearly all, naturally, to be obtained only by mining: this led him to express very different views from Ronsard on the supposed sacrilege of rifling treasure which mother Nature had intended to remain hidden. Thus he said of the magnet:

> se nourrist és minieres,
> Prend la force et le pois des terres ferronnieres:
> Nature ne voulant cacher dedans son sein
> Le bien qui sert à l'homme, et qui luy fait besoin.[2]

Olivier de Magny, finding himself committed to praising *Monseigneur le garde des seaulx de France*, in 1553, availed himself of the convention by which legal dignitaries were credited with having reinstated the Age of Gold (this being particularly the age of justice, symbolised by Astraea), and assured him that:

[1] *Poètes du XVIᵉ siècle*, ed. A. M. Schmidt, pp. 548–9.
[2] *Ibid.* p. 588.

> en ton chef la belle Astrée gist,
> Et prudamment en la Gaule regit...[1]

A more ambitious development of this theme is to be found in Magny's *Ode de la Justice*, 'A Monsieur d'Avanson, premier président au Grand Conseil du Roy, en faveur de Pierre de Paschal', the first poem in Book II of his *Odes* (1559).[2] The first fourteen stanzas paraphrase the story of the Four Ages as told by Ovid. After this, the character of Astraea is introduced, at the moment of her flight to Heaven. She and her retinue appear before the throne of Jupiter in indignation. The father of the gods eventually pacifies her by prophesying how Henry II, with D'Avanson at his right hand, will restore her to her rightful place on Earth. The poem ends with praise of D'Avanson and with a plea for his support of Paschal, who was engaged in a troublesome lawsuit. The ode shows some affinities with Ronsard's *Ode à Michel de l'Hospital* (1552)[3] with its account of the Muses' visit to Jupiter, and even more affinities with the *Hymne de la Justice* (1555);[4] while we have no terminus a quo for the composition of Magny's *Ode de la Justice*, it is likely that he had in fact read both these poems of Ronsard by the time he wrote it. It is the more noticeable that the description of the Age of Gold lacks the more distinctive elements beloved by Ronsard. Mankind lived happily without travail or care, for the earth gave abundantly whatever was required without trouble. But early man's bliss was untouched —a Hesiodic touch—by devouring fever or by wan old age, and the landscape was frankly fanciful—rivers running nectar, the fountains milk, streams honey, and a climate without winter. The woodland scene, the explicit diet of raw food, the absence of settled homes or private property—these features, beloved of Ronsard, have no place here.

Magny was also capable of referring to the age in which he lived as an Age of Iron:

---

[1] *Les Amours*, ed. Courbet, p. 119.
[2] *Les Odes*, ed. Courbet, I, 74 ff.
[3] Lau. III, pp. 118–63.
[4] Lau. VIII, pp. 47–72. Cf. above, pp. 21–2.

> Le siècle où nous vivons est voirement de fer,
> Et le fer voirement est venu de l'enfer...[1]

and of implying that Health is the great giver of well-being in whatever age we live.[2]

Magny made a more novel use of the convention in writing against Pope Julius III, whose reign he denounced so heartily as an Age of Iron that his death was in itself a portent of the return of the Age of Gold—something of an inversion of the usual compliment.[3] He was also capable of using formulae normally associated with the Age of Gold to describe not merely the Elysian Fields but the Christian after-life, for he wrote to François Pesloe an ode 'on the death of his sister' evoking the blessed state of the holy souls:

> Toujours la saison y est une,
> Et toujours le Soleil, la Lune,
> Et les Astres y sont tous uns:
> Mesmes de fruictz & fleurs les plaines,
> Y sont toujours largement pleines,
> Et les biens y sont tous communs.[4]

This extension of the Age of Gold idea is never found in Ronsard.

Most of these poets show a professional interest in the concept of the Age of Gold as a literary Golden Age.

Du Bellay did not hesitate to represent the work of a friend and fellow-poet—Ronsard—as a manifestation of the Age of Gold returning:

> Le siecle d'or qui pour se redorer
> Dore tes vers du plus fin or du monde
> Me faict ici par l'or de ta faconde
> En mon esprit ton esprit adorer...[5]   (1552.)

Magny praised Hugues Salel, the translator of Homer, for his contribution to the overthrow of ignorance and the restoration

---

[1] Magny, *Les Odes*, ed. Courbet, I, 47. For the play on words, cf. Ronsard, *Les Armes*, 'Quiconque a le premier des enfers deterré / Le fer, estoit, Brinon, lui mesme bien ferré' (1555).
[2] Magny, *Les Odes*, ed. Courbet, I, 39.   [3] *Ibid.* I, 138 (*Sur la mort de I.P.T.*).
[4] *Ibid.* II, 70.   [5] Lau. IV, p. 179.

of the Age of Gold in terms which made the brilliant activity
of the nine Muses the particular characteristic of that age:

> ...Qui as destruit & combatu
> Le superbe monstre ignorance,
> Faisant par ton savoir encor
> Renaistre ce beau siecle d'or
> Où plus brilloient les estincelles
> De la fureur des neuf Pucelles...[1] (1553.)

and Jacques Tahureau frankly congratulated the children of the
royal family on their good fortune in living at a time when
there were so many gifted men of letters available to sing their
praises:

> Heureux, vrayment, de voyr cet age d'or
> Je vous estime...[2] (1554.)

Pontus de Tyard alluded to the return of the Age of Gold as
being in progress under the reign of Henry II, because the king
gave honours and rewards in equal share to valour and to
learning: this allusion was made as an encouragement to poets,
in his *Chant en faveur de quelques excellens poetes de ce temps*:

> Qui l'honneur deu va baillant
> Et au docte & au vaillant:
> Et qui le siecle peri
> (Siecle d'or,) va recueillant.[3] (1555.)

But he looked for the return of the Age of Gold above all as
an age when greed and dissimulation would be banished, as
well as ignorance, when the goddess of Hate, Até, 'who, in the
age we live in, paves her floor with the scalps of men', would
flee before the radiant advent of Astraea, and would return to
Hades whence she came:

---

[1] *A Monseigneur de Saint-Cheron*, printed in the group of odes following the
sonnets to Castianire, *Les Amours*, ed. E. Courbet (1878), p. 127.

[2] Tahureau, *Les premieres poésies*, f. B8ᵇ.

[3] Tyard *Œuvres poétiques complètes*, éd. John C. Lapp (STFM), 1966,
pp. 157–8, where the text is based on the collected edition of Tyard's
Œuvres poétiques (1573). The original edition was *Erreurs amoureuses, augmentées d'une tierce partie, plus Un livre de Vers Liriques*, Lyon (Jean de Tournes),
1555, 8°, where the text is the same for this ode apart from differences of
spelling (p. 103).

> Mais je desirerois bien
> Que la verité cachée,
> Songneusement arrachée
> Du noir Puits Cimmerien,
> Avec l'or Saturnien,
> Veinssent redorer nostre aage,
> Qui par l'altéré souci
> De l'Avarice, et l'outrage
> De l'ignorance est noirci...

> La molle deesse Até
> Qui fait au siecle où nous sommes
> Son pavé des chefs des hommes,
> Gluant à l'humanité
> La triste calamité,
> Dans les Abismes r'entrée
> Fuiroit l'esclair radieux
> Duquel l'equitable Astrée
> Viendroit esclairer noz yeux.[1]

That intellectual uprightness and clear-headedness would be characteristic of the Age of Gold is an idea natural to a neo-Platonist like Tyard. His conception of it was none the less different from that of, say, Lorenzo de' Medici,[2] in that it related to his own age (not to a lost age in the remote past, never to return) and indeed he denounced specific intellectual and moral failings which were poisoning society.[3]

Ronsard was very conscious of the revival of French poetry which was taking place in his time and to some extent under his leadership. Nowhere, however, does he speak of this in terms of a 'Golden Age' of French poetry; the idea is quite absent from such a poem as the *Elégie à J. de La Péruse* (1553) in which he records the achievements up to date of himself, Du Bellay, Tyard, Baïf, Des Autels, and Jodelle.[4]

Were Ronsard's favourite picture of the Age of Gold to be the obvious one to poets of his generation and upbringing, we

---

[1] Ode, *Du Socratique, ibid.* pp. 172–3.
[2] See above, pp. 86–8.
[3] Cf. *LeSiècle doré* of Guillaume Michel (see above, pp. 3–5), which was published in 1521, the year of Tyard's birth.
[4] Lau. v, pp. 259–65.

should expect to find it, if we find it anywhere, in the sylvan songs and eclogues of Jean Vauquelin de La Fresnaye, *Les Foresteries*, published in 1555, the same year as *Les Armes* and the *Hymne de la Justice*. Vauquelin, stimulated by the provincial literary circles he had been frequenting at Poitiers, combined some real naturalistic freshness with ambitions to follow fashions set by the Pléiade. The only specific reference to the Age of Gold in the *Foresteries* occurs in fact in the quatrain:

> Mon cher Buquet dont la doctrine sainte
> Comme en tableaus aus Forests je voi peints:
> Forests vraiment qui chanteront encor'
> Le divin siecle d'or,[1]

in which it seems to be rather the virtues of Buquet's works, displayed on votive tablets hung upon the trees, which will cause the forests to sing, than their own recollections of having been the scene of that happy state. There is indeed a reference to the 'siecle ancien' when humanity lived on acorns, but Vauquelin is naive enough to show why such a state of things could not normally be acceptable to him and his contemporaries as the Age of Gold: addressing the Hollow Oak of Perrin, he praises its acorns, and asks:

> Pourquoi n'en vivroit on bien
> Puisque le siecle ancien
> En faisoit sa nourriture
> Comme les porcs leur pâture?[2]

Acorns were pig-food. So strong was the association (when the sole alternative for winter feeding was grain, fed only to beasts intended for the luxury market), and so familiar the spectacle of the pigs feeding in the forests, that Vauquelin's remark is wholly natural. Experts like Malleville solemnly quoted Aristotle for the opinion that acorns were the true diet of pigs, noxious to other animals.[3]

[1] J. Vauquelin de La Fresnaye, *Les Foresteries*, ed. Bensimon, p. 134.
[2] *Ibid.* pp. 83–4.
[3] Claude de Malleville, *In regies aquarum et silvarum constitutionis commentarius* (1561), f. 22ᵇ. Cf. M. Devèze, *La vie de la forêt française au XVIᵉ siècle* (1961), I, 88–92.

Acorns (edible to human beings, but very nasty) were by the same token the last resort of people desperate with hunger. The eating of them thus also had the association of famine or of direst poverty. The twelfth-century poet Béroul, telling of the hardships endured by Tristan and Iseut in the forest in hiding from King Mark, was careful to describe how their food was supplied by Tristan's prowess as a hunter. He could go no further, to represent Tristan's utter infatuation with the queen, than to make him say, 'Rather would I be a beggar, and live on grass and acorns, with her, than own the realm of King Otran' (the fabulously wealthy Saracen despot of legend).[1]

Only a poet with a very personal vision of the earliest and happiest state of man would have braved the risk of ridicule to the extent that Ronsard did, in making this despised and bitter food the diet of the Age of Gold.

The sight of a handful of acorns was enough to set Don Quixote off on his famous oration on the Age of Gold:

Happy times, and happy ages! those to which the ancients gave the name of golden, not because gold (which in this our iron age is so much esteemed) was to be had in that fortunate period without toil and labour; but because they who then lived were ignorant of these two words, *meum* and *tuum*. In that age of innocence all things were in common: no one needed to take any other pains for his ordinary sustenance than to lift up his hand and take it from the sturdy oaks, which stood inviting him liberally to taste of their sweet and relishing fruit...[2]

No wonder the goat-herds, whose hearty meal he had just shared, thought he was mad. Would even he have been able to produce this particular association of ideas, had Ronsard not pioneered it a generation before?

[1]
> Mex aim o il estre mendis
> et vivre d'erbes et de glan,
> qu'avoir le reigne au roi Otran.

Le Roman de Tristran, by Béroul, ed. A. Ewert (Oxford, 1939), I, lines 1404–6.

[2] *Don Quixote*, Book II, chap. III (Jarvis's translation). For Cervantes' ironical reference to the sweetness of the acorn, cf. Part II, chap. LXVII, 'The oaks with a bounteous hand shall give their sweetest fruit', etc.

Other representations

Ronsard spoke of himself in the early poem, *A son luc*, as

> Poëte de nature,
> Idolatrant la musique, & peinture...[1]

Two of the 1550 Odes refer to paintings, both of mythological subjects. In *A son lict* (II, xxvii), the lines beginning

> Qui a point veu Mars & Venus
> Dans un tableau portraits tous nus...[2]

sound distinctly like a recollection of a picture he had seen, and the following *Des peintures contenues dans un tableau* (II, xxviii) describes a picture celebrating the Entry of Henry II into Paris by an elaborate political allegory. The latter is also mythological, in its treatment of the subject: the Cyclops are seen at work forging the armour of the gods, while Jupiter sits in the clouds directing a thunderstorm at the fleet of the Emperor Charles V; another episode shows Juno, with the help of Venus and the Amores, persuading Jupiter to make love to her and so ensuring the return of spring. Ronsard emphasises particularly the lifelike representation of the exertions of the Cyclops at their forge, and the colouring of the sea.[3]

He counted at least one painter, though not of the first rank, among his circle of friends: Nicolas Denisot of Le Mans,[4] and praised him for being painter and poet too. He indeed represented himself in the *Amours* carrying round with him a miniature which Denisot had painted for him of Cassandre.[5] To François Clouet, called Janet, the King's Painter, he gave detailed instructions for a portrait of Cassandre. This may be no more than an amusing device for enumerating the lady's

---

[1] Published in the *Bocage* (printed after the *Odes*) of 1550. Lau. II, p. 157, lines 25–6, cf. pp. 160–1, lines 81–100 on the art of painting. Cf. Jean Adhémar, 'Ronsard et l'Ecole de Fontainebleau', *BHR*, xx (1958), 344–8.

[2] Lau. I, p. 258, lines 9–16.   [3] *Ibid.* pp. 259–64.

[4] See Lau. III, p. 47, n. 4, and p. 182, n. 2. For Ronsard's Ode to Denisot, *ibid.* pp. 177–83.

[5] Sonnet, 'Le plus toffu d'un solitaire boys' in the *Amours* (1552), Lau. IV, pp. 13–14.

charms, and not even an original device at that, but the poet's chatter to the artist shows 'how seriously he conceived the whole figure in terms of actual painting' and of actual paintings by Clouet.[1]

The opportunities which he enjoyed of seeing the great paintings of the period were admittedly few, in comparison with those open to anyone who had been in Italy. The riches of the palace of Fontainebleau he must, however, certainly have known. The poet who wrote *La défloration de Lède*[2] in 1550 could there have seen the lost masterpiece of Leonardo da Vinci, Leda and the Swan.

In view of this interest in the visual arts, and of his own lively visual imagination, it may be useful to inquire how the Age of Gold theme was treated by artists.

The only representations of the subject likely to have been available to him, at the period when his own conception of it was first formed, were illustrations in books.

Most significant among these are perhaps the miniatures which he might have seen in manuscripts of the *Roman de la Rose*.[3]

Most manuscripts do not illustrate this episode at all. It does not figure, for instance, among the sixty-four miniatures in Cod. 2592 in the National Library, Vienna, carried out in the first half of the fourteenth century in Paris.[4] On the other hand, it is given particular prominence in another splendid copy, also in the National Library, Vienna, Cod. 2568, dating from the first thirty years of the fifteenth century. Here, on f. 63ᵃ, under the heading 'Cy fait mention du bon temps de jadis de l'aage dorée', a panoramic scene of Golden Age life appears above the

---

[1] *Elégie à Janet peintre du Roi*, in the *Meslanges* (1555), Lau. VI, pp. 152–60. See R. A. Sayce, 'Ronsard and Mannerism: the *Elégie à Janet*', *L'Esprit Créateur*, VI (1966), 234–47.

[2] Lau. II, pp. 67–79 (*Odes*, III, xxv).

[3] For the Age of Gold in the *Roman de la Rose*, and for Ronsard's acquaintance with the poem, see above, pp. 78–81.

[4] See A. Kuhn, 'Die Illustrationen des Rosenromans', *Jahrbuch der kunsthistorischen Sammlungen in Wien*, XXXI (1912), and, for the MSS of the *Roman* in general, see E. Langlois, *Les manuscrits du Roman de la Rose: description et classement* (Paris, 1911).

opening lines of Jean de Meung's description, 'Jadis au temps des premiers peres, etc.' (lines 8355 ff.). This occupies almost half the page, and is more than twice the size of all the other miniatures in the manuscript, except the frontispiece. The artist has, in fact, whether on his own initiative or on the instructions of his patron, gone to special trouble to illustrate this subject.[1] Under a bright blue sky, against a background of distant hills and abrupt pink rocks, a stream winds its way among green meadows strewn with flowers into the centre foreground, where a tree bearing golden fruit stands upon its bank. Human beings, clad in skins leaving bare the legs and arms, converse with one another from the entrances of wattle shelters or from caves, or move about the meadow gathering food and eating; a man climbs the tree in the foreground and picks its fruit. Men, girls and children are included in the scene. Following Jean de Meung, the artist shows no family life. On the other hand, he does not in any way emphasise love-making: only one couple is shown, standing some way up the stream, in close conversation or perhaps actually kissing. This reticence antici-pates Ronsard's treatment of the theme. But the scene preserves one feature of Jean de Meung's Age of Gold quite alien to Ronsard's: the provision of artificially constructed human dwellings. And the scenery is very different to the forest which feeds and shelters Ronsard's Age of Gold people. The stylised hills in the miniature recall the jagged crags of Giovanni di Paolo's Sienese landscapes,[2] rather than the glades of oak-trees evoked by Ronsard's poetry. The proximity of the woods is, on the other hand, emphasised in the very pretty miniature representing the same subject in Douce 195 in the Bodleian Library, a manuscript prepared, probably by Robinet Testard, for Louise of Savoy, the mother of Francis I:[3] the grove of brilliant green trees on the left of the picture, with their scarlet fruit, and the trees on the hill-side on the right, under a cloud-

---

[1] See Plate 2.
[2] E.g. *St John Baptist entering the Wilderness*, National Gallery, London.
[3] Otto Pächt and J. J. G. Alexander, *Illuminated manuscripts in the Bodleian Library, Oxford*, I, German, Dutch, Flemish, French and Spanish Schools (Clarendon Press, Oxford, 1966), cat. no. 787 (f. 59[b]). Cf. BM Harley MS 4425, f. 70[b].

less sky, occupy indeed most of the scene, since the artist has restricted himself to truly miniature dimensions for this subject (though the manuscript includes several illustrations on a larger scale). Indications of Golden Age life have to be correspondingly selective. On the side nearest the grove, an old man holds a long stick (presumably to knock down the fruit) while a fat boy walks away from him carrying some of the fruit in a bag slung round his neck. On the opposite slope a girl and a young man sit embracing, in front of a cave which may or may not be their dwelling. Interest is thus evenly divided between food-gathering and love-making. In addition, animals are introduced into the scene: two sheep graze on the hill-side (possibly suggesting the beginnings of a pastoral society), and in the foreground stands a lamb, in the attitude usually chosen for representations of the Agnus Dei, and perhaps symbolising innocence. The clothing of the human figures is similar to that of the miniature in Vienna Cod. 2568—loose tunics of skins or fleece—but the style of it is more elegant and the girl wears a green garland on her head. Other artists, confronted with the task of depicting the Age of Gold on so small a scale, standardised on a scene of love-making: 'three pairs of youths and maidens...among trees with birds in them' is the courtly formula adopted by one fourteenth-century miniaturist.[1]

Though a miniature such as one of these, if seen by Ronsard, might have helped to arouse his interest in the theme, they do not suggest a concept of it very like his, nor indeed any uniformity of tradition in their iconography. The illustrated printed editions of the *Roman*[2] offered at best a crude picture of people sleeping huddled together on the ground fully dressed.

Illustrations in the printed editions of Ovid's *Metamorphoses*, of which the most important set was that of Bernard Salomon for *La métamorphose d'Ovide figurée*,[3] offer some scope for comparison. They were, however, conceived as a series illustrating the Four Ages. The Age of Gold may thus be shown

[1] *Pierpont Morgan Library Catalogue* (1909), no. 112, miniature no. 25, f. 59.
[2] See F. W. Bourdillon, *The early editions of the Roman de la Rose* (1906).
[3] Lyon (J. de Tournes), 1557, 8°. See Fig. 8, *a, b, c*.

Figure 8*a*. Bernard Salomon's illustrations of the
Four Ages: Age of Gold
La vita e metamorfoseo d'Ovidio figurato, Lyon, 1557, 8°

simply as a countryside in which pairs of comely lovers sit or
walk or pluck fruit from the trees. The Age of Silver is represented by a scene of ploughing. The Age of Iron is characterised
by armies setting out to war and brigands attacking defenceless
travellers, against a background of walled cities and of sea-
coasts crowded with sailing ships.

The Four Ages would appear to form, like the Four Seasons,
a scheme which might appeal to the artists of the Fontainebleau
School with their lavish use of mythological subjects for
decorative purposes. The subject does not, however, seem to
have been treated by French artists in Ronsard's lifetime except
in the medium of book illustration.

Humanist circles were on the other hand sufficiently inter-

L'età dell' Ariento.   4

In tal beatitudine terrena
(*Ciò che fan l'otio & l'abbondanza infieme*)
L'ingrata gente, di fuperbia piena,
Pofe in fe ftiffa (Iddio lafciando) ffeme.
Ond' ei tofto turbò l'aria ferena,
Et tolfe al campo il natural fuo feme,
Tal che fu forza all'huom, primo d'amore,
Viuer' al caldo, e al giel del fuo fudore.

Figure 8*b*. Bernard Salomon's illustrations of the
Four Ages: Age of Silver

national for any artist working under their patronage to provide
a point of comparison with the picture of the Age of Gold
offered by his poetry. And Lucas Cranach the Elder produced
about 1530 an easel picture of the subject, which was evidently
popular, for there are no less than three extant versions of it.[1]
All these, with minor variations, show a gay and graceful
scene of elegant couples in a walled garden full of flowers and

[1] M. J. Friedländer and Jacob Rosenberg, *Die Gemälde von Lucas Cranach*
(Berlin, 1932), recorded two (nos. 213 and 214), of which the first was then
in Dresden (Samml. O. Weissenberger) and the second in Oslo (National-
galerie). The first was also reproduced by Hans Posse, *Lucas Cranach der Ä.*
(Vienna, 1942), plate 90 and pp. 32 and 62; it was by then in Berlin (Galerie
Haberstock). A third, dated 1534 on the fountain, was lent to the exhibition
Between Renaissance and Baroque at the City Art Gallery, Manchester, 1965
(cat. no. 78) by Col. W. R. Crawshay.

L'età del Rame & del Ferro.   5

L'insolito trauaglio & la pigritia
Moleftar tanto i miseri mortali,
Che, prepofto all' Aratro la militia,
Diuentar i'vn dell' altro micidiali.
Crefcendo poi con l'oro l'auaritia,
Sentì la Terra innumerabil' mali,
Quai furno (ai dura & mal cangiata forte)
Odio, inganno, timor, dolore, & marte.
                                                    b

Figure 8c. Bernard Salomon's illustrations of the
Four Ages: Age of Bronze and Iron

shrubs and fruit-trees, all the figures being nude (except for
necklaces worn by some of the ladies). Three men and three
women, holding hands, dance round a tree; other couples sit
and eat fruit and converse, and another pair bathe in the stream
which runs down into the foreground, the lady roguishly
splashing the gentleman with water. The animal creation enters
into the spirit of the party: couples of birds and beasts may be
seen fondling each other, including a lion and lioness who may
symbolise peace between all creatures. The presence of the
wall, and of feudal castles on the distant mountain-tops, suggests
no very serious attempt to depict some early stage of human
history: if the knights and ladies of the castles had cast off their
clothes and their inhibitions and determined to spend a summer

114

afternoon playing at the Age of Gold, they would not have looked much different. The conception is primarily that of a paradise of lovers. The *hortus inclusus* depicted has some affinities with the *paradiesgärtlein* beloved of late gothic painters. More than thirty years later, in Florence, a pen and ink drawing of the Età dell'Oro was produced by Giorgio Vasari,[1] only some fourteen years older than Ronsard and belonging to a world of humanist learning and classical taste even closer to Ronsard's than to that of the court of Wittenberg. The *invenzione* for this drawing was provided by Vincenzio Borghini and was dated 1567. Vasari and Borghini had collaborated in planning the pageant of the Genealogy of the Gods which took place in Florence, 21 February 1566, as part of the festivities for the wedding of Francesco de' Medici and Joanna of Austria, Vasari being responsible on that occasion for the design of the twenty-one floats and the costumes of the 392 mythological or allegorical figures forming the procession. Vasari was very familiar with the ceremonies attending the previous Medici ducal marriage, that of Cosimo I and Eleanor of Toledo in 1539, and the motto displayed at the top of his drawing of the Age of Gold, 'O begli anni dell'oro', is a quotation of a canzonetta sung at the 1539 festivities.[2] The 1566 pageant included a float symbolising the reign of Saturn (in whose suite featured the Golden Age),[3] and it is not surprising that the subject of the Age of Gold was in his mind in 1567, though the picture presumably planned in the drawing was never (as far as is known) carried out.

Vasari sketched a smiling landscape of hills, woods, meadows and streams, in which graceful human figures (all nude) are dispersed in such a way as to suggest not only pairs of lovers but also parties dancing, bathing or picnicking, children playing alone or together, and in one case a group of three different generations, suggesting a family. The ease with which food is got is shown by the child who has climbed a tree on the right

[1] Louvre, Inventory No. 2170. See P. Barocchi, *Il Vasari pittore* (Florence, 1964), pl. 92, and notes on pp. 141–2.
[2] See above, p. 7.
[3] See A. M. Nagler, *Theatre festivals of the Medici 1539–1637*, pp. 13–48.

of the picture and is throwing fruit down from it to other children, whose eager faces can be seen upturned, looking through the foliage. Peace between the animals, and peace between man and beast, is symbolised by a hound and hart lying down together, and by a long-suffering lion who submits to being kissed by a rabbit and ridden by a small boy who whacks his flanks with a bunch of flowers; the closeness of the gods to men is seen in the river divinity who presides on a distant mountain side over the source of the stream running down through the landscape into the foreground of the picture, and by the figures of Apollo, etc. floating just above the horizon, while a scroll is held forward by the winged figure, bearing the words 'O begli anni dell'oro'. Apart from the shepherd on a hillside who pipes for the dancers circling round a nearby tree—a small concession to the pastoral tradition—the picture consistently depicts humanity in an idle and idyllic 'natural' stage.

It is quite distinct, in its classical grace and serenity, from the weird and wild life of early man as Piero di Cosimo had represented it with 'primitivist' realism,[1] a generation before. This is not surprising, when it is remembered that Vasari's *Life* of Piero described that artist's way of life, dictated by the same almost atavistic obsession with the 'natural' as his pictures, as 'una vita da uomo piuttosto bestiale che umano'. On the other hand, in his attempted abstention from showing even the beginnings of technological progress, Vasari differs also from the artist who had illustrated the Como edition of Vitruvius, *De Architectura* (1521), and who had represented the stage of evolution described by Vitruvius when men first learnt the use of fire, of speech, of dwellings, and of family life, by a camp-fire scene which he calls *Aurea aetas*.[2]

The painting by Vasari's disciple Jacopo Zucchi,[3] one of three

---

[1] E. Panofsky, *Studies in iconology: humanistic themes in the art of the Renaissance* (New York, 1939), chap. ii, 'The early history of man in two cycles of paintings by Piero di Cosimo'.
[2] *Ibid.* pp. 39–44 and pl. x.
[3] See H. Voss, *Die Malerei der Spätrenaissance in Rom und Florenz*, 2 vols. (Berlin, 1920), ii, p. 319 and fig. 113.

small pictures now in the Uffizi (the other two showing the Age of Silver and the Age of Iron) follows the general plan of the Vasari drawing, including the display of the motto 'O begli anni dell'oro' on a scroll. Zucchi too showed a ring of dancers (in this case back to back, holding hands) and made much of the stream, in which people embraced or bathed. Unlike Vasari he included no group which could be regarded as a family; the fact indeed that he depicted two cases of a woman alone with a baby—one on the river-bank in the foreground, the other further up the hill-side—might be held to suggest that family life had not yet been instituted. The other figures are arranged much as in the drawing, some sitting by themselves, others with companions: in the foreground, children play with birds.

Translation of the theme into pictorial terms produces in all these cases certain resemblances to Ronsard's treatment of it. Moralising or satire are virtually excluded: the carefree, gentle way of life, and the benignity of nature, are dwelt upon with pleasure for their own sake.

On the other hand, the artists give prominence to individuals or pairs, or at any rate to small groups, which Ronsard does not do. And they do not depict a forest scene. Woods appear in the background, but the setting is open parkland. In addition to acorns and beech-nuts, delicious fruits of every kind are at hand in profusion, as well as flowers to delight the eye. The introduction of a dance, and of bathing in the stream, are social elements quite absent from Ronsard's Age of Gold.

The passage in *Les Isles Fortunées*, describing the life Ronsard and his friends are to lead there,[1] and the passage in the *Epitafe de Hugues Salel* describing the life of the poets in the Elysian Fields,[2] are a good deal closer to the scenes depicted by the artists. These passages, however, though important for the development of the theme in his poetry,[3] do not purport to deal with the Age of Gold as such, and it is the more noteworthy that he did not apply a description of this sort to the Age of Gold itself.

[1] Lau. v, pp. 182–3, lines 93–114, and p. 190, lines 231–49.
[2] Lau. vi, pp. 34–5, lines 43–72.   [3] See above, p. 16.

Given his insistence on the forest scene, it was logical to limit his selection of food to the fruits of the forest, and to sacrifice the tempting spread (and the riot of flowers) which park or garden could provide. This was in accordance, too, with the more spartan conception of the Age of Gold popularised by Boethius.

Would not the introduction of dancing and music, on the other hand, have been compatible with living in the forest?

There is, here too, a sort of logic about Ronsard's choice. The Age of Gold, for him, was a state of nature—certainly not a Hobbesian state of nature, since it was essentially benign and amicable, but still a state of nature. Was it not already improving upon nature for six human beings to arrange themselves (as Cranach made them do) alternately men and women, to join hands, and perform steps together round a tree, not to mention the still more sophisticated sport represented by Vasari which involved the organization of no less than twelve people and the co-operation of a piper? Once even so simple an artefact as a shepherd's pipe is admitted, where is one to draw the line? Vasari shows what looks suspiciously like a basket being used by one of the picnickers to bring in the fruits that have been collected, carried on the picker's head, and he can hardly have thought that the majestic hair-styles worn by the women could be achieved without recourse to art... Ronsard is more radical. The humblest tool, the simplest pastime, presupposes a plan, and planning was to him the antithesis of the Age of Gold.

In so far as there existed at all in Ronsard's time an iconography of the Age of Gold, it was evidently not calculated to suggest a picture at all like this. Pleasure in the scene depicted, for its own sake (as distinct from pointing a moral) is indeed to be found there, and so is the absence of agriculture and the dependence on Nature's bounty. But the artists do not conceive it as a state of things when man was so much part of nature that there were neither dwellings nor dances, and when the individual was unimportant.

A landscape, particularly a forest landscape, in which the

human beings were presented as nothing more than part of the natural scene, would hardly have been shown by any artist whose work Ronsard could have known.

Albrecht Altdorfer had expressed a love of the forest which offers some parallel to Ronsard's. The *Satyr Family* (1507), in Berlin, represents a woodland scene: a satyr watches with concern, and his wife clings to him in alarm while clutching the baby satyr to her, at the passing of a man (unaware of their presence), naked and holding a stick, who is wading up through a pond or brook in the glade below them. The *St George* (1510), in Munich, is a true forest landscape, in which the presence of the horse and rider—and even of the dragon—dwarfed as they are by the surrounding trees with their massive foliage, serves only to emphasise the immensity of the woods, through which there is the barest hint of a glimpse through to a more open landscape.[1] A tendency to see the forest as the habitat of early Man is discernible perhaps in the *Satyr Family*, and also in the drawing of the *Wilder Man* (1508) passing on a marshy track under enormous spruces with broken branches, and of the *Waldmenschen* (undated, *c.* 1510).[2] The technical difficulties of representing the forest in the medium of painting were considerable, and Altdorfer was somewhat exceptional in his time in possessing both the wish and the skill to overcome them. It seems improbable that Ronsard had seen his forest paintings, or even heard about them.

In France, the painting of landscape was still indeed an unfamiliar notion.[3] Ronsard could have seen a picture such as the *Landscape with the death of Eurydice* (now in the National Gallery, in London), by Niccolo dell'Abbate, an Italian artist who came in 1552 to assist Primaticcio in the decoration of

[1] L. von Baldass, *Albrecht Altdorfer* (Zürich, 1941), pls. 229, 234, and pp. 42, 48, 62, 198–9.

[2] The two drawings (the first in the British Museum, the second in the Albertina, in Vienna) are reproduced *ibid.*, pp. 43 and 60 respectively.

[3] Denis Rouart, introduction to the catalogue of the Exhibition, *La Forêt dans la peinture ancienne* (Nancy, Musée des Beaux Arts, 1960), regards the Parisian artist appropriately called Jean Forest (1635–1712) as the first native French painter to give pride of place to the landscape, and especially forest landscape, in his pictures.

Fontainebleau, and who is known to have done a set of four large landscapes for the palace, of which this may be one.[1] But his landscape—apart from being in this particular case a view on the sea coast, which is very unlike anything in Ronsard's poetry—is not much more than a skilfully constructed setting for a mythological episode. The groups of trees are carefully chosen and carefully executed elements in the composition. It has nothing likely to inspire with enthusiasm for untouched nature a poet who beheld it. Among native French artists, there was no one who could offer even this degree of understanding of landscape. It has indeed been said: 'France at that time expressed her passion for Nature not in line or colour but in words. Ronsard was the first French landscape painter, and outside his work we shall find nothing to equal the *Elégie aux Bûcherons de la Forêt de Gâtine.*'[2]

[1] Exhibition, *Landscape in French Art* (London, Royal Academy of Arts, 1949), no. 17. See L. Dimier, *Le Primatice* (1928), pp. 39–43. Niccolo collaborated, as did Ronsard, in the preparations for the Entry of Charles IX into Paris in 1571; see above, p. 45.

[2] *Landscape in French Art*, Introduction (by Bernard Dorival), p. ix. The *Elégie*, 'Quiconque aura premier la main embesognée', first appeared in the 1584 collected edition of Ronsard's works. In particular the lines,

tes bois
Dont l'ombrage incertain lentement se remue,

are celebrated for both their musical and their pictorial character (Lau. XVIII, I, pp. 143–7).

4

Traditional and contemporary influences
affecting Ronsard's idea of the Age of Gold

LUCRETIUS, SENECA, NATURAL LAW

Ronsard's favourite picture of the Age of Gold represented a society of 'gatherers' living under ideal conditions but essentially wild or primitive in character. His Golden Age men are not peaceful Neolithic farmers (like those of Aratus); they are not shepherds except in the *Bergerie* where the task in hand and the models chosen forced him into the pastoral tradition; they are not even hunters, for all his awareness of the sport and the setting of the chase.

Is this preoccupation with humanity in the earliest 'wild' state to be accounted for by the treatment given to the Age of Gold by classical poets? It appears not. Ovid alone perhaps, among the poets who avowedly celebrated the Age of Gold, could have provided him with the starting-point for such a picture.

Is the explanation then to be sought for among writers who had written about the history of Early Man, without celebrating the Age of Gold or even believing in it?

The origins of civilised life were already a subject of serious inquiry in Greek antiquity.[1] If belief in an Age of Gold was respected as a myth of profound significance, it was generally assumed, in practice, that the human race, as we know it, lived at first a brutish and laborious existence, gradually alleviated by the discovery of speech, the use of fire, the building of dwellings, the domestication and breeding of animals, and the sowing of crops. Gods or heroes were often credited by

---

[1] See A. O. Lovejoy and G. Boas, *Primitivism and related ideas in antiquity*, passim.

tradition with the gift to men of these techniques. Prometheus was revered for giving fire; Demeter or Triptolemus (in Italy, Ceres or Saturn; in Egypt, Osiris, etc.) for teaching agriculture; Hephaestus or Athene for revealing all the arts of civilised life. These figures might come to be regarded as personifications of human ingenuity, or identified with an élite or with a single genius.[1]

This train of thought could inspire great poetry. The heroic act and punishment of Prometheus, for instance, already related by Hesiod, was celebrated by Æschylus. Ronsard, however, consistently took sides against Prometheus: far from praising the discovery of fire and its consequences, he joined the select band of authors—mostly poets—who deplored it as the beginning of all evils:

> Maudit soit Prométhé par qui fut desrobbé
> Le feu celestial...

he cried, in the *Exhortation pour la Paix*.[2] Yet we are assured by Ronsard's first biographer that one of the great moments in his poetic experience had been when his tutor Dorat read right through the *Prometheus Vinctus* with him in the original, translating it as he went into French.[3]

Nor were attempts lacking in sixteenth-century France to use the early progress of man as material for epic: Maurice Scève, the Lyonese poet, who was some twenty-five years older than Ronsard, was writing such an epic almost at the same time as Ronsard's poems dealing with the Age of Gold, *Le Microcosme* (published in 1562).[4] This was no masterpiece, but it

[1] See R. Johnson, 'The Promethean commonplace', *JWCI*, xxv (1962), 9–17.
[2] See R. Trousson, 'Le mythe de Prométhée et de Pandore chez Ronsard', *Bulletin de l'Association Guillaume Budé* (1961), pp. 351–9, and *Le thème de Prométhée dans la littérature européenne* (1964).
[3] '...luy leut de plain vol le Promethée d'Æschyle, pour le mettre en plus haut goust d'une Poesie qui n'avoit encor passé la mer de deçà, et en sa faveur traduisit cette Tragedie en François, laquelle, si tost que Ronsard eut goustée: Et quoy, dit-il à Dorat, mon maistre, m'avez vous caché si long temps ces richesses?', Claude Binet, *Vie de Ronsard* (1586), ed. Laumonier (1910), pp. 12–13.
[4] *Le Microcosme* (Lyon, 1562, posthumous), accessible in the *Œuvres poétiques complètes*, ed. G. Guégan (1927).

showed keen awareness of the poetry latent in the early struggles of mankind.

Another aspect of man's early history in which Ronsard refused to find inspiration was that of the beginnings of the arts.

The legend, for instance, of Orpheus bringing men together in communities by the power of his poetry and song[1] might have been expected to appeal to him, as other aspects of the Orpheus myth undoubtedly did; the *Ars Poetica* of Horace and writers of the Italian Renaissance had made it famous. The civilising influence of Love, and of the arts, was featured in Bembo's *Gli Asolani* (1504)[2] in a positively anti-primitivist picture of the history of human happiness. Thus Bembo expounds the advance of virtue as well as of civilisation which took place when mankind, under the influence of the poets and especially of Orpheus, renounced their wild ways:

Poets...the first teachers of conduct, at a time when rough and savage men were not yet well banded in societies, were instructed by nature, which had given them powers of expression and of mind fit for the task, to find verses with whose sound they might soften the brutality of those who, having come forth from trees and caves without other knowledge of themselves, still lived like beasts; and scarcely had these first teachers uttered their songs when, wherever they went singing, they began to lead the savage men who were enchanted by their voices...Men...would still be wandering up and down the mountains and the woods, as naked, wild and hairy as the beasts, without roofs and human converse or domestic customs, had love not persuaded them to meet together in a common life. Then abandoning their cries, and bending their glad tongues to speech, they came to utter their first words; and scarcely could they talk to one another when, condemning the tree trunks and jagged caves which had been their homes, they began to build their crofts and, leaving their wild nuts, to hunt the savage beasts with which they had once lived.—Little by little as men lived in this new way, love gathered strength and with love grew the arts. For the first time fathers knew their children from those of other

---

[1] See A. Buck, *Der Orpheus-Mythos in der italienischen Renaissance, Schriften und Vorträge des Petrarca-Instituts Köln*, xv (Krefeld, 1961).

[2] Translated into French by Jean Martin under the title *Les Azolains de Monseigneur Bembo de la nature d'amour*, Paris (1545), 8°.

men... Then villages were newly filled with houses and cities girt themselves with walls for their defence and laws were made to guard praiseworthy customs.[1]

On the other hand, authors who were attempting simply to reconstruct the life lived by the first men and women tended, reasonably enough, to suppose that much of it was lived in the woods.

And here we recognise one of the most conspicuous features of the Age of Gold in Ronsard, a feature not accounted for by any of the poets who celebrated the Age of Gold as such: the sylvan setting.

Thus Cicero, in a well-known passage of *De inventione rhetorica*[2] describes the first decision of human beings to live together in a fixed home as the work of a wise man, who persuaded his fellows to adopt this habit when they had been hitherto 'scattered in the fields and hidden in the shelter of the woods' (dispersos homines in agris et in tectis silvestribus abditos)'.

Cicero takes it for granted that mankind was better off under the new dispensation than the old. Far from romanticising the earlier state or identifying it with the Age of Gold, he calls it 'wandering like the beasts (passim bestiarum modo vaga-bantur)'. But it had potentially a romantic aspect to it, and this aspect was revealed in one of the most anti-Age of Gold writers of antiquity: Lucretius.

Lucretius in Book v of *De rerum natura* derided those who believe in a legendary age in the world's youth when streams of gold flowed over the land and trees blossomed with jewels. Expounding the Epicurean theory of evolution, he told the early history of mankind as an epic of upward struggle, from the beginning when they wandered in search of roots and

---

[1] Bembo, *Gli Asolani*, trans. Rudolf B. Gottfried (1954), Book I. Cf. the evolutionary representation of this stage of human history in Lucretius and Vitruvius; see above, pp. 27–8. For the concept of the Age of Gold as the Age of Poetry see E. E. Reed, 'Herder, Primitivism and the Age of Poetry', *Modern Language Review*, LX, 4 (Oct. 1965), 553–67.

[2] *M. Tullii Ciceronis Artis Rhetoricae Libri Duo*, ed. A. Weidner, pp. 76–7 (Book I, 2).

berries, sheltering as best they could in caves or under brush-wood from weather and from beasts of prey. He used the same terms to describe their way of life as Cicero in the passage just quoted—'vitam tractabant more ferarum'. But, being a great poet, he could not conjure up even the terrible hardships of early man without communicating to the scene a sort of wild beauty which could not fail to impress any reader who was himself a poet:

> Nor was there any sturdy steerer of the bent plough, nor knew anyone how to work the fields with iron, or to plant young shoots in the earth, or cut down the old branches off high trees with knives. What sun and rains had brought to birth, what earth had created unasked, such gift was enough to appease their hearts. Among oaks laden with acorns they would refresh their bodies for the most part; and the arbute-berries, which now you see ripening in winter-time with scarlet hue, the earth bore then in abundance, yea and larger. And besides these the flowering youth of the world then bare much other rough sustenance, enough and to spare for miserable mortals. But to slake their thirst streams and springs summoned them, even as now the down rush of water from the great mountains loudly summons far and wide the thirsting tribes of wild beasts. Or again they dwelt in the woodland haunt of the nymphs, which they had learnt in their wanderings, from which they knew that gliding streams of water washed the wet rocks with bounteous flood, yea washed the wet rocks, as they dripped down over the green moss, and here and there welled up and burst forth over the level plain.[1]

Lucretius argued, earlier in the same Book, that nature, far from being designed by a divine providence to favour human life, is more favourable to beasts than men. The cultivation of crops, on the relatively few parts of the earth suitable for growing them, is a life-and-death battle with nature:

> Of all the field-land that remains, yet nature would by her force cover it up with thorns, were it not that the force of man resisted her, ever wont for his livelihood to groan over the strong mattock and to furrow the earth with the deep-pressed plough. But that by

[1] *Titi Lucreti Cari De Rerum Natura Libri Sex*, ed. and trans. Cyril Bailey, I, 481 (Book v, lines 933–52).

turning the fertile clods with the share, and subduing the soil of the earth we summon them to birth, of their own accord the crops could not spring up into the liquid air.

How easy, by contrast, is the life of animals, who fend for themselves from birth without the attentions required by children, without clothing, without weapons, etc., all their needs supplied by nature's care:

since for all of them the earth itself brings forth all things bounteously, and nature, the quaint artificer of things.[1]

Lucretius does not conclude that men would be happier if they could live in the wild state, like animals, let alone imply that the tilling of the earth is perverse and impious. This passage might none the less appeal to a reader already disposed to be sentimental about the earliest food-gathering state of man.

The whole passage describing the life of the earliest men, beginning at l. 925, is full of evocations of a forest scene.[2]

Ronsard's fondness for forests and streams as the characteristic setting for the Age of Gold may well owe something to the woodland scenes thus evoked by Lucretius in connection with the life of early Man, and to this recurrent use of words for forest, grove, etc. Nothing like this emphasis is to be found in any poet dealing with the Age of Gold.

De Rerum Natura is not in itself an improbable source for Ronsard to have drawn upon.

His friend Lambinus—Denis Lambin[3]—produced an important edition of Lucretius. As the first edition of it was printed in 1561, the period when he was working on it overlaps with the period when Ronsard was writing about the Age of Gold.

---

[1] *Op. cit.* pp. 443–5 (Book v, lines 206–12 and 233–4).

[2]
glandiferas inter curabant corpora quercus
plerumque... (939–40).
denique nota vagis silvestria templa tenebant
nympharum... (948–9).
sed nemora atque cavos montis silvasque colebant (955).
et Venus in silvis iungebat corpora amantum (962).
consectabantur silvestria saecla ferarum (967).
silvestria membra
nuda dabant terrae nocturno tempore capti,
circum se foliis ac frondibus involventes (970–2).

[3] For this friendship, see P. de Nolhac, *Ronsard et l'humanisme*, pp. 154–65.

Lucretius, Seneca, Natural Law

Book II was actually dedicated to Ronsard.[1] An inscribed copy
of the third (1570) edition, presented by Lambinus to Ronsard,
has recently come to light.[2]
Though Ronsard never acknowledged indebtedness to
Lucretius, and was careful to express his abhorrence of the
poet's atheism, he claimed, in the posthumously published
Préface sur la Franciade: Au lecteur apprentif, that Lucretius was
the only Latin poet worthy to be named in the same breath as
Virgil, and called some of his lines 'non seulement excellens,
mais divins'.[3] Some familiarity with the doctrines of epicurean-
ism as taught by Lucretius, and with certain parts of *De Rerum
Natura*, has been detected in the poetry of Ronsard by all scholars
who have sought it, particularly in the *Hymne de la Mort*.[4]
Ronsard could easily have read Lucretius, before Lambinus
(and Dorat, Ronsard's old tutor, to whom Lambinus dedicated
Book VI of his edition, acknowledging his help) brought *De
Rerum Natura* to the general attention of his friends and fellow-
students of the classics: numerous editions,[5] both Italian and
French, circulated in France already when he was a boy, and so
avid a reader of the classics would scarcely have overlooked the
work. There is at least one clue, which appears to have been
hitherto overlooked, to early interest in Lucretius among the
Pléiade poets: Jacques Tahureau, whom Ronsard included
among the friends invited to sail with him to *Les Isles Fortunées*
(1553),[6] spoke of 'les beaux vers de ce hautain Lucrèce' in his
Premières poésies (1554).[7]

---

[1] Reprinted *ibid.* p. 159.
[2] M. Morrison, 'Another book from Ronsard's library: a presentation copy of
Lambin's Lucretius' (with facsimile of title-page, showing Lambinus'
inscription 'Pour Monsieur de Ronsard / dono ipsius Lambini ut sit amicitiae
monumentum' and Ronsard's signature), *BHR*, xxv (1963), 561–6.
[3] Lau. XVI, 2, p. 338.
[4] Lau. VIII, pp. 161–79, commentary. Cf. F. Neri, 'Lukrezio e la poesia di
Ronsard', an essay in *Il maggio delle fate* (Torino, 1944); Eleanore Belowski,
'Lukrez in der französischen Literatur der Renaissance', in *Romanische
Studien*, XXXVI (1934), (pp. 20–35 on Ronsard); Simone Fraisse, *Une
conquête du rationalisme; L'influence de Lucrèce en France au XVIe siècle* (pp.104–
20 on Ronsard).
[5] See C. A. Fusil, 'La Renaissance de Lucrèce au XVIe siècle en France', in
RSS. xv (1928), 134–50.   [6] Lau. V, p. 178, line 68 and n. 4.
[7] Tahureau, *Les Premières Poésies* (1554), f. EI[a].

The possibility that Ronsard may have been influenced by Book v of *De Rerum Natura* has, however, scarcely been considered. Mademoiselle Fraisse, who mentions it, considers the picture of early man one of the Lucretian myths which can be disregarded as an influence upon the Pléiade:[1] a few lines of the *Elégie des Armairies* and a reference to *Les Armes* is all the evidence cited. The assumption that the Age of Gold is a mere literary commonplace, and that it invariably prescribed acorns and water, etc., has stultified further investigation. And the strophe of Desportes, which in her view sums up all the use made of Book v by the school of Ronsard—

> Nos ancestres grossiers, qui vivaient aux bocages
> Hideux, velus et nus comme bestes sauvages...

is very different in emphasis from anything Ronsard wrote upon the subject.

What has probably obscured the relationship between Ronsard's Age of Gold people and Lucretius' early Man, is that the notion of evolution, so characteristic of Lucretius, is wholly ignored by Ronsard. He is content to picture to himself this earliest era of human history, without committing himself to the view that subsequent discoveries and improvements constitute Progress.

Many other differences exist between Ronsard's picture of the Age of Gold and Lucretius' picture of early man, besides the whole idea of evolution. Lucretius claimed that man then lived 'sponte sua' and deduced from this that each man lived for himself and could not think of the common good; Ronsard believed that men had all things in common and were essentially sociable. Lucretius speculated on the chance matings which

---

[1] 'Ecartons enfin du nombre des mythes empruntés à Lucrèce le tableau des premiers âges. Au premier abord d'ailleurs aucune confusion n'est possible. Ronsard et ses disciples, en quête d'un thème plus poétique que vraisemblable, préfèrent les fables d'Hésiode, d'Ovide et de Tibulle sur l'âge d'or, au réalisme de Lucrèce dans son Livre V. Parfois, il est vrai, quelques détails relèvent des deux traditions: celles-ci s'accordent pour nourrir l'humanité primitive de glands, la faire boire aux sources et aux fontaines, la loger dans des cabanes de feuilles. Mais ces traits étaient dès l'antiquité d'une extrême banalité.' (Fraisse, *op. cit.* p. 100.)

[2] Fraisse, *loc. cit.*

Sponte sua, satis id placabat pectora donum.
Glandiferas inter curabant corpora quercus
Plerunque, & qua nunc hiberno tempore cernis
Arbuta pœniceo fieri matura colore,
Plurima tum tellus etiam maiora ferebat.
Multáque præterea nouitas tum florida mundi
Pabula diua tulit, miseris mortalibus ampla.
At sedare sitim fluuij, fontésque vocabant:
Vt nunc montibus è magnis decursus aquäi
Clarior accitat sitientia sæcla ferarum.
Denique noctiuagi siluestria templa tenebant
Nympharum, quibus exibant humore fluenta
Lubrica, proluuie larga lauëre humida saxa:
Humida saxa super viridi stillantia musco:
Et partim plano scatëre, atque erumpere campo.
Nec dum res igni scibant tractare, neque vti
Pellibus, & spoliis corpus vestire ferarum:
Sed nemora, atque cauos monteis, siluásque colebant,
Et frutices inter condebant squallida membra,
Verbera ventorum vitare, imbreísque coacti.
Nec commune bonum poterant spectare, neque vllis
Moribus inter se scibant, nec legibus vti.
Quod cuique obtulerat prædæ fortuna, ferebat,
Sponte sua, sibi quisque valere, & viuere doctus.
Et Venus in siluis iungebat corpora amantum,
Conciliabat enim vel mutua quanque cupido,
Vel violenta viri vis, atque impensa libido,
Vel pretium glandes, atque arbuta, vel pira lecta.

Figure 9. Lucretius on early Man

De Rerum Natura, Book v, Paris, 1561, 4° (edition by Ronsard's friend Lambinus)

would occur before fixed homes and families existed; Ronsard is obstinately silent on the role of love. Lucretius celebrates man's first successes in hunting the wild beasts; Ronsard makes no reference to hunting.

Nor is Ronsard tempted to treat as a sort of Age of Gold the next stage of human society described in Book v, when men first worked together to practise the use of fire or the building of a hut, when they first wore skins as clothes and cared for their women and children. This episode was famous, not only for the almost idyllic character conferred upon it by Lucretius, but through the treatment it received from his disciple, Vitruvius, in his treatise *De Architectura*. Here Vitruvius attributed the origins of society to the chance discovery of the use of fire, followed by the invention of speech, and by the erection of the first buildings. The artists commissioned to illustrate the first printed editions of Vitruvius represented the men and women of this era not as brutish, but as noble in physique and serene in expression: the illustration of an early community grouped round the camp fire, in the Como edition of 1521, is actually entitled *Aurea Aetas*.[1] There is no sign that this view of early human society appealed at all to Ronsard, with its assumption that the Age of Gold could not have come until some technological progress had been made.

If the description of the earliest men in *De Rerum Natura* influenced Ronsard in his preference for an Age of Gold *before* technology, the effect of it may have been reinforced by the passage in the *Fasti* where Ovid evoked the period 'before Jove' when the Arcadians occupied the earth:

> Vita feris similis, nullos agitata per usus;
> Artis adhuc expers, et rude vulgus erat.
> Pro domibus frondes norant, pro frugibus herbas:
> Nectar erat palmis hausta duabus aqua.
> Nullus anhelabat sub adunco vomere taurus,
> Nulla sub imperio terra colentis erat...[2]

[1] See E. Panofsky, *Studies in iconology: humanistic themes in the art of the Renaissance*, pp. 33–67, and pl. x (19). Cf. above, p. 116.
[2] *Fasti*, II, lines 291–6.

though Ronsard abstains from comparing the life of his Age of Gold to that of wild animals, and gives it a rudimentary moral basis by emphasising the friendly sharing of all benefits in common.

'Primitivism'—the belief that men were better off *without* civilisation—indeed manifested itself already in antiquity as a fashionable affectation or a moralist's gibe.

This might take two forms. What has been designated 'soft' primitivism assumed that primitive human life was lived under favourable conditions: a benign climate, a fertile country, and no predisposition to work or to quarrel. What has been called 'hard' primitivism recognised that the lot of primitive man must have been one of great hardship and privation (at least in any conditions known to Europeans since the Ice Age) but claimed that, just because of this, he was strong, daring, frugal, and full of manly virtues, a reproach, in fact, to 'civilised' society.[1]

Unpoetic as this latter concept may appear to be, it was urged with eloquence by would-be reformers of society who believed passionately in the need to reassert true values and who denounced the corrupting quest for wealth and luxury. A spokesman of this creed was Seneca, preaching a spartan and puritan virtue which he found (though in an imperfect because unreasoning state) in primitive man. In principle, he indeed held that early man was innocent through ignorance. 'Ignorantia rerum innocentes erant. Multum autem interest utrum peccare nolit an nesciat...virtus non contingit animo nisi instituto et edocto.'[2]

This would apply too to Ronsard's Age of Gold American Indian in the *Complainte contre Fortune*. 'Qui ne connait les noms de virtus ni de vices'.[3]

There is also a good deal of emphasis on the abundance of nature's gifts and on men's willingness to share them with each other:

[1] See Lovejoy and Boas, *Primitivism and related ideas in antiquity*, pp. 1–11.
[2] *Ad Lucilium Epistulae morales*, trans. R. M. Gunmere, II, 428 (Ep. XC, 46).
[3] Lau. X, p. 34, line 358. See above, p. 27.

What race of men was ever more blest than that race? They enjoyed all nature in partnership. Nature sufficed for them, now the guardian, as before she was the parent, of all; and this her gift consisted of the assured possession by each man of the common resources...But avarice broke in upon a condition so happily ordained...[1]

and on the woodland setting:

The men of that day, who had found in some dense grove protection against the sun, and security against the severity of winter or of rain in their mean hiding-places, spent their lives under the branches of the trees and passed tranquil nights without a sigh.[2]

Ronsard might also have found in this Epistle a hint for a detail, conspicuous in two of his descriptions of early man drinking from the stream: that he drank not from a vessel but in his cupped hand, or even with his mouth to the water. For Seneca here introduces, in close conjunction with his picture of early man before the invention of tools, etc., the story of Diogenes who threw away his drinking-cup (the only private possession he had retained, believing it to be indispensable)when he saw a boy drinking water in his cupped hand ('cum vidisset puerum cava manu bibentem aquam').[3]

We may take it for granted that Ronsard knew of the ideas here expressed. The whole period was full of neo-Stoic teaching, Seneca was constantly reprinted and translated, and Marc-Antoine Muret, Ronsard's commentator and friend,[4] was working on an edition of Seneca in the last years of his life.

Seneca's picture of early man in Epistle XC is not called the Age of Gold, but it contained a reference to the Age of Gold

[1] Seneca, *op. cit.* II, 423–5 (Ep. XC, 38).
[2] *Ibid.* II, 427 (Ep. XC, 41).
[3] *Ibid.* II, 403 (Ep. XC, 14). Cf. 'Les hommes tiroient l'eau dans le creus de leurs mains', in *Les Armes* (Lau. VI, p. 205, line 14), and

> Qui sans charger sa main d'escuelle ou de vaisseau
> De la bouche tiroit les ondes d'un ruisseau,

in *Au Seigneur Baillon* (Lau. XII, p. 90, lines 59–60). Ovid's line about the Arcadians, 'Nectar erat palmis hausta duabus aqua' in the *Fasti* (see above, p. 130) may also have been in Ronsard's mind.
[4] See P. de Nolhac, *Ronsard et l'humanisme*, pp. 146–52.

which might have helped to associate the two themes in the reader's mind: it was written to refute the teaching of Posidonius, that the Age of Gold was the age of the great technological inventions and hence under the rule of 'the wise men'.[1] The philosopher's sneer at all devices which make human life less laborious and precarious may seem ungracious: they can be explained as a revolt against the opposite tendency, that of prizing material show, comfort and convenience as if nothing else mattered. The worth of the individual human person, irrespective of his means and status, was a truth which Stoic teaching was determined to assert.

It was largely under this Stoic influence that Roman jurists developed the concept of Natural Law (what was inherently rational and equitable) as distinct from the laws which might be found necessary in any particular community to regulate human life. Thus the principle was laid down, 'Quod ad jus naturale attinet, omnes homines aequales sunt', notwithstanding the inequalities of wealth and rank which existed in all states known to the writers, and even the legality of slavery. It was doubted by some whether private property was founded in Natural Law. It was recognised indeed that man, in his present condition, could not live by Natural Law alone, and needed the restrictions of man-made laws as well, but this was considered by Stoics and by Christians as a sign of his corruption.[2] The sole rule of Natural Law might thus be thought of as something like the Age of Gold or (by Christians) like the Age of Innocence in the Earthly Paradise. For, although the distinction is one of principle, and was quite familiar as such to all students of law, many people found it convenient to symbolise or dramatise it as two successive stages in man's history.

If the concept of Natural Law played any part in forming Ronsard's picture of the Age of Gold, the expression itself takes a long time to make an appearance in his poems on this theme. It is stated that the people of the Age of Gold:

---

[1] 'Illo ergo saeculo, quod aureum perhibent, penes sapientes fuisse regnum Posidonius iudicat...' (Seneca, *op. cit.* II, 396 (Ep. XC, 5)).

[2] See A. J. and R. W. Carlyle, *A history of medieval political theory in the West*, I, 23–134.

gardoient la loy saincte
De Nature & de Dieu, sans force ny contrainte,

in the *Elégie au Seigneur Baillon* (1564).[1]
Possibly by this period the subject was 'in the air' to a greater extent than when Ronsard began to write about the Age of Gold in 1555. Bodin was in Paris from 1561 onwards, though the *Methodus* was not published until 1566, and the *Six Livres de la République* not until 1576. The application of the term to the Age of Gold at any rate seems to be peculiar to Ronsard. The connection of the two ideas may have been made in his mind before it was explicitly stated in his poetry. The same can be said of the connection between the Age of Gold and the New World, first specifically stated in the *Complainte contre Fortune*.

The possible influence of Lucretius upon Ronsard, and the possible influence of Stoicism and of the idea of Natural Law, are very different in kind: the first is the influence of a poet upon a poet—a matter of a mood or a picture rather than of borrowing ideas—while the second is a set of ideas filtering through to a highly intelligent man who knew of them because he was a man of his time. They may, however, in their various ways, have prompted the interest in early man, and the almost romantic picture of his way of life, which Ronsard associated consistently with what he called the Age of Gold.[2]

THE NEW WORLD

Speculations on the life of early Man, and visions of the Age of Gold, had both been affected by contact with the New World and with its inhabitants, in the first half of the sixteenth century.

The first writer to publicise the discoveries of Columbus, the Italian humanist Pietro Martiro d'Anghera (Peter Martyr Anglerius), working at the Spanish court, drew a number of comparisons between the Indians and the Age of Gold.

In his *Decades of the New World*, of which the First Decade

---

[1] Lau. XIII, p. 91, lines 69–70.
[2] It may be noted that Lucretius, Cicero and Seneca were read or reread by Ronsard in the preparation of *Les Hymnes* (1555 and 1556). Lau VIII, p. xv.

was printed in 1504, he popularised, from the first, these comparisons. The natives of Hispaniola were found by Columbus naked, 'lacking weights, measures and money': they lived in the Age of Gold, without laws, without judges and without books, content with Nature and careless of the future: admittedly, they were tormented by the lust for power and waged war upon one another but this was a plague from which (in the author's opinion) it was hard to believe that even the Age of Gold itself was free.[1] Of the Cubans, too, he asserted that the present was their Age of Gold, particularly emphasising the absence of private property and of enclosures.[2] In the original, and in vernacular versions, the *Decades* were already known in Ronsard's boyhood. A translation of part of the *Decades* into French appeared in 1532, handsomely printed, and dedicated to Charles, Duke of Angoulême (afterwards Duke of Orleans), third son of Francis I, to whom Ronsard was a few years later a page: this renders as follows the opening lines of the passage on the Cubans, the words *Aage d'or* being printed in the margin:

Ces gens là ont la terre entre eulx commune comme le soleil, l'air et l'eaue. Ceci est mien, & cela est tien (qui sont cause de tous discords) ne se treuve point entre eulx: & vivent contens de si peu de chose, qu'en si grande amplitude de terre, les champs & biens superfluent plus que aulcune chose defaille à aulcun. Ilz ont l'aage d'or, ilz ne fossoyent ny enferment de hayes leurs possessions, ilz laissent leurs jardins ouvertz...[3]

[1] 'Sed Hispaniolos nostros insulares illis beatiores esse sentio, modo religionem imbuant: quia nudi, sine ponderibus, sine mensura, sine mortifera denique pecunia, aurea aetate viventes, sine legibus, sine calumniosis iudicibus, sine libris, natura contenti vitam agunt, de futuro minime soliciti. Ambitione & isti tamen imperii causa, torquentur, & se invicem bellis conficiunt: qua peste auream aetatem haudquaquam credimus vicisse immunem' (*Decades*, I, Lib. 2, f. 5ᵃ).
[2] 'Compertum est apud eos, velut solem & aquam, terram esse communem, neque Meum aut Tuum, malorum omnium semina, cadere inter ipsos. Sunt enim adeo parvo contenti, quod in ea ampla tellure magis agri supersint, quam quicquam desit. Aetas est illis aurea, neque fossis, neque parietibus aut sepibus praedia sepiunt. Apertis vivunt hortis' (*ibid.* Lib. 3, ff. 9ᵇ–10ᵃ).
[3] *Extraict ou recueil des Isles nouvellement trouvées en la grand' mer oceane* (1532), f. 23ᵃ. The colophon is dated 12 January 1532. This is probably 1532 Old Style (i.e. 1533), as S. de Colines seems to specify 'calculo romano' when dating a book New Style.

Another passage, in the eighth book of the Third Decade, speaks of reports, heard by the explorers, of wild men who lived in mountain caves and were content to eat the fruits of the forest, without any settled homes or any crops, 'as we read of the Age of Gold'.[1] In view of the determination of the author to remind his readers thus of the Age of Gold theme as they read about the New World, it is worth remembering that there is frequent mention, in these accounts of the islands, of the forests with which they were covered: one particularly romantic moment in the first book of the First Decade tells how the sailors, coasting along some of the islands, 'ouyrent'— in the words of the French translator—'au mois de Novembre entre forestz espesses chanter le Rossignol'.

Even first-hand experience of America did not necessarily bring disillusionment to educated men familiar with this association of ideas.

Vasco de Quiroga, one of the jurists sent from Spain to Mexico in 1531 to open the Second Audiencia, and destined to become Bishop of Michoacan, wrote in a report in 1535, advocating a Utopian system of government for the Indians to which he believed their natural simplicity best suited: 'with much cause and reason is this called the New World, not because it is newly found, but because it is—in its people and in almost everything—as was the first and golden age'.[2]

If the Noble Savage[3] was already to hand as a model for the people of the Age of Gold, he none the less differed in some respects from Golden Age Man as Ronsard chose to picture him. Even Peter Martyr described the Indians as living in fixed settlements and supplementing Nature's bounty by some cultivation or by hunting; 'gatherers' are mentioned, from hearsay,

---

[1] '...homines vivere aiunt, montium cavernis & sylvestribus fructibus contentos, qui nunquam mansueverint,...sine certis sedibus, sine sationibus aut cultura ulla, uti legitur de aurea aetate' (*Decades*, III, Lib. 8, f. 62ᵃ).

[2] Silvio Zavola, 'The American Utopia of the sixteenth century', *Huntington Library Quarterly*, X (1947), 339.

[3] The term 'Noble Savage', at least in English, seems to date from Dryden's *Conquest of Granada*. On this whole subject, see the excellent work by H. N. Fairchild, *The noble savage: a study in romantic naturalism* (New York, 1928).

but not with any particular approval, and most of the tribes were admitted to be warlike.

The Entry of Henry II into Rouen, 1 October 1550, included a spectacular show purporting to represent a Brazilian forest. A whole area on the banks of the Seine was put into fancy dress for the purpose, a model Brazilian village was built, exotic trees and plants were simulated round it, and some three hundred participants (a nucleus of real Indians, the rest local volunteers suitably dressed—or undressed) enacted typical activities of the natives. While a crowned couple swung unconcernedly in a hammock, other couples strolled or sat in conversation, a group of seven men and women danced round a tree holding hands, isolated figures shot with bow and arrows at birds, climbed trees in search of fruit, or hastened into their huts; groups of men fought each other with bows and arrows, clubs and shields, and others prepared to set off from the bank in canoes to trade with the ships in the river. The printed account of the Entry contained a woodcut illustration of this scene, which must therefore have been available to a wide public.[1] There are, it will have been noticed, certain points in common between it and some pictorial representations of the Age of Gold, such as the dance, and the tree-climbing to pick fruit.[2] As the Age of Gold theme was used in the decorations of the Entry into the city,[3] some association between that and the Brazilian forest may have been suggested to onlookers and readers. The Brazilians are not, however, shown as very primitive or very peaceful.

The Brazilians as described by André Thevet in *Les singularitez de la France Antarctique, autrement nommée Amerique* (1558), based on his own observations while with the French expedition under Durand de Villegagnon in 1555, indeed formed a far from idyllic society; not only did they live in tribal communities and practise a rudimentary agriculture, but

---

[1] *C'est la deduction du sumptueux ordre et magnifiques theatres dressés par les citoiens de Rouen à Henry second* (1551), ff. K2ᵃ–K3ᵇ. Cf. J. Chartrou, *Les entrées solennelles et triomphales à la Renaissance* (Paris, 1928), pp. 111–12 and fig. facing p. 112, and pp. 130–40.
[2] See above, pp. 110–18. [3] See above, p. 8.

they displayed a variety of vices ranging from pipe-smoking to cannibalism. Thevet's own attitude to them was usually one of hearty contempt—'ceste canaille' is typical of his terminology—tempered by some admiration for their physical bravery.

It is true that some of the artists employed by Thevet presented a more romantic picture than did the text. Some (no doubt under his instructions, and possibly from crude sketches done on the spot) were content to provide a homely woodcut showing simple activities of the Indians, in which the figures, while by no means squalid or repellent, are slightly comical. Others, perhaps given a more general directive to illustrate a subject like a battle between Indian tribes, evidently consulted their sketches of classical friezes and sarcophagi, and composed heroic scenes of lithe warriors in action:

> girt
> With feathered cincture, naked else and wild
> Among the trees on isles and woody shores,

the feathers being indeed the only indication that the participants are American Indians. Such pictures had their own part to play in the development of the Noble Savage.[1]

Certainly Ronsard was not the only reader of the book to disregard both the tone and the trend of Thevet's comments on the Indians.

Etienne Jodelle, a friend and former fellow-student of Ronsard's, in an Ode to Thevet printed in *Les singularitez,* asserted that his fellow-countrymen had no reason to think themselves less barbarian than Thevet's Brazilians: if they go about naked, we go about disguised to each other, painted, masked; if they do not fall in with our idea of piety, we treat our own religion with disdain and deceit; if they have less power of reason than ourselves, is it not plain that our own abundance of it serves us only to harm one another?[2] This was

---

[1] See Gilbert Chinard, *L'exotisme américain dans la littérature française au XVIᵉ siècle* (1911), pp. 99–103.
[2] '...Ces barbares marchent tous nuds, / Et nous marchons incognus, / Fardez, masquez. Ce peuple estrange / A la piété ne se range. / Nous la nostre nous mesprisons, / Pipons, vendons & desguisons. / Ces barbares pour

a moral which Thevet himself was far too prosaic to draw from his observation of Brazil.

Clearly the book, and the publicity which attended Thevet's preparation of it, aroused interest: his appointment as chaplain to Catherine de' Medici and as Cosmographer Royal made him personally known to men of letters who frequented the court. Ronsard wrote the *Complainte* the year after Thevet published *Les singularitez*; a year later, he eulogised him in the *Ode à André Thevet*, while praising also Gilles Bourdin who patronised them both.[1] It seems possible that Ronsard, like Jodelle, found his imagination stirred by the talk occasioned by the expedition to Brazil and by the publicity given to it by *Les singularitez*, but, like Jodelle, was more interested in his own reactions than in what Thevet actually said.

Jean du Thier, who died in September 1559 (within a few months of the *Complainte contre Fortune* being published), invited comparison between the New World and the Age of Gold, and deplored the destruction of the latter by colonisation, in his adaptation in French of the Italian work *La Pazzia* (itself translated and adapted from the *Praise of Folly* of Erasmus). The Indians are said to have been happy without laws or letters, and to have held gold and precious stones of no account, to have lived on the fruits which the earth brought forth of its own accord, and to have had all things in common, like the commonwealth of Plato, 'ainsi qu'au siecle heureux qui fut dit l'aage doré du vieil Saturne'—a way of life which the coming of the 'avaritious and ambitious Spaniards' had brought to a miserable end, as if the colonists had carried with them overseas the box of evils of Pandora.[2] A few pages later,

se conduire / N'ont pas tant que nous de raison, / Mais qui ne voit que la foison / N'en sert que pour nous entrenuire?...' (Estienne Jodelle, seigneur du Limodin, à M. Thevet, in André Thevet, *Les singularitez de la France Antarctique* (1558), f. ã 4ᵃ).

[1] *A André Thevet, Angoumoisin*, 'Hardi, celuy qui le premier' (*Les Œuvres*, 1560, Livre v, xxi), Lau. x, pp. 265–71.

[2] *Traicté fort plaisant des Louanges de la Folie, traduict d'Italien en François par feu messire Jean du Thier* (1567), f. 18ᵃ. The edition published by Barbe, Paris, 1566, appears to be the first: the work was in any case posthumous. The authorship of *La Pazzia* (published at Venice in 1550 (B.M. 8405 b. 53 [1])) itself is uncertain: on the attribution of it—accepted by the B.M. Catalogue

the author evokes the happy state of the wild animals, as opposed to those domesticated by mankind ('errans par les delectables pasturages, ou par l'air, selon leur instinct naturel, sans aucune fatigue vivent toujours en liberté et à leur plaisir...'), a description which has affinities with Ronsard's poem to Robert de La Haye published the following year.[1] Du Thier was a friend and patron of Ronsard at the time when the *Complainte contre Fortune* was being composed: an Eclogue called after him, with a preceding eulogy of him, was in fact printed in the *Second Livre des Meslanges* immediately after the *Complainte*. The subject may thus have been 'in the air' at that time, particularly in the circles in which Ronsard moved. Ronsard's originality can be all the better appreciated when his treatment of the theme is compared with Du Thier. Sympathy with the natives, particularly as an expression of anti-Spanish sentiment, is not unusual by this period: belief that they were better off in a state of nature is not so common.

To arrive at his peaceable, wandering food-gatherers, however, he had to renew the Age of Gold inspiration first used in *Les Armes* and to recollect not so much the account of Thevet as impressions of the Indians gleaned from such sources as the most favourable passages of Peter Martyr, describing the gentle peoples of the West Indies whose fate it was to perish under the impact of European rule, rather than the tribes whose martial prowess had impressed even Thevet. Tomahawks did not suit his notions of the Age of Gold any better than swords or guns, and he suppressed them. He was left with an America invested with all that the concept of inviolate nature meant to him, heightened with all the associations of leisure, pleasure and innocence which the Age of Gold tradition could afford. The thought had an immediacy which the Age of Gold in the past could never have. The result was a moment of insight: he was able to imagine a time when even a colonist like Villegagnon, whose intentions towards the natives were avowedly philan-

of Printed Books—to Vianesio Albergati, see the article on Albergati by G. Alberigo in the *Dizionario biografico degli Italiani*, vol. I. On Du Thier, see Lau. x, p. 38, n. 2.

[1] *Ibid.* f. 28b. Cf. above, p. 28.

thropic, would find them execrating the day when the Europeans' sails first whitened on their horizon.

It is only in this, the most feeling of all Ronsard's passages on the Age of Gold theme, that the association of ideas between that theme and the New World is explicit. The part that accounts of America may have played in shaping his mental picture of the Age of Gold *before* 1559 cannot be determined: it cannot be wholly discounted. The train of thought and sentiment in *Les Isles Fortunées* suggests that the two subjects were coming together in his mind in 1553, before he began to celebrate the Age of Gold as such.

PARADOX, AND GUY DE BRUÉS' 'DIALOGUES'

The Fortunate Isles, where the earth brought forth the most lavish presents of its own accord, and where work, old age and illness were unknown, were the birthplace of Folly, as reported by Erasmus in his *Moriae Encomium* (1509). Not surprisingly, therefore, Folly claimed to know something about the Age of Gold. Science, scholarship and wisdom had then not been invented (she told her congregation), Folly being the natural and healthy state of Man.

The simple folk of the Golden Age, unequipped with any arts, lived only by the guidance and promptings of Nature. What use could they have for grammar, when all had the same language, and asked nothing of speech except to understand one another?... What need was there for legal learning, when evil conduct (surely the origin of good laws) was lacking?[1]

Such a passage, if lifted from its context, might easily appear to preach an anti-intellectual and primitivist conception of the Age of Gold. A primarily satirical and even paradoxical inten-

---

[1] 'Siquidem simplex illa aurei seculi gens, nullis armata disciplinis, solo naturae ductu instinctuque vivebat. Quorsum enim opus erat grammatica, cum eadem esset omnibus lingua, nec aliud sermone petebatur, nisi ut alius alium intelligeret?...Quorsum requireretur legum prudentia, cum abessent mali mores, ex quibus haud dubie bonae leges prognatae sunt?' (*Opera* (1540), IV, 365).

tion[1]—and the whole *Praise of Folly* is of course a paradox in form—may thus lead to the expression of nostalgia for a remote ideal society, and so become part of the store of ideas upon which a poet could draw.

In so far as Ronsard's favourite Age of Gold picture was a primitivist one, it confronted the reader with a paradox: that Man was better off without the laws, skills and comforts which seem to us desirable. In reconstructing the context in which he came to imagine it thus, it is worth recalling that paradox, as a distinct literary form, was then in fashion. The *Paradossi* of Ortensio Landi (1543) were translated into French by Charles Estienne in 1553: these purported to demonstrate, for the benefit of young lawyers or rhetoricians, how defending some apparently hopeless proposition might serve to exercise his ingenuity. The *Circe* of Giovan Baptista Gello (1549), translated into French by Denis Sauvage (1550),[2] used the paradox technique in a more searching and specialised way, to query facile generalisations about man's superiority over the other creatures. Ulysses obtains Circe's consent to persuade the hapless human beings whom she has turned into animals to resume their rightful shape; those who wish it, she agrees to release from her spells. He is astounded to hear from his first would-be convert, the oyster, that he is blissfully contented with his animal existence, only concerned to open at suitable moments to sip dew—we are reminded of *L'huitre* of Rémy Belleau dedicated to Ronsard in 1556—and remembering with horror his toils and fears in his former vocation as a fisherman. Still more eloquent is the case brought forward by his next interlocutor, the mole (a former farm-labourer). He finds himself defending, against the mole, the natural endowments of mankind, and claiming that man too in his natural state is well provided for: 'Ne dit-on pas', he rhetorically asks, 'que ces premieres bonnes vieilles gens de cest aage, que l'on nommoit

---

[1] Professor Rosalie Colie's important study, *Paradoxia epidemica: the renaissance tradition of paradox* (Princeton University Press, 1966), provides much information on the subject.
[2] *La Circe, nouvellement mise en Francoys par le seigneur du Parc.* Cf. Plutarch, *Gryllus*.

doré, vivoyent ainsi que j'ay dit?' to which the mole replies: 'Comment, Ulysses, qui te mesles tant de faire le sage, croys tu en telles fables?'...[1] In the end, Ulysses accounts himself lucky to be able to persuade the elephant, the most intelligent of beasts, that it is worth his while to become a man once more.[2]

There is an element of paradox too in the *Dialogues contre les nouveaux academiciens* of Guy de Brués (1557),[3] where the happy state of animals, or of primitive man, is among the subjects under discussion. This work is closely connected with Ronsard and his circle. The participants in the *Dialogues* speak in the character of Ronsard himself, of Jean-Antoine de Baïf, of Guillaume Aubert of Poitiers, and of Jean Nicot the future author of the *Thrésor de la langue française*. In the first Dialogue, Baïf is made by the author to assert that Man is worse off than the animals, for having taken it into his head to distinguish between vice and virtue, which are in reality a matter of opinion, and to make laws. Challenged to justify this sceptical point of view, Baïf invokes 'l'aise et le bonheur que nous avions, lors qu'un chascun vivoit selon son appetit, et selon son innocence, et bonté naturelle', and quotes the passage on the Age of Gold from Book 1 of the *Metamorphoses* of Ovid. The ensuing discussion is conducted mainly by Baïf and Ronsard, Ronsard arguing for the dignity of human reason and the moral foundations of society. In the following two Dialogues, Aubert is made to defend even more radical views than those of Baïf, denying that the most revered human institutions have any moral or rational basis. In particular, Aubert affects to regard the setting up of laws as the downfall of mankind, since it introduced concepts like property and gain. 'Nous avons délaissé nostre liberté naturelle', he declares in the Second Dialogue, and then eulogises the animals who have not done so:

Vous vivez heureusement le temps que le destin vous veut prester la vie. Vous n'avez aucunes loix qui donnent plus d'autorité à un

[1] *Ibid.* f. C4ᵃ and ᵇ.
[2] On this subject, see G. Boas, *The happy beast in French thought of the seventeenth century* (1933).
[3] Guy de Brués, *Dialogues*, ed. P. P. Morphos (Baltimore, 1953).

de vostre espece qu'à l'autre, et qui vous enseignent d'invahir et usurper les biens que nature vous despart egalement...Vous n'avez jamais voulu abandonner vostre simplicité naturelle pour sçavoir cognoistre l'honeste et le deshoneste, le vice et la vertu...Vous n'avez jamais entretenu des advocats qui au pris de vostre misere vous ayent vendu leur audacieux caquet...Vous n'avez jamais ouy ces mots *mien* et *tien*.[1]

Plato, he claims, was proposing a contradiction in terms, in instituting laws in his republic and at the same time desiring that the words 'mine' and 'thine' should never be heard in it: since 'après les loix introduittes, toutes les miseres desquelles nous sommes affligez nous aviendroient'.[2] And although it is Ronsard who, in the *Dialogues* of Brués, presents the moral and rational point of view about the laws, Aubert quotes Ronsard's *Hymne de la Justice* (lines 67–70 and 53–56) in support of his own opinion.

How far do the *Dialogues* reflect conversations which could really have taken place between the characters in question? Guy de Brués was not one of the inner circle of the Pléiade, but in 1555 Ronsard addressed to him one of the sonnets in the *Continuation des Amours*,[3] and the dedication stood unchanged in all the editions published in his lifetime: as Ronsard was notoriously quick to erase the name of anyone mentioned in his poems with whom he had subsequently fallen out, this authorises us to suppose that Ronsard knew and approved of him in 1555 and did not withdraw his favour from him when the *Dialogues* were published in 1557. In the first Collected Works of Ronsard, in 1560, a footnote to the sonnet by Rémy Belleau, another member of the group, explained carefully who Brués was and referred politely to his *Dialogues*.[4]

---

[1] Brués, *op. cit.* pp. 185–6 (152–3 of original edition).
[2] *Ibid.* pp. 260–1.
[3] Sonnet, 'Veus-tu sçavoir, Brués, en quel estat je suis?', Lau. VII, pp. 166–7. In the posthumous editions, the name of Brués is replaced by that of Claude Binet, Ronsard's biographer.
[4] 'Il adresse ce sonet à Brués, homme fort docte, & des mieus versez en la cognoissance du Droit et de la Philosophie, comme il fait paroistre par certains dialogues qui se lisent aujourd'huy'. Quoted by Laumonier, Lau. VII, p. 166, n. 4.

Guillaume Aubert could quite well have participated in discussions with Ronsard and Baïf at this time. He was a Poitiers jurist, practising in Paris, and, though more particularly a friend of Joachim du Bellay (then in Italy), knew the other poets of the Pléiade too. Ronsard bestowed upon him, in the *Continuation des Amours* of 1555,[1] one of the finest of his anacreontic odes, 'Versons ces roses...', which contained a tribute to the memory of Jean Brinon who had been the patron of them both; in 1556 he addressed to him the sonnet, 'Penses-tu, mon Aubert, que l'empire de France...'[2] In that same year, 1556, Aubert himself published a poem called *Chant de la Justice*,[3] dedicated to Jean Brinon, which (as Brinon died early in 1555) was probably composed at about the same time as Ronsard's *Les Armes* (1555)—also dedicated to Brinon—and a little earlier than Ronsard's *Hymne de la Justice* (late 1555). Aubert's *Chant de la Justice* is spoken by Astraea escorted by 'les pucelles/Qui présidoient au siècle d'or', notably Faith, Peace and Humanity.[4] As to the 'primitivist' point of view which Aubert is represented as defending, he may well have been, or appeared at least to Brués, the most suitable of the four speakers, as the only professional advocate among them, to plead a controversial and even paradoxical case, while being in real life a staid and even conventional figure. If, on the other hand, Brués makes Baïf and Aubert expound the views of the 'nouveaux académiciens', or sceptics, it is (ostensibly at least) for the express purpose of refuting them, for Ronsard and Nicot are represented as converting the other two in the end to the more orthodox opinions. Thus, the choice that Brués makes, to argue for one or the other point of view, among the four

[1] *Ibid.* p. 189.
[2] *Ibid.* p. 310 (after the *Nouvelle Continuation des Amours*, 1556).
[3] In his edition of Guillaume Michel, *De la justice et de ses espèces* (Paris, 1556, f. A4ᵇ). See below, p. 149.
[4] Morphos was unable to find 'any concordance between his true ideas and feelings and the position he is represented as holding in the *Dialogues*; the point of his poem *De la Justice* was to uphold the concept that the individual conscience of a virtuous person is on a higher plane than positive human laws, not to preach ethical and juristic scepticism as Aubert is made to do by Brués in the *Dialogues*' (Brués, *op. cit.*, introductory study, pp. 72–3).

protagonists, in the debate, may be quite arbitrary. The possibility remains that some discussion of such topics as those treated in the *Dialogues* had indeed taken place among Ronsard and his friends at the period indicated by Brués, that is during the summer following the reconciliation between Ronsard and Baïf (1555).

From the point of view of Guy de Brués, such discussion (if it took place at all) was no more than the starting point of the *Dialogues*, for which he obtained a privilege, 30 August 1556, and published eventually in 1557. The familiarity with philosophical literature and with the technique of philosophical discussion which he attributes to Ronsard and Baïf is no doubt much in excess of what either could in real life have commanded; that they were represented as the protagonists in the discussion shows more concern to imitate the literary form of the philosophical dialogues of antiquity than to respect the real character of the poets. Not surprisingly, the modern editor of Brués, who points this out, has found no trace of the influence of the *Dialogues* upon the poetry of Baïf or of Ronsard, whether before or after their publication.[1] He concludes, very judiciously,

From this contact, Baïf remains impervious to any speculative thinking, from what we can gather from his writings. As for Ronsard, the views which he presents in his philosophic poems are significant by their imaginative conception of the celestial spheres rather than by any philosophic system consistently held together. In his love poems he continues to express mainly the variations of his own moods, not any integrated set of moral attitudes that might be related to the influence of the *Dialogues*. We may conclude that Ronsard, who was exposed to philosophic ideas from other sources also, was primarily a poet: he was moved by the poetry of philosophic visions rather than by the convincing force of philosophic explanations of the world, and in his marked eclecticism he was led by his temperament more than by any logical congruity of his thinking.[2]

Influence upon the poets of an actual conversation on these ideas, held in the summer of 1555, would not, however,

---

[1] Brués, *op. cit.* pp. 71 ff.   [2] *Ibid.* pp. 81–2.

necessarily have taken the form of philosophical discussion in their poetry. Just as Brués, after hearing such a conversation, or hearing of it, may have seen in it an elegant setting for a serious philosophical debate, the poets may in retrospect have let their imagination dwell upon the primitive state of man, the Age of Gold, and so on, and have been reminded of other discussions or celebrations of these themes which they had read.

For what it is worth,—the sonnet of Baïf 'Que le siecle revinst de celle gent dorée',[1] dates from the year, 1555, in which Brués represents these conversations as having taken place.

As to Ronsard, the first of his descriptions of the Age of Gold, in *Les Armes*, appeared in the *Meslanges* (1555, printing completed 22 November 1554[2]), and the *Hymne de la Justice* in the first book of *Hymnes* (1555).[3] The only poem he addressed to Nicot, the Odelette 'La Nature a donné des cornes aus toreaus', appeared in the *Bocage* of 1554,[4] and it deals (though jokingly) with the subject of the relative endowment of man and the animals by Nature, a theme which comes under discussion in the *Dialogues* of Brués.

Thus these, and Baïf's sonnet to Francine on the Age of Gold, and Aubert's *Chant de la Justice*, were published during the two years preceding the completion of Brués' *Dialogues* and within a few months of the time when Brués represents Baïf and Ronsard holding discussions with Aubert and with Nicot.

I am therefore inclined to think that conversations on some of the subjects dealt with in the *Dialogues* really had been taking place in 1554 and 1555 among Ronsard and his friends. Whether the conversations were stimulated by Ronsard's composition of *Les Armes*, etc., or whether the poems were stimulated by the conversations, is another question.

---

[1] See above, p. 98. Baïf is represented as deeply interested in the question, what animal he would have wished to be had he been given the choice of rebirth as man or animal (cf. Menander in Stobaeus, *Florilegium*, CVI, 8), Brués, *op. cit.* [5], p. 95. He treats this theme in the poem 'Maury, si quelque Promethée', *VII Livre des poemes* (*Œuvres en rime*, ed. Marty-Laveaux, II, 366–8), published in his collected works of 1573, date of composition uncertain. Cf. Ronsard, *Elégie à Robert de La Haye*, 'Si j'estois à renaistre au ventre de ma mère' (1560). See above, p. 28.

[2] Lau. VI, pp. 131–2.   [3] Lau. VIII, pp. 47 ff.
[4] Lau. VI, p. 115. Brués, *op. cit.* pp. 185–7, etc.

To someone like Brués, the notion of an Age of Gold, or of natural man, was only incidental to the argument, and the argument (however genuinely based on reports of the conversations) was a serious philosophical exercise. To the poets they were themes capable of setting in motion a creative process. The cleverness to see how such a theme could be used, whether paradoxically or not, in a debate on juristic and sociological relativism, and the skill to argue for it, is one thing: the power and the inclination to imagine humanity really living in such conditions is another. Baïf, in a single sonnet, and Ronsard, in several eloquent passages, used their imagination thus, perhaps stimulated by participating in discussions on the subject with their friends: Ronsard's response was on a larger scale, and quite different in character from Baïf's.

BÉRANGER DE LA TOUR; GUILLAUME POSTEL

A description of 'La forme de vivre de ceulx du bon temps, qu'on appelloit l'aage doré' featured prominently in the allegorical work composed by Jean Bouchet to commemorate the passing of the age of Francis I, *Triomphes du treschrestien roy de France François premier*, published in 1550. For Bouchet, the Age of Gold did not lie in the remote past. Its society was not structurally different from that of his own time, any more than it had been for Guillaume Michel when he wrote *Le siècle doré* in 1521. But it was already past. It was—duly idealised—the relatively stable and prosperous society which the 74-year-old Bouchet could remember in his boyhood, and which he thought of with nostalgia:

> Quelques temps fut que de ces habitacles,
> Les habitans par les divins oracles
> Vivoient en paix, se donnoient du bon temps
> Joyeusement, sans guerres ne contends:
> Chascun faisoit ce qu'estoit tenu faire,
> Sans l'un à l'autre aulcunement forfaire...[1]

Bouchet was still a personality in the literary and intellectual life of Poitiers, a centre familiar to many young poets and

---

[1] Bouchet, *Triomphes du treschrestien roy de France François premier* (1550), f. 85.

students of law, and it is unlikely that Ronsard and his friends failed to look at this his last work, royal in subject and handsomely printed. Ronsard himself had a personal reason to feel interest in anything that Bouchet wrote: his father, who died in 1544, had been for some forty years a friend and benefactor of Bouchet, who always wrote of him with affection and gratitude.[1]

Were there any other works which came out for the first time immediately before the period of Ronsard's greatest interest in the Age of Gold, which might have directed his attention to the theme? Any such work would, it is true, have been equally available to all the other French poets of the time: yet Ronsard was particularly sensitive to literary fashions, and probably had a keener professional interest than most of his contemporaries in keeping abreast of new publications.

Certainly two books actually entitled 'The Age of Gold' appeared in French bookshops 1551-3. One was a volume of verse, *Le siècle d'or et autres vers divers*, by Béranger de La Tour d'Albénas.[2] The other was *La doctrine du siècle doré* by Guillaume Postel.[3]

It may be added that Guillaume Aubert of Poitiers was preparing for posthumous publication the work *De la justice et de ses espèces*,[4] which he was to dedicate (with a *Chant de la Justice* of his own) to Jean Brinon (1556), and *De la justice et de ses especes* was the last work of Guillaume Michel. Were this to be the same man as the author of *Le siècle doré* of 1521,[5] we should have a direct link between *Le siècle doré* and members of Ronsard's circle of friends who might have talked to him about it.

The poem of Béranger de La Tour is by no means insignificant. In seventy-one stanzas, of six decasyllabic lines each, he

[1] A. Hamon, *Un grand rhétoriqueur poitevin: Jean Bouchet, 1476-?1557* (Thèse), Paris, 1901, pp. 53, 137, and 231.
[2] Lyon 1551, 8°. Not signed with the author's name but only with his motto 'Souspir d'espoir', and dedicated Albenas 1 May 1551 to M. de Bresé, Bishop of Viviers. [3] Paris (1553), 16°.
[4] Paris 1556, 8°. Cf. above, p. 145.
[5] Weinberg, 'Guillaume Michel, dit de Tours, the editor of the 1526 *Roman de la Rose*', queries this but, I think, unnecessarily (see my forthcoming note in BHR).

LE SIECLE
D'O R.

*

A V A N T *moymesme, auant*
l'homme formé,
Vn vil Chaos, en soy, tenoit fermé
Le pur Neant dont prouint tou-
te chose:
Infuse estoit l'humidité au sec.
Le chaud au froid, le bien au mal auec;
Et l'vnion en guerre y estoient close.

Le hault, le bas, le mylieu, & l'extreme,
Le plus, le moins alors estoient vn mesme:
L'amer, le doux, le mol, l'aspre, & le dur
Se compartoient ensemble sans contendre
Le cours du temps ne se pouuoit estendre,
Car le passé, se ioingnoit au futur.

En mesme place illec faisoient seiour
L'obscurité, & la clarté du iour:
Mort, vie aussi en paix contregardees,
Le plein le vuide ensemble se mettoient:
Et en ce creux massif cachez estoient,
Les haults secrets des premieres Idees.

a 4 *Mais*

Figure 10. First lines of Béranger de la Tour's poem
on the Age of Gold
Le Siècle d'or, Lyon, 1551, 8°

---

develops a monologue spoken (as the reader gradually comes
to understand) by the First Man, who has presided over the
Age of Gold, recalling his immensely long and idyllically
happy life, as he awaits the end of the reign of Astraea and of the
rule of Saturn which he knows to be imminent, and with it

his own removal to some higher form of existence. This is not the Garden of Eden, though the poem is strongly religious in tone, but rather a Christian and neoplatonist dream of what the Garden of Eden would have remained but for the Fall. The speaker has lived in perfect obedience to God, in perfect love and companionship with the woman given him by God, with the unending interest and joy of his children and his children's children and unending delight in the animals and birds with whom he lives in perfect trust and friendship.

Béranger's technique, like that of Héroët, seems amateurish when compared with Ronsard's own, but he is quite able to say what he wants, and that is not without a touch of real romantic imagination.

At a humbler level, Béranger does as Lorenzo de' Medici did in the *Selva Seconda* (which indeed he is likely to have known): he indulges in a long series of stanzas elaborating at leisure and in detail a personal picture of a human life in the Age of Gold. Like Lorenzo, he makes much of the happy relationship with the animals, and like him too he describes the mastery enjoyed by man over his own mind and body. More adventurously, he actually pictures the love, innocent of passion, which Lorenzo had specified, in an idyllic account of the first marriage and the first birth.

If much of the poem lies outside the range of Ronsard's interests and sympathies, it includes features dear to him:

> Terre administre & produit d'elle mesme
> Fruits differents, sans que je plante ou seme,
> Comme ayant pris de me nourrir la charge...[1]

> Je suis mon Roy, mon directeur & guide,
> Entreteneur de ma franchise, & cuide
> Que loy ne peult en oster ou distraire...[2]

> Durant mon regne equalité conduit
> Tous les vivans: ce que plus les induit
> De ne porter l'un contre l'autre envie...[3]

> Gland ma faim chasse, & ma soif le rivage.[4]

[1] *Le Siècle d'or*, p. 12.   [2] *Ibid.* p. 13.
[3] *Ibid.* p. 14.   [4] *Ibid.* p. 14.

There is, moreover, considerable emphasis on the woodland setting of this Age of Gold:

> Apres ayant cueilli assez dequoy
> Pour me nourrir, je m'en entre à requoy
> Souz le couvert de mes vertes maisons.[1]

> Loing de voisins sont noz maisons natales,
> Ormeaux branchuz servent de toict, ou sales,
> Et au pavé les motes verdoyantes:
> Et comme à nous, ce lieu demeure ouvert,
> Ouvert aussi est aux bestes errantes.[2]

The Age of Gold according to Guillaume Postel is a very different story. A pioneer of the study of oriental languages and customs, particularly of Hebrew and Arabic, he became deeply interested in the elements of true religion common to Jewish, Christian and Moslem belief. Adopting opinions recalling those of Joachim of Flora, he began to preach the coming of a further revelation of God to man, in which men of all creeds and sects would be united in brotherhood by the Holy Spirit. In this revelation, in which the French nation was to play a special part, a series of divinely inspired women (among whom, interestingly for the period, he numbered Joan of Arc) had already begun to supply leaders and prophets. By 1552 books and pamphlets on these lines were being published almost monthly, and in 1553 they reached a climax, including *La doctrine du siecle doré, ou l'évangélike regne de Jésus, roy des roys*,[3] printed both by itself and as a sequel to the yet wilder discourse entitled *Les tres merveilleuses victoires des femmes du nouveau-monde*. A commentary on the Fourth Eclogue of Virgil came out the same year under the title, *Sibillinorum versuum a Virgilio in quarta Bucolicorum ecloga transcriptorum ecfrasis commentarii instar*,[4] in which Virgil's prophecy of the return of the Age of Gold was interpreted in terms of Postel's teaching.

In such works, Postel promised the return of the Age of Gold through the agency of France and of the kings of France,

---

[1] *Le Siècle d'or*, p. 13.　　　　[2] *Ibid.* p. 15.
[3] Paris (J. Ruelle), 1553, 16°.　　[4] Paris (J. Gueullart), 1553, 4°.

not as a courtier's compliment but with a visionary's conviction:

Comme il pleut à Dieu soubz le Gallique nom jadis instituer l'aage doré, donnant trescertaine persuasion, tant par les livres Sibyllins comme aussi par les Sacréz, qu'il fault que tel Siècle soit Restitué au monde, aussi fault il tenir pour tout certain que Dieu immuable de dedans ledict Gallique peuple Restituera toutes choses par son adversaire Satan destruictes, faisant fondement par les deux premiers Espritz du monde...[1]

Although Postel withdrew for some time to Bâle in the summer of 1553, it was not until 1562, the year which saw the appearance at Lyons of Matthieu d'Antoine's *Responce aux resveries et hérésies de Guillaume Postel*, that he was detained at the monastery of Saint-Martin-des-Champs where he remained until his death in 1581.

In Ronsard's *Les Isles Fortunées*, however, published the same year as *La doctrine du siecle doré*, 1553, there is a very hostile reference to him and his influence. One of the blessed immunities of the Fortunate Isles is said by the poet to be that

Ni là, Postel de sa vaine science
N'a point troublé la simple conscience
Du populace: ains sans manquer de foi
D'un seul Jesus reconnoissent la Loi.[2]

Thus, if Ronsard disapproved of Postel, at least there can be no doubt whatever that he knew, or knew of, his recent writings.

Postel is, indeed, too absorbed in preaching the imminent return of the Age of Gold to explain what it had been like in the past. Even had he done so, it would probably have provided little material for such a picture as Ronsard's. And had Ronsard wished to represent the Age of Gold as a world of religious revival, he had earlier and more orthodox precedents to follow.[3]

[1] *Les tres-merveilleuses victoires des femmes du nouveau monde. A la fin est adjoustée la Doctrine du siecle doré*, p. 45. This is dedicated to Marguerite, Duchess of Berry (sister of Henry II, afterwards Duchess of Savoy).
[2] Lau. v, pp. 186–7, lines 189–92.
[3] E.g. Jean Raulin. See above, pp. 5–6.

It may at least be said that the phrase 'Age of Gold', and the idea (however differently conceived to Ronsard's) were 'in the air' at the time when he turned his attention to the theme, first in *Les Isles Fortunées* and then in the series of passages beginning with that in *Les Armes*, and that it was used, by no means only in the conventional manner, to denote a coming period of material and artistic prosperity.

THE FOUR AGES AND PROGRESS

Ronsard's poetry shows an obvious tension between at least two conceptions of the Age of Gold, the 'primitivist' and the 'civilised'. This tension reflects a subject of disagreement which became in his lifetime a burning issue among writers both in France and England: the idea of Progress.[1]

'You suppose the first age was the goulde age. It is nothing soe,' protested Gabriel Harvey in a letter to Spenser. 'Bodin defendith the goulde age to flourishe nowe, and owr first grandfathers to have rubbid thorowghe in the iron and brasen age at the beginninge when all thinges were rude and unperfitt in comparison of the exquisite finesse and delicacye that we ar growen unto at these dayes.'[2]

This rebuke did not prevent Spenser from writing in the introductory stanzas of Book v of the *Faerie Queene*, published in 1596:

> For from the golden age, that first was named,
> It's now at earst become a stonie one,

and from going on to celebrate 'Saturne's ancient raigne' when Justice—the subject of Book v—reigned supreme.

Jean Bodin, to whose authority Harvey appealed, was especially critical of the tradition which represented all human

---

[1] J. B. Bury, *The idea of progress: an inquiry into its origins and growth* (1924), is still useful for this subject though mainly concerned with later periods.

[2] *Works*, ed. A. B. Grosart (1884), I, 146 (Letter-book of 1573–80). On the use of the theme in sixteenth-century English literature see P. Meissner, 'Das goldene Zeitalter in der englischen Renaissance', *Anglia*, LIX (1935), 351–67, and Professor H. Levin's important essay 'The Golden Age and the Renaissance' in *Literary Views: critical and historical essays*, ed. C. Camden, published for Rice University (Chicago University Press, 1964), pp. 1–14.

history as occurring within the scheme of the Four Ages, Gold, Silver, Brass and finally Iron, and which identified each with the successive empires which had dominated the civilised world, Babylon, Persia, Greece and Rome. A full exposition of this scheme may be found in the *Historia de duabus civitatibus* of Otto von Freising,[1] which was read and studied from the twelfth to the sixteenth century, and survives in no less than fifty manuscripts, receiving the honours of first edition in print in 1515 at the hands of the humanist Cuspinianus, who dedicated it to the Emperor Maximilian I. In particular, Otto accused Aeneas of having inaugurated the Age of Iron, by overthrowing in Italy the last remains of the peaceful era inherited from Saturn, and by committing Rome to a policy of war and conquest; St Augustine had already denounced that policy in chapters IX–X of Book III of the *City of God* and quoted the lines from Virgil describing the end of the Age of Gold:

deterior donec paulatim ac decolor aetas,
et belli rabies et amor successit habendi.[2]

To Bodin such preconceived ideas prevented history from being properly written and masked the improvements which had in reality taken place in the course of time.[3] He was not alone in thinking 'the goulde age to flourishe nowe', but his arguments were more challenging than were the easy assertions of Renaissance eulogists.

Belief in the reality of human progress, and doubts or fears about it, could both be naturally expressed at this period in terms of the Age of Gold, as can be seen in the case of the disagreement between Gabriel Harvey (quoting Bodin) and Spenser. It was not yet only poets who used the symbol, nor was it, for them, yet necessarily an empty phrase. Pascal was to

[1] *Ottonis Episcopi Frisingensis Chronica sive Historia de duabus civitatibus*, ed. A. Hofmeister (1912), Prologus; Lib. I, xxv–xxvi: Lib. II, xiii; Lib. VI, xxxvi. The identifications are related to the prophecy in the Book of Daniel, ii, 31–45, arising out of Nebuchadnezzar's dream of the idol with the feet of clay (whose head, made of gold, symbolises the kingdom of Babylon). [2] *Aeneid*, VIII, 326–7.
[3] *Methodus ad facilem historiarum cognitionem* (1566), cap. VII. On Bodin, cf. also above, p. 134.

stigmatise it as part of the jargon which his contemporaries believed to constitute poetic beauty.[1] It is in fact arguable that it could still for at least another century symbolise a genuine personal vision of happiness, and survived even Voltaire's mockery in *Le Mondain*:

> Regrettera qui veut le bon vieux Tems,
> Et l'Age d'Or et le Régne d'Astrée,
> Et les beaux jours de Saturne et de Rhée...[2]

Satisfaction or discontent with the present were usually at hand to set up a state of emotion about the idea of progress, and to give character to the consequent attitude of the writer towards the Age of Gold. Ronsard's career in France, and Spenser's in England, coincided with a period of considerable economic distress which for most individuals and families would compare badly with the conditions they knew to have existed earlier in the century: factors such as these helped to sharpen the controversy on the question, whether human history was a progress or a regress, and whether the Age of Gold was accordingly to be located in the past, the present or the future. Spenser, always deeply concerned with moral values, placed it firmly in the past, as an era primarily of justice and of virtue, though one in which 'all things freely grew out of the ground'. Ronsard, fundamentally hedonistic, was more concerned with material and aesthetic criteria. Hence the duality in his attitude towards the idea of progress. Acceptance of the present, or imminent future, as the Age of Gold, reflects moods of appreciation of the 'exquisite finesse and delicacye' of his age, in moments of success and pleasure at the brilliant Valois court. Celebration of the Age of Gold in the remote past or in remote America, among wandering woodland foodgatherers, reflects moods of revolt against that age, not only against the court but against many political and economic trends. Among the symptoms of

[1] '...On ne sait ce que c'est que ce modèle naturel qu'il faut imiter et à faute de cette connaissance on a inventé de certains termes bizarres: "siècle d'or, merveille de nos jours, fatal", etc., et on appelle ce jargon beauté poétique' (*Pensées*, ed. L. Brunschvicg, no. 33).

[2] A. Morize, *L'Apologie du luxe au XVIIIᵉ siècle et Le Mondain de Voltaire* (1909), p. 133.

The Four Ages and Progress

the latter which aroused his indignation, we know to have been the destruction of the forests, to bring financial gain to needy kings and princes, and to supply the ever-increasing demands of towns and industries. We are told that there are many instances of English writers in the sixteenth and seventeenth centuries 'who, in invoking the Golden Age, or more often a golden world, couple the allure of greenwoods or gardens together with their fears of enclosure, industry and urbanisation'.[1] This is a salutary reminder of the strong feelings which could find expression in references to the Age of Gold, and may be a clue to the state of mind in which Ronsard became attracted to the theme, and began to elaborate the elegiac or 'primitivist' interpretation of it. 'Aucun poète', declared Pierre de Nolhac, 'n'a été plus que Ronsard mêlé par sa carrière aux choses de son époque...il en a connu tous les aspects, fréquenté tous les milieux et hardiment partagé les passions.'[2] The insistent preference for a forest scene, a wandering life, and total abstention from interference with Nature, which his poetry at one period shows, may, however, require further explanation.

[1] H. Levin, *op. cit.* p. 10.
[2] *Préface du catalogue de l'exposition Ronsard à la Bibliothèque Nationale* (Paris, 1925).

5

✤ ✤

Ronsard's natural surroundings, tastes and temperament idealised in his image of the Age of Gold

THE COUNTRY

Intellectual as Ronsard was, he was first and foremost a poet. His conception of the Age of Gold was determined not only by reading and discussion, but by factors more intimate and more difficult to classify. Among these, account must be taken of taste and temperament.

Why did he, at least for a few years and in certain moods, choose to idealise a state of nature, when men lived in the forests, without homes, herds or crops? Is there a possible clue in his attitude to nature itself?

The starting point, in studying this question, must be the realities of the natural scene amid which he was brought up. This was the valley of the Loir, the river which flows through Illiers, Châteaudun and Vendôme, to join the Sarthe below La Flèche. Both join the Mayenne above Angers to become the Maine for a short distance, and eventually run into the Loire, which meanwhile has been taking its stately course parallel with the Loir but south of it and separated from it by a high ridge. Ronsard was born at the manor-house of La Possonnière, just above the village of Couture (Loir-et-Cher), on the left bank of the Loir between Montoire and La Chartre, in the Bas-Vendômois. This was his home until the death of his father in 1544, though by that time he had been absent from it for considerable periods of time, first as a schoolboy, then as a page at court, and then as a student. His elder brother Claude, who came into La Possonnière, died in 1556, and his duties as a

guardian of his nephews and nieces thenceforth took him there
from time to time. When the opportunity came to secure the
ecclesiastical benefices he needed for his livelihood, he was
careful to arrange that they should be in this district, which
suggests an enduring affection for it.[1]

At first, his nature poetry is a faithful reflection of the
countryside where he grew up, the valley of the Loir below
Vendôme. From his sparkling ode on the source,

> Source d'argent toute pleine,
> Dont le beau cours éternel
> Fuit pour enrichir la plaine
> De mon païs paternel...[2]

he celebrated its course in terms of almost topographical
precision, as it passed through his homeland,

> Deus longs tertres t'emmurent,
> Dont les flancs durs & fors
> Des fiers vents qui murmurent
> S'opposent aus effors.

> Sur l'un Gâtine sainte
> Mere des demidieus,
> Sa teste de verd painte,
> Envoie jusque aus cieus,

> Et sur l'autre prend vie
> Maint beau sep, dont le vin
> Porte bien peu d'envie
> Au vignoble Angevin.

---

[1] See above, p. 44. The principal source of information about Ronsard's
early life is his *A Pierre de Paschal*, published in the *Bocage* of 1554 Lau. vi,
pp. 61–70 and Laumonier's footnotes, and Cl. Binet, *La vie de Pierre de
Ronsard*, ed. Laumonier. Cf. H. Longnon, *P. de Ronsard, essai de biographie:
les ancêtres, la jeunesse*.

[2] *A la source du Loir, Odes* (1550), IV, xv; Lau. II, p. 129. The source is in the
Bois de Gâtine (Etang de Gâtine) close to the village of Saint-Denis-des-
Puits, above Illiers (Eure-et-Loir). Ronsard's road from his home to Paris,
which he must often have travelled, lay for the most part along the course
of the Loir as far as Châteaudun; he had relatives at Illiers, his paternal
grandmother being a member of the Illiers family, so it would have been
easy for him to make the detour necessary to visit the source. The Bois de
Gâtine celebrated in his poetry is, however, a different wood, of the same
name, within walking distance of his old home. See Map, p. 195.

Natural surroundings, tastes and temperament

Le Loir tard à la fuite
En soi s'ebanoiant,
D'eau lentement conduite
Tes champs va tournoiant,
Rendant bon & fertile
Le pais traversé,
Par l'humeur qui distile
Du gras limon versé.[1]

The visitor to this part of the Loir valley at the present day has no difficulty in recognising the subject of this passage. The little river winds its way along the course it has made for itself through the plateau of tufa, leaving the meadows away from the steep side rich and fertile; on the slopes or *coteaux* facing south, above the right bank, there are still vineyards on favourable sites, and on the hill-sides facing north there are still woods; by going down the valley as far as Le Lude, one can still see majestic trees coming right down to the river.

Among the odes of 1550 which celebrated this district, or special features and places in it, are some of his most beautiful poems: *A la fontaine Bellerie*,[2] *A la forest de Gâtine*,[3] and *De l'élection de son sepulcre*.[4] The latter, in its original form, included a particularised description of the place he had chosen in fancy to be buried in, the Green Island, surrounded by the waters of the Loir where it is joined by its tributary, the Braye, at Couture. Already in 1555 he deleted the stanzas giving these details. At twenty-five—he was at most that age when he wrote the ode—the sensibility to nature, which had moved him to pray for a grave in the open air rather than a marble tomb even near those of kings, was still closely linked to the actual places where he had become aware of it. Five years later he was evidently moving already towards the classical ideal expressed in a poem published posthumously:

[1] *Les louanges de Vandomois, à Julien Peccate, ibid.* II, xvii, Lau. I, pp. 222–3, lines 9–28.
[2] Lau. I, pp. 203–5. ('O Déesse Bellerie...' in 1555 rewritten to read, 'O fontaine Bellerie'.)
[3] *Ibid.* p. 243. ('Donque forest, c'est à ce jour...' in 1555 rewritten to read, 'Couché sous tes umbrages vers...')
[4] Lau. II, pp. 97–103. ('Antres, & vous fontaines'.)

5. The garden of the Château du Lude, by the Loir (spring 1960).

J'ayme fort les jardins qui sentent le sauvage,
J'ayme le flot de l'eau qui gazoille au rivage...

Responce aux injures

6. The tomb of Guillaume du Bellay in Le Mans Cathedral.

Je veil, j'enten, j'ordonne,
Qu'un sepulcre on me donne,
Non pres des Rois levé,
Ne d'or gravé.

7. The Loir at the Ile Verte (spring 1960).

> Mais en cette isle verte
> Oú la course entr'ouverte
> Du Loir, autour coulant,
>   Est accolant.
>   De l'élection de son sépulcre

8. The Forest: Midsummer's dawn.

Dans les hautes forets des hommes reculées,
Dans les antres segrets de frayeur tout couverts...
Discours à Pierre l'Escot

Le general est ferme, et ne fait place au temps,
Le particulier meurt presque au bout de cent ans;[1]

the reference to:

> cette isle verte,
> Où la course entrouverte
> Du Loir, autour coulant,
> Est accolant,

> Là où Braie s'amie
> D'une eau non endormie,
> Murmure à l'environ
> De son giron,

was suppressed in 1555, no doubt as detracting from the universality of the poem's appeal. Where such references were allowed to remain, it was chiefly in contexts where the classical models evoked by Ronsard themselves contained allusions to a well-localised neighbourhood. Thus the ode *A la fontaine Bellerie* in Book II in 1550, celebrating a spring on a farm close to his birthplace, was preserved, though with many alterations, in all editions of his works, saved perhaps by its obvious appeal to the ode *O fons Bandusiae* of Horace (III, xiii) as well as by the haunting 7-line stanza form specially devised for it by Ronsard in his most exquisite lyrical mood; another ode with the same title, beginning 'Argentine fonteine vive', in Book III in 1550, was suppressed in 1553, but reinstated with alterations in 1555.[2] The evolution of his nature poetry is not merely towards the general and universal: it is also towards those aspects of nature which meant most to him. The scenery of the Loir valley, in

---

[1] *Elegie II, A Philippes des-Portes, Chartrain*, Lau. XVIII, 1, p. 249, lines 35–6.

[2] Lau. I, pp. 203–5, and Lau. II, pp. 14–15, and footnotes and variants. Cf. *A sa lire, Odes* (1550), I, xx, Lau. I, p. 165, lines 49–52:

> Mais ma Gastine, & le haut crin des bois
> Qui vont bornant mon fleuve Vandomois,
> Le Dieu bouquin qui la Neufaune entourne,
> Et le saint Chœur qui en Braie sejourne...

These allusions, laboriously explained in the *Breve exposition de quelques passages du premier livre des odes* by 'I.M.P.' (Lau. II, p. 211), corresponded to those of Horace to Tibur, etc. in the Ode, *Quem tu Melpomene*, IV, iii, which Ronsard was here imitating.

which his taste for landscape had been formed, offered him
considerable variety: forests, river-meadows, vineyards, gardens
and cornfields. His observations of these became, like the
experiences he derived from his reading, the object of a process
of selection. His picture of the island in *De l'election de son
sepulcre* is already significant in this respect. We know from the
suppressed stanzas the exact place he had in mind, the *île verte*
at the junction of the Loir and the Braye: it is in fact, while very
pretty and secluded, less than a mile from the centre of Couture
(a thriving village even in the sixteenth century) on one side,
and from Pont de Braye (on the main road from Vendôme to
Angers) on the other, and the mill of Le Pin, just up the Loir,
overlooks it. The opening lines of the poem, invoking caves,
waterfalls running over high rocks, and forests, before mentioning streams meandering through meadows, suggest a
decidedly more romantic landscape than this. The episode too
in which he pictures 'the shepherds who live near there' coming
once a year to his grave to honour his memory might suggest,
to a reader who did not know the place, that a few shepherds
were the only human beings in the neighbourhood. By the
time he began to celebrate his distinctive picture of the Age of
Gold, this process was being carried a stage further. The passage
of time, the development of his study of poetry and of his
poetic sensibility, and absences from his native countryside,
sifted the elements which had affected him most deeply in his
early impressions of his physical environment.

The early ode *Des roses plantées pres un blé*, 'Dieu te gard
l'honneur du printens', seems to record a recollection of having
seen roses growing against a background of green corn:

> D'assés loin tu vois redoublé
>> Dans le blé
> Ta joue de cinabre teinte,
> Dans le blé qu'on voit rejouir
>> De jouir
> De ton image en son verd peinte.[1]

[1] Lau. II, p. 125, lines 7–12.

On the other hand, the rose (always an important symbol in
Ronsard's poetry) appears in a sonnet of 1555 in a garden near
a lonely forest:

> Douce, belle, gentille, & bien fleurente Rose...
>
> Hé Dieu, que je suis aise alors que je te voi
> Esclorre au point du jour sur l'espine à requoy,
> Dedans quelque jardin pres d'un bois solitere![1]

He might indeed have seen a rose growing in a garden on the
edge of a wood: the woods come down to the end of the
garden at La Possonnière. The emphasis on its seclusion ('à
requoy', 'bois solitaire') make the woods, however, not merely
the background to the rose, but part of the scene in which it is
set.

The third edition of the *Odes*, also published in 1555,
contains a poem of particular significance in this respect,

> Quand je suis vint ou trente mois
> Sans retourner en Vandomois,
> Plein de pensées vagabondes,
> Plein d'un remors, & d'un souci,
> Aus rochers je me plains ainsi,
> Aus bois, aus antres, & aus ondes...[2]

The four following stanzas address in turn each of the natural
features here evoked: 'Rochers...', 'Bois...', 'Antres...',
'Ondes...', contrasting their permanence with the rapid decay
of a human body—his own—as it ages; the last stanza defiantly
proclaims his preference for having been a human being, and
not one of them, since otherwise he would not have known the
experience of being in love with Cassandre. The woods, so
often in poetry a symbol of change, are here remembered for
their perpetual self-renewal: the trees lose their leaves in the

---

[1] Lau. VII, p. 184 (*Continuation des Amours*, LXVII). The conjunction of the rose-
garden and the lonely forest seems to have appeared to Ronsard incongruous
when he reread it much later: 1578–87 editions give the reading 'Aux
jardins de Bourgueil pres d'une eau solitaire'.

[2] *Ibid.* pp. 98–9. The ode took its place, as Ode xiii, in Livre IV (that containing *Au pais de Vandomois, De l'election de son sepulchre, Au fleuve du Loir,
A la source du Loir*, etc.).

winter, but are reclothed with fresh foliage every spring; they are accompanied, as the objects of Ronsard's recollection, by rocks, caves and streams.

In the *Quatre livres des Odes* of 1550 Ronsard showed some fondness for picturing the life of farm and field. The ode 'Argentine fonteine vive' (III, vi) evokes the season of harvest, and the rhythmic thud of threshing with the flail:

> Quand l'esté ménager moissonne
> Le sein de Ceres devétu,
> Et l'aire par compas resonne
> Dessous l'épi de blé batu.[1]

De la venue de l'esté (III, x)[2] is rather like an episode in a series of miniatures showing the work of the different months or seasons of the year, with the careful picture (under the sun in Cancer) of the 'diligente troupe/Des ménagers' working all day in the heat to get the harvest in, and of their wives walking through the fields to them, carrying on their heads wooden platters or casks to bring them their lunch. The shepherd's day too is described, from the moment, before dawn, when he rises to lead his flock to pasture,

> Parmi les plaines découvertes,
> Par les bois, & les rives vertes.

In the hymn *A Saint Gervaise et Protaise* (III, ii) Ronsard affirmed in a different way his solidarity with his fellow countrymen. Celebrating the martyrdom of these saints under the persecutions of Nero, Ronsard asked in the name of the villagers (whose parish church at Couture was dedicated to them) for their intercessions, which were to extend to the

---

[1] Lau. II, p. 14, lines 5–8. The Ode is addressed to *La fontaine Bellerie*, like II, ix.
[2] Lau. II, pp. 23–8. The footnote 1 on p. 23 argues that the ode was written in 1547 (1548 at the latest), and refers to the ode on *Les grans chaleurs de l'année 1547* of Jacques Peletier du Mans. The originality of this ode is emphasised by Laumonier, *Ronsard, poète lyrique*, p. 439. W. H. Storer, *Virgil and Ronsard*, pp. 39–42, points out many parallels with the *Georgics*, and, while admitting that 'it is so cleverly arranged and filled with incidents gained in part from observations in Vendomois that it cannot be called a paraphrase of Virgil', concludes 'if it is not a translation, or paraphrase, it is certainly an imitation' (p. 39).

temporal blessings of prosperity of the corn, the vines and the flocks:

> Faites que des bleds l'apparance
> Ne démente nostre esperance,
> Et du raisin ja verdelet
> Chassez la nue menassante,
> Et la brebis aus champs paissante
> Emplissez d'aigneaus, & de laict.[1]

In a poem published only after his death—written, therefore, at an uncertain date—Ronsard invoked Saint Blasius in a 22-stanza hymn on behalf of the 'pères de famille' of the parish, in this case the parish of Montrouveau (not far from Couture), in which lay the priory of Croixval, one of Ronsard's favourite residences in the last years of his life. A yet more homely and particularised concern was here allowed expression, in a touching rustic litany, for the flocks to be spared the depredations of disease, wolves, thieves and snake-bites and spells; the crops and the vines to be spared excessive heat and cold; the orchards and kitchen-gardens, the houses and children, to be protected; the daughters to find good husbands; the chickens to be safe from foxes, the bees to prosper in their hives, the sheep and goats to have plentiful winter fodder; the farmer himself to be protected against the violence of soldiers, the horrors of lawsuits and the wiles of moneylenders; his labourers to be sturdy and uncomplaining, free from illness and accidents...[2]

The life and work of the countryside does not inspire so much of his mature poetry as might be expected from a man so familiar with it as Ronsard evidently was. No poem of any magnitude is devoted to the subject, and, while he was ready to write an imitation of the *Aeneid*, and completed four books of *La Franciade* in this endeavour, he attempted nothing like

---

[1] Lau. II, pp. 5–7. This ode was retained in all editions of Ronsard's poetry until 1567. Saint Gervaise and Saint Protaise had another claim on Ronsard's attention, as well as their patronage of the parish of Couture: they are the subject of a splendid tapestry in the cathedral of Saint Julien of Le Mans, of which Ronsard was a canon from 1560 and with which he must have been familiar from his boynood; see above, pp. 92–3.

[2] Hynne XII, *Des pères de famille à Monsieur S. Blaise, Sur le chant: 'Te rogamus, audi nos'*, first published in the *Œuvres* of 1587, vol. VII, and edited separately with a commentary by Nicolas Richelet in 1618. Lau. XVIII, 1, pp. 275–80.

the *Georgics*. It would have been quite possible to plan such a work: there was even the recent Italian example of Luigi Alamanni's *La Coltivazione* (1545) dedicated to Francis I and published in Paris.

There were other possible poetic forms open to him, had he wished to celebrate country life. One, of which he was well aware, was a tale with a rustic setting. He went as far as experimenting with this, in *Le voiage de Tours* (1560), a semi-autobiographical story, told in the first person, running to 346 lines.[1] He and Jean-Antoine de Baïf set off one day from Couture to go to a country wedding at Saint-Cosme below Tours on the Loire: the bride was a cousin of the village girl Marie, of Bourgueil, whom Ronsard was courting, and they hoped to see both her and Baïf's Francine, with whom he had fallen in love when he was at Poitiers. Walking up through the forest of Gâtine, they reached the castle of Beaumont-la-Ronce in time to dine there with Ronsard's cousin Philippe de Ronsart, and spent the night at L'Angennerie, apparently in the open air under some willows; by starting at dawn, they arrived at Saint-Cosme to find the wedding festivities in full swing, and joined in the dancing with Marie and Francine. The girls, however, gave them no encouragement and Baïf, after complaining that Francine would not accept the present of two pigeons he had brought her, nor even link her finger with his finger as they danced together, exhausted himself in reproaches and fell fainting with emotion. Ronsard at this moment saw with mortification that Marie's mother was taking her off to the river bank where their boat was tied up to a willow, to go home to Bourgueil at the end of the party, and he sang sadly of his love to the wind that was wafting her down the Loire. Finally, restraining Baïf from a vain attempt to follow Francine home, he took his friend into Tours to spend the night.

[1] Lau. x, pp. 214–30. The poem was published in Book II of the *Amours*, in the first collected edition of his works (1560). The Saint-Cosme which features in the story was the site of the abbey of which Ronsard was subsequently prior *in commendam* and which became his principal country residence. It was then an island in the Loire: the branch of the river which separated it from the left bank was filled in during the eighteenth century.

Ronsard and Baïf are represented as shepherds, and bear diminutive versions of their Christian names—Perrot and Thoinet—and some of their speeches are inspired by Theocritus. There is, however, a good deal of realism. When Thoinet recalls how he first set eyes on Francine in the spring, he characterises the season not only by the traditional signs, like the swallows' return, but also by more detailed and homely observations:

> Quand la lymace, au dos qui porte sa maison,
> Laisse un trac sur les fleurs, quand la blonde toison
> Va couvrant la chenille...[1]

When he was in doubt whether she would return his love, he consulted a witch called Janetton at Crotelles, (near Poitiers), whose antics he describes, and then himself tried forms of divination well known in folklore of the region—the behaviour of two reeds cut for Midsummer Night, and of leaves of hazel grasped in his hands.[2] When he threatens to throw himself into the river, he is careful to mention that he will first take off his 'jaquette et souquenie', the latter being an old-fashioned form of 'souquenille', the proper word for the peasant's smock, and points out the exact spot on the bank, 'Où tu vois ce garçon à la ligne pescher',[3] where he proposes to jump in.

A group of verse-tales such as this one, based on episodes in his own experience, might have provided a vehicle for his powers of observation of country life: it would certainly have been quite a novelty in French literature at the time. Though story-telling was not his strong point—his weakness for long monologues was fatal—he evidently enjoyed writing *contes* of a few hundred lines and never wholly loses the thread of the narrative. The reason for failing to follow up *Le voiage de Tours* is, I think, the same as the reason for his lack of interest in pastoral poetry in general: he could not solve the dilemma which this kind of subject presented him with, since he could neither be satisfied with an artificial convention which bore no

[1] *Ibid.* p. 217, lines 75-7.   [2] *Ibid.* pp. 218-19, lines 95-126.
[3] *Ibid.* p. 222, lines 174-7.

relation to reality, nor find any way of his own of treating
imaginatively the realities of country life.

The mythological symbols of country life were on the other
hand alive and real to him; indeed, he found it natural to think
of all natural phenomena in terms of mythology. This may well
reflect his response to the pictorial art of his time, of which he
must have known well the work of Rosso and Primaticcio at
Fontainebleau: the decoration of the Galerie d'Ulysse by the
latter artist showed not only the whole story of the Odyssey, in
fifty-eight pictures on the walls, but a series of over ninety
mythological subjects on the vaulted ceiling.[1] Poussin, whose
painting (a generation after Ronsard) is in some respects the
counterpart or even the ultimate fulfilment of Ronsard's art,
at once so learned and so brilliant, said that he knew nothing
more proper than this gallery to educate a painter and to fire
his genius.[2] The ballroom (or Galerie de Henri II), for which
Primaticcio designed the wall-paintings, also displayed a vivid
series of mythological compositions, sixty-two in all: among
those for which his original drawing survives is Ceres, showing
the corn-goddess presiding over scenes of cutting and carrying
the harvest and of baking bread.[3]

Whether or not such works of art played any part in forming
Ronsard's mental picture of the natural world, he displays a
similar vigour in handling mythological and allegorical themes,
and it is often in these that he reveals best his power to evoke
realistic country scenes.

The *Hymne de l'Automne* (1563), for instance, has as its subject
the end of summer, with the harvest and the vintage. Of the
Hymnes on the four seasons, it is the most elaborate, and the
longest (470 lines). Only once, however, is a real harvest scene
evoked. Autumn, personified as a young woman, finding her

[1] L. Dimier, *Le Primatice*, chap. III. The Galerie d'Ulysse was demolished in 1736: the existence of the original drawings for about one-third of the subjects, and some copies, plus an engraving of Du Cerceau showing the whole decorative scheme of one bay, give some idea of the effect.
[2] Quoted by L. Dimier, *op. cit.* p. 27.
[3] *Ibid.* pp. 37–40, and pl. XI. The drawing is in the Cabinet des Dessins at Chantilly. The paintings, which survive but heavily restored, were carried out by Niccolo dell'Abbate, to Primaticcio's design.

way through the universe to the palace of her mother Nature,
calls first on her brother Spring, and (finding him away) pillages
his flowers, and then arrives at the palace of Summer: there,
Ceres, with Summer, leads the festivities, dancing with poppies
in her hand and ears of corn upon her head—and, quite suddenly,
the scene becomes a real country house, with a real farmyard;
with the work of the harvest in full swing:

> cette garse entra dans le chasteau:
> Dedans la basse court elle vit meint rateau,
> Meinte fourche, meint van, meinte grosse javelle,
> Meinte jarbe, toison de la moisson nouvelle,
> Boisseaux, poches, bissacs, de grands monceaux de blé
> En l'aire çà & là l'un sur l'autre assemblé.
> Les uns batoient le grain de sur la terre dure,
> Les autres au grenier le portoient par mesure,
> Et soubs les tourbillons les bourriers qui voloyent
> Pour le joüet du vent, parmy l'air s'en alloyent.[1]

But this is short-lived, and the vintage, which Ronsard could
conjure up so vividly for purposes of imagery,[2] is represented
purely in the form of an allegory, the meeting of Autumn and
Bacchus.

Imagery drawn from country life is indeed frequent in his
poetry, even where the theme in hand seems least likely to
suggest it. Thus in the *Responce aux injures* there are similes
referring to a bull maddened by a gadfly, to the bellows in a
blacksmith's shop, to threshing, to a bee going from garden to
garden, and to the taking of a hornets' nest.[3] Even where these
comparisons are modelled upon an example in Virgil or some
other classical poet, they often show a distinct element of

[1] Lau. xii, pp. 60-1, lines 311-20. Van = winnowing-basket, riddle;
javelle = swathe (loose bundle of corn on the threshing-floor); jarbe
(dialect form of gerbe) = sheaf; boisseau = bushel; poche = sack; bis-
sac = double sack (for carrying like saddle-bags); bourrier (old word) =
chaff. Cf. the comparison with threshing and winnowing in the *Responce aux
injures*, Lau. xi, pp. 159-60, lines 851-62.
[2] E.g. the famous comparison of the poet's youthful inspiration, 'Comme on
void en septembre, ez tonneaux Angevins...' in the *Elégie au seigneur
L'Huillier* (*Œuvres*, 1560), Lau. x, pp. 293-4, lines 23 ff.
[3] Lau. xi, p. 119 (lines 47-50), p. 126 (lines 176-8), pp. 159-60 (lines 851-62),
p. 161 (lines 881-6), p. 172 (lines 1106-16).

original observation. In the last-named example, for instance, Ronsard probably had in mind Apollonius Rhodius (as suggested by Laumonier) describing the rout of the Berbycians at the hands of the Argonauts, or Virgil describing the turmoil among the Latins after Aeneas called on them to surrender the town, or both; both use the comparison of angry bees being smoked out. It is not quite correct, however, to say that Ronsard 'uses the same image substituting wasps for bees'.[1] The situation is different: instead of a beekeeper or a shepherd finding a swarm of bees in a cranny of a rock, and using smoke to stupify them or drive them out (in order to take the honey), Ronsard imagines a husbandman, careful of his grapes which are just beginning to ripen, noticing a hornets' nest in a decaying oak nearby, and who, fearing the damage to be expected from their depredations, goes out armed with lighted straw to take the nest (at night—when they will all be in the nest—because the object is to destroy as many as possible).

Ronsard evidently did not think the countryside as a whole (much as he loved it), and the seasonal ritual of rural life and work, sufficiently poetic to inspire him with the main inspiration for a major work, in their own right.

His direct observations of these were used, like the open-air sketches of the old masters, in the studio, to provide elements in a carefully calculated composition depicting a mythological, allegorical or pastoral scene.

'When he came to paint,' says Sir Kenneth Clark of Rembrandt, 'he felt that all these observations were no more than the raw material of art. For him...landscape painting meant the creation of an imaginary world, vaster, more dramatic, and more fraught with associations than that which we can perceive for ourselves.'[2]

That imaginary world, for Ronsard, could not be given an

---

[1] Cf. Apollonius Rhodius, *Arg.* II, 130, and *Aeneid*, XII, 587, and W. B. Cornelia, *Classical sources of the nature references in Ronsard's poetry* (New York, 1934), p. 163. The latter, though limited by definition to what is derivative in Ronsard rather than looking for what is original, is perhaps the most useful repertory available of his nature-imagery.

[2] *Landscape into Art*, p. 31.

agricultural setting. He had lived all his boyhood, and much of his later life, at close quarters with village life. He knew how desperately hard was the work of the *vigneron* and the farmer; when he invoked it in his poetry, it was often to symbolise toil, struggle and fatigue. As to the shepherd, and the cowherd, no one who knew so well what the daily care of flocks and herds involved, could be satisfied for long to write as if they had no trouble except the occasional refusal of a shepherdess to return their love. Ronsard was essentially a poet of the summer, and, as he sat in his rooms in Paris, or Le Mans, or at Court, thinking of the summer countryside of the Loir valley, his thoughts did not turn for long at a time to the fields and vineyards where his fellow-countrymen were working, but to the sensation of resting or wandering in shady gardens, among cool streams and springs and caves, or in the green heart of the forest.

INVIOLATE NATURE

Ronsard's interest in the Age of Gold coincides with a period when he wrote some of his most exquisite poems addressed directly to objects in nature: the *Nouvelle continuation des amours* of 1556 includes:

> Dieu vous gard, messagers fidelles
> Du printemps...[1]

acclaiming in turn the birds, flowers, butterflies and bees, the harbingers of spring, and:

> Bel aubepin verdissant
> Fleurissant
> Le long de ce beau rivage...[2]

with its delicate observation of all the wild life which the tree shelters, the ivy growing up it, the ants' nest under its roots, the bees who have colonised a half-decayed place in its trunk, and the pair of nightingales who return to it each year. His solicitude for natural beauty, often expressed on the subject of flowers,

---

[1] Lau. VII, pp. 294-5. [2] *Ibid.* pp. 242-4.

where he had the support of tradition, is very marked also in his poems to trees.[1]

Ronsard's response to the world of nature round him might on occasion be mingled with thoughts of his love for Cassandre (or for whomsoever was the object of his affections for the moment). It might be mingled too with reflections on art as against nature, or on the court as against the country. It could also be, however, the purest interest and admiration and solicitude for what he saw. In this he was probably exceptional among French poets of his time. He was able, unlike most of his contemporaries, to feel the personality (as it were) of particular woods, rivers, plants and animals, and to appreciate in them a life of their own, in their own right, independent of their significance or usefulness to man.[2]

Exploitation of the land for the use of man might thus be seen in certain moods almost as a desecration, even at its most innocent and necessary: farming is the first step in industrialisation, and Ronsard's daydream puts the clock back to the period when Western Europe was covered with the primeval forest, long before the countryside had acquired the pattern of alternating field and woodland which generations of human effort had already given it in prehistoric times.[3]

The siting of the Age of Gold could not therefore be for him in agricultural or even pastoral society, however idealised: it tended to the scene where man can still see—or think he sees—nature as it was before man set out to master his environment: the forest.

[1] Full appreciation of this aspect of Ronsard's poetic sensibility, and comparison with his contemporaries, would be assisted by more research on the treatment of natural scenery and objects in the French poetry of this period. At present such subjects seem to be rarely chosen for theses. A quite modest dissertation, such as Johanna Lehmann, *Baïfs dichterische Vorstellung von Meer und Wasser* (Romanisches Museum, Greifswald, 1917), makes a really useful contribution to literary criticism in such a field: a study of the treatment of trees and plants, on the lines of Hélène Naïs, *Les animaux dans la poésie française de la Renaissance* (Paris, 1961), would be invaluable.

[2] N. H. Clement, 'Nature and the country in sixteenth and seventeenth century French poetry', *PMLA*, XLIV (1929), 1005–47 (on Ronsard, see especially pp. 1018–24); H. Guy, 'Pierre de Ronsard peintre et interprète de la nature', *Bull. Acad. Delphinale*, XV (1924), 151–64.

[3] Cf. G. Roupnel, *Histoire de la campagne française* (Paris, 1932).

Among the most conspicuous features of the Age of Gold in Ronsard's poetry is the notion of a natural scene untouched by any work of man. For him, in this mood, the ploughshare and the axe are not only symbols of man's perverse determination to improve on nature, but instruments whose effect upon the face of mother earth is felt as a wound by the earth and (on her behalf) by the poet.

This idea is first found in *Les Isles Fortunées* (1553):

> Là, sans navrer, comme ici, nôtre aïeule
> Du soc aigu...[1]

the word 'navrer' still having in sixteenth-century French the full force of its original meaning of violent injury, the cutting edge of the ploughshare being imagined as a weapon.

There are hints of such an idea in the Latin poets, and particularly in the lines of Ovid:

> Ipsa quoque immunis, rastroque intacta, nec ullis
> Saucia vomeribus, per se dabat omnia tellus.[2]

By the following year, the idea of the ploughshare and its effects makes its appearance in poems where it is more strange.

The first instance appears to be the ode to a nightingale, published in the *Bocage* of 1554, where the nightingale is instructed to tell his mistress how her youth and beauty must wilt with the passage of time,

> Et toute la face seichée
> Devient comme une fleur touchée
> Du soc aigu,[3]

which may be contrasted with the gentler picture, of the rose fading and dropping after the heat of a summer day, which he had used in the ode to Cassandre, 'Mignonne, allons voir si la rose', written the previous year.[4]

In an ode in *Les Meslanges* of 1554, also addressed to a bird, this time the skylark, he speaks of the gladness of the plough-

[1] Lau. v, p. 182, lines 97–8.   [2] *Metamorphoses*, I, 101–2.
[3] Lau. vi, p. 72, lines 27–9.   [4] Lau. v, p. 196.

man and of the land itself at the lark's song, but of the earth itself as being, at that season of the year,

> couroussée de la playe
> Du soc, qui l'estomac lui fend.[1]

The *Hymne de la Justice* (1555) takes up the same theme:

> quand les laboureurs du soc ne tormentoient
> Par sillons incongneuz les entrailles encloses
> Des champs...
>
> Il faudra que les bœufz aux champs tu aiguillonnes,
> Et que du soc aigu la terre tu seillonnes...[2]

and the *Hymne de l'Or* echoes the latter thought:

> Il faut à coup de soc & de coutres trenchans
> Deux ou trois fois l'année importuner les champs...[3]

which in turn is echoed by the description of the Indian way of life in the *Complainte contre Fortune* (1559):

> Qui à grands coups de soc la terre n'importune...[4]

The prophecy of the Age of Gold in the *Bergerie* (1565) speaks of a time when the earth

> ne sera comme devant ferüe
> De rateaux bien dentez ny de soc de charüe,[5]

and extended the idea to cultivation of the vines in similar terms:

> Les vignes n'auront peur de sentir les faucilles,

elaborated in the 1584 edition as the couplet:

> Les moissons n'auront peur des faucilles voutées
> Ny l'arbre de Bacchus des serpettes dentées...[6]

The tree-felling theme is found at first in the context of ship-building, a skill which enabled men to visit countries over the

---

[1] Lau. VI, p. 246, lines 11–12.
[2] Lau. VIII, p. 50, lines 54–6 and 139–40, p. 54.
[3] *Ibid.* p. 187, lines 177–8.   [4] Lau. X, p. 34, line 365.
[5] Lau. XIII, p. 109, lines 663–4.   [6] *Ibid.* line 667 and variants.

water and to buy goods not available in their own, hence in
antiquity a symbol of commerce and commercial values. Thus
in *Les Isles Fortunées* the pines are never cut down for this or
any other purpose:

> ni d'un effort de bras
> Avec grand bruit, les Pins on ne renverse
> Pour aler voir d'une longue traverse
> Quelqu'autre monde...[1]

but the moralising anti-commerce emphasis is already balanced
by solicitude for the trees themselves:

> ains jamais decouvers
> On ne les voit de leurs ombrages vers,
> Par trop de chaut, ou par trop de froidure.[2]

In the *Elégie au Seigneur Baillon* (1564), one of the last evocations of the Age of Gold in Ronsard's poetry, the pines are
said to have *felt* the impact of the axe, just as the vines in the
Bergerie were said to have *felt* afraid of the pruning-knife—

> Les hauts pins, qui avoient si longuement esté
> Sur la syme des monts plantés en seureté,
> Sentirent la congnée...[3]

With this may be compared the description of the tree-felling
and the building of the fleet of Francus in Book I of *La Franciade*,
published in 1572. An army of wood-cutters set out,

> pour renverser à bas
> Meint chesne vieil ombragé de ses bras,

and after selecting the finest trees, set to work:

> Contre le tronc sonne meinte congnée
> D'un bras nerveux à l'œuvre embesongnée,
> Qui meinte playe & meinte redoublant,
> Coup dessus coup contre l'arbre tramblant,
> A chef branlé d'une longue traverse
> Le fait tomber tout plat à la renverse,
> Avecq grand bruit.[4]

[1] Lau. v, p. 183, lines 116–19.   [2] *Ibid.* lines 119–22.
[3] Lau. XII, pp. 89–90, lines 47–9.   [4] Lau. XVI, pp. 56–7, lines 533–47.

More rarely, the theme is touched upon with no sentiment of loss or damage to the earth, and with, if anything, a suggestion of praise of the skill and energy of the workman. The verses entitled *Les poemes* ('Poëme et Poësie ont grande différence...') compare the poem, as a work of art, in the vast field of poetry, with a single tree selected to be made into a plough or a ship:

> comme en des Forés
> Un seul Chesne, un seul Orme, un Sapin, un Cyprés,
> Qu'un nerveux Charpentier tourne en courbes charrues,
> Ou en carreaux voutez des navires ventrues...[1]

Mining, and the working of metals—not only of iron, but of gold—might be regarded too as an outrage to mother Earth, and the source of all the ills arising from the power to make weapons and to coin money: in the *Metamorphoses* of Ovid, this was treated as specially characteristic of the end of the Age of Gold. Virgil had already implied that the men of the age 'before Jove' used no metals, since he described them as having been dependent, for felling and splitting timber, upon wooden wedges. (Curiously enough, the ingenuity with which generations of men made tools and even weapons of *stone* seems to pass unnoticed by the poets.) In reality, gold (and after it silver) was the softest metal and the one most easily obtained and worked in prehistoric conditions, and the order of the metals which gave their name to the Four Ages in antiquity may owe something to the actual order in which mankind mastered the use of them.[2] But the ovidian presentation of the myth lumps together all use of metals as equally pernicious and equally characteristic of a degenerate age. Ronsard adopts this attitude towards the use of mining and metals, in the principal passages he wrote upon the Age of Gold, beginning with a long development in *Les Armes* to include the added horrors brought to weapons and warfare by the use of gunpowder. Denunciations of men or devils who

---

[1] Lau. XVIII, I, pp. 283–4, lines 7–10. *Nerveux* here and in the foregoing quotation of course has its etymological meaning of sinewy or vigorous.
[2] See J. Gwyn Griffiths, 'Archaeology and Hesiod's Five Ages', *Journal of the History of Ideas* (1956), pp. 109–19.

with impious hands
Rifled the bowels of their mother Earth
For treasures better hid...

were already familiar to George Agricola, who in his pioneer treatise on mining and metals, *De re metallica* (published in 1556, the year after *Les Armes*), devoted almost the whole first book to refuting these wrong-headed notions. That Gold, in the form of money, and Iron, in the form of weapons, can be pernicious to mankind he did not deny, but blamed man's cupidity and violence, not the metals themselves, for these evils. Quoting the well-known passage from Ovid, and the opinion of certain high-minded thinkers that metals are unnecessary for food or clothing, and therefore not intended by Nature for the use of man but with good reason hidden in the ground, he painstakingly showed that metals are essential for the tools needed in any effective farming and gardening, and in the making of clothes and shoes and houses, and contended that Nature grew them in the ground not to 'hide' them from impious hands but to provide the conditions in which they best could be produced. Without metals, he concluded, men would lead a wretched existence, at the mercy of weather and wild beasts, dependent for food upon the acorns, fruits and berries of the forests, or on herbs and roots grubbed up with their finger-nails, roving the woods and plains at random like wild beasts. That any one—even a poet—should be so far gone as to regard such an existence as the Age of Gold, did not enter the head of the sensible Dr Agricola, seeing that (as he put it) 'this condition is utterly unworthy of humanity with its splendid and glorious natural endowment'.[1]

Ronsard, who in this mood thought even ploughing impious, naturally took over the Ovidian denunciations of mining and metal-working, accepting the consequences (as described by Agricola) for early man—and the Age of Gold—without misgiving.

Interference with the natural scene by mining or quarrying

[1] G. Agricola, *De re metallica*, trans. H. C. Hoover and L. H. Hoover (New York, 1950), Book I, pp. 6–17.

could, of course, have roused emotions in Ronsard as strong as those inspired by the sight of trees being felled and woods turned into plough-land. As his strictures on mining occur only in passages on the Age of Iron, and appear to contain no new element, such personal emotions do not seem to have entered into his treatment of the subject. It is probable that no landscape dear to him had ever been threatened by such disfigurement, and possible that he had never even seen a mine. His dislike for the idea of it was therefore one of principle.

The idea of sea-faring also being an outrage to Nature, likewise traditional to the Age of Gold theme, did arouse emotions in him, but not emotions of concern and admiration for the sea itself. The dangers and discomforts of sea travel were what gave animation to his strictures on it. Two crossings to Scotland in his boyhood, the second of which encountered a storm lasting three days,[1] seem to have contributed to a hatred of the sea which is expressed with particular violence in the poems written to Mary, Queen of Scots, after she sailed from France, on the death of her husband the young king Francis II. Nothing would induce the poet to bring her his homage in person in her kingdom over the water. The utmost he could contemplate was metamorphosing himself into a bird or star to accompany her ship,[2] or hoping that Scotland might float free of its foundations and take a cruise to the coasts of France,[3] or praying that the sea might be turned to dry land.[4] In another discourse to her, he protested at the myth showing Venus being born from the waves of the sea, 'des flots couverts d'horreur et de peril', and can explain it only as an allegory meaning that Love is deceitful, bitter, cruel and terrible.[5] He frankly confessed that, while it was within his skill to sing the praises of

[1] See the autobiographical poem *A Pierre de Paschal*, Lau. VI, pp. 66–8, lines 59–74.
[2] *Elégie à H. L'Huillier*, 'L'Huillier, si nous perdons cette belle princesse', Lau. XII, pp. 191–2, lines 43–8.
[3] *Elégie sur le départ de la Royne d'Escosse*, 'Comme un beau pré dépouillé de ses fleurs', Lau. XII, pp. 197–8, lines 75–92.
[4] *Elégie à la royne d'Escosse*, 'Le jour que vostre voyle aux vagues se courba', Lau. XII, p. 283, lines 103–8.
[5] *Elégie*, 'Bien que le trait de vostre belle face', Lau. XIV, p. 159, lines 163–74.

a river, to praise the grandeur of the sea was quite beyond him.[1]
Nor does he use imagery taken from the sea, except time-
honoured conceits about ports and shipwrecks in the *Amours*.
Significantly, his most famous elegy to Mary, Queen of Scots,
contains almost the only exception: the sight of her pacing
alone along the paths of the park of Fontainebleau, the veils
and draperies of her widow's dress billowing out round her—
they were white, following the special convention of the *dueil
blanc* observed by the French royal ladies at that period—struck
him at a moment when his mind was full of her impending
voyage home, and suggested a formal comparison with a ship's
sails.[2]

His concern for the forest is quite different. It is aesthetic, and
emotional.

FREEDOM

The moods in which Ronsard was ready to disparage not only
sea-faring, mining and metal-working, but even the calling of
the farmer and the shepherd, may possibly have owed something to an aristocratic disdain for manual work. The *Responce
aux injures* on 1563, which may count as expressing his feelings
with particular frankness, contains the following proud and
vehement declaration:

> J'aymerois mieux ramer sur les ondes salées,
> Ou avoir du labeur les deux mains empoulées,
> Ainsi qu'un vigneron, par les champs incogneu,
> Qu'estre d'un gentilhomme un pipeur devenu.[3]

The *Hymne de l'Autonne*, written the same year, provides
another example of this attitude, though this time the speaker
is not Ronsard himself but an allegorical figure:

> ne pense pas estre
> Fille d'un laboureur qui de coultres tranchans
> Fend la terre & la seme & engrosse les champs,

---

[1] *Sur le trespas d'Adrian Turnèbe*, 'Je scay chanter l'honneur d'une rivière',
Lau. XIII, pp. 194–5.
[2] *Elégie*, 'Bien que le trait...', Lau. XIV, p. 153, lines 19–40.
[3] Lau. XI, p. 152, lines 695–8.

Et raporte au logis les deux mains empoulées…
Tu es bien d'autre sang plus genereux issue,
Et de parens plus grands & plus nobles conceue.[1]

Ronsard moreover expressed distaste for any occupation which restricted his freedom to spend his time as he pleased, and admitted that this was one of the attractions to him of the profession of poetry, though, even there, he would not write a line if it did not please his mind to do so:

La poësie est plaine de toute honneste liberté, et, s'il faut dire vray, un folastre mestier, duquel on ne peut retirer beaucoup d'avancement, ny de profit. Si tu veux sçavoir pourquoy j'y travaille si allegrement: pource qu'un tel passetemps m'est aggreable, et, si mon esprit en escrivant ne se contentoit, je n'en ferois jamais un vers, comme ne voulant faire profession d'un mestier qui me viendroit à desplaisir.[2]

The account he gave, in the *Responce aux injures*, of the way he spent his day, is in this respect revealing. He spent four or five hours of every morning in study, went to church, spent an hour in conversation, had midday dinner, and spent the rest of the day as the spirit moved him, according to whether it was wet or fine:

Car si l'apresdinée est plaisante & sereine,
Je m'en vais promener tantost parmy la plaine,
Tantost en un village, & tantost en un boys,
Et tantost par les lieux solitaires & coys,
J'ayme fort les jardins qui sentent le sauvage,
J'ayme le flot de l'eau qui gazoille au rivage.
Là, devisant sur l'herbe aveq' un mien amy
Je me suis par les fleurs bien souvent endormy
A l'ombrage d'un saule, ou lisant dans un livre
J'ay cherché le moyen de me faire revivre…[3]

---

[1] Lau. xii, p. 52, lines 122–5 and 129–30.
[2] *Epistre au lecteur par laquelle l'Autheur respond à ses calomniateurs*, preface to *Les Trois Livres du Recueil des nouvelles poésies* (1564). Lau. xii, p. 8, lines 106–13. I have modernised the punctuation.
[3] *Responce aux injures* (1563), Lau. xi, pp. 144–5, lines 531–40. His occupations when the weather was wet included playing cards, and various forms of exercise such as fencing; he also volunteered the information (withdrawn in later editions) that he enjoyed making love and writing about it, and took pleasure in dancing, masques and music. *Ibid.* p. 145, lines 545–54.

The only routine apart from this to which he submitted was,

> quand je suis aux lieux où il faut faire voir
> Ce que peut un tressaint & tresjuste devoir,[1]

that is, his spells of residence as a Canon of Le Mans cathedral
where he had succeeded to a stall (Du Bellay's) in 1560. These
cannot have been very irksome, as he had many friends in Le
Mans and could enjoy the society offered by a provincial
capital. As to the duty of attending the services, he admitted
his pleasure in wearing rich vestments, burning delicious
incense, and hearing the singing of the liturgy.

His preference was clearly marked for the open air, and for
walking in the countryside, when he was not pursuing his
self-imposed daily task of study and writing (though even then
he often took a book with him). Echoes of a similar routine
can be heard in some of his later poems, such as *La Salade*
(1569), though here it is more homely and domestic as befitted
an invalid, living in seclusion at his priory of Croixval on the
edge of the forest of Gâtine, attended by his friend and secretary, Amadis Jamyn. The expedition in *La Salade* is only in
search of plants for their salad at dinner, but this little ritual is
described with zest: Jamyn is to wash his hands, and bring a
clean napkin, before they set off: and for a few moments they
might almost be mistaken for the people of the Age of Gold...

> D'un vague pas, d'une veuë escartée,
> Deçà delà jettée & rejettée,
> Or' sur la rive, ores sur un fossé,
> Or' sur un champ en paresse laissé
> Du laboureur, qui de luy-mesme aporte,
> Sans cultiver, herbes de toute sorte,
> Je m'en iray solitaire à l'escart.
> Tu t'en iras, Jamyn, d'une autre part...[2]

until they return together to the house, reading Ovid on the
way, and, having rolled up their shirt-sleeves, wash their salad

[1] *Ibid.* pp. 146–8, lines 565–600.
[2] Lau. xv, pp. 76–7, lines 5–11. *La Salade* was published in *Le sixiesme livre
des Poëmes* (1569). Laumonier's reasons, given in the footnotes to the poem,
for thinking it refers to Croixval, seem conclusive.

by plunging it in the water of the 'belle fonteine' before bringing it in to dress it with salt, vinegar and olive oil of Provence.

The theme of wandering in a forest did not lose its attraction for Ronsard when his interest waned in the Age of Gold theme. It is, for instance, introduced into two poems of 1569, both among those written to entertain himself when he was an invalid and both frankly retelling a story to be found in the Latin poets.

Le Satyre recounts the discomfiture of Faunus, who conceived a desire for Iole, the companion of Hercules, and, attempting to ravish her in the cave where the pair had gone to sleep the night, stumbled instead in the darkness (misled by their having as a joke exchanged clothes) on the hero himself. As told by Ovid, in the *Fasti*, there is no counterpart to Ronsard's lines,

> Come ilz erroient en cheminant tous deux
> Par tertres, bois, par bocages ombreux...[1]

though of course the whole episode takes place in the woods, the habitat of Faunus.

The *Hylas* describes how Hercules landed with the heroes on the coast of Achaea and went inland into the woods to seek a tree suitable to make an oar, his own oar having broken:

> Hercule estant pensif & fantastique,
> Bien loing il erre en la forest rustique,
> Haute maison des oyseaux...[2]

Meanwhile his cup-bearer Hylas goes in another direction to find water to draw for his master, and is trapped by the water-nymphs:

> come son pié le meine,
> Dans la forest umbreuse se pourmeine
> Errant par tout...[3]

---

[1] Lau. xv, p. 68, lines 19–20. Cf. Ovid. *Fasti*, ii, lines 305–56. *Le Satyre* was published in *Le sixiesme livre des Poëmes* (1569).
[2] *Ibid.* p. 240, lines 149–51.
[3] *Ibid.* p. 243, lines 201–3.

The description of the pool in the heart of the forest, overhung by trees, is in its turn linked to the passages evoking the poet's encounter with the magic of the woods:

> Meint chesne vieil ombrageoit l'onde noire,
> Faunes, Sylvains n'y venoient jamais boire,
> Ains de bien loing s'enfuyoient esbahiz:
> Maison sacrée aux Nymphes du pais...
>
> Là carolloient à tresses decoiffées,
> De main à main les Nymphes & les Fées,
> Foulant des pieds les herbes d'alentour...[1]

In an elegy published the year before he died, in additions to the *Sonnets pour Hélène*, Book II, he described his perfect contentment before he fell in love, as consisting in leisure to walk as he pleased, sometimes with a book, sometimes looking at and enjoying the forms and colours of the flowers and foliage; here we have one last celebration of the theme of wandering in the forest:

> Tantost j'errois seulet par les forests sauvages,
> Sur les bords enjonchez des peinturez rivages,
> Tantost par les rochers reculez et deserts,
> Tantost par les taillis, verte maison des cerfs...[2]

There is therefore a connection between the wandering habit of his Age of Gold people[3] and his own fondness for wandering, as being the essence of perfect freedom to spend one's time and choose one's place.

THE FOREST SCENE

We are without a full scale study of the forest as a subject of poetry in the sixteenth century. Were such an inquiry undertaken, it would in all probability confirm the conclusion reached by Michel Devèze, in the chapter 'La forêt: lieu poétique et esthétique' included in his great book on the French

---

[1] *Ibid.* p. 244, lines 229–32, and p. 245, lines 245–7. There is less emphasis on a forest setting for this episode in his sources (Theocritus, *Idyll*, XIII; Propertius, I, 20, and Valerius Flaccus, *Argonautica*, III, 481–597).
[2] Lau. XVIII, 1, p. 34, lines 25–8.   [3] Cf. above, pp. 28–30.

forests in this period:[1] 'Ronsard reste évidemment le plus expressif des poètes qui aiment la forêt.'

Circumstances favoured this vocation. La Possonnière, where he was born and spent his childhood, was on the edge of the forest of Gâtine; the house is, to this day, surrounded by trees, and the garden still leads straight up into the woods on the hill-side above. The forest of Gâtine, still considerable, especially between Montrouveau and Les Hermites, was some six times larger when Ronsard was a boy. A survey made in 1573 for Henry of Navarre, who, as Count of Vendôme, was the owner of it, estimated the total area as about 2200 *arpents royaux*, though not quite all of this was actually covered by woods.[2] Ronsard's father, Loys de Ronsard, was the *sergent fieffé* or hereditary Head Forester of it. In this capacity,[3] he was not obliged to supervise the care of the forest in person as were the ordinary *sergents*—he was indeed often absent from La Possonnière for months at a time, taking his turn of service at court as a member of the royal household—nor was he paid, but he enjoyed certain rights in the forest and took the final responsibility for it.

Three of Ronsard's collections of poetry were given the title *Bocage*, the word still used in French to describe a countryside of green meadows, enclosed by hedges, with trees growing freely in the hedges and in coppices. This term, which it seems to have been his own fancy to apply to a volume of verse, was chosen for the fourteen miscellaneous poems, mostly early compositions, appended to the *Quatre premiers livres des Odes* of 1550.[4] It was adopted also for the miscellany dedicated to Pierre de Paschal, which Ronsard published in 1554;[5] this included six poems from the original *Bocage* of 1550 (among

[1] M. Devèze, *La vie de la forêt française au XVIᵉ siècle*, II, pp. 193–7.
[2] R. Caisso, 'La forêt de Gâtine au temps de Ronsard', pp. 276–8. Cf. Devèze, *op. cit.* I, p. 255. The *arpent royal* was slightly smaller than an English acre. Caisso calculates the size of the forest, converted into metric measurements, as 1139 hectares.
[3] Devèze, *op. cit.* I, pp. 313–15.   [4] Lau. II, pp. 155–202.
[5] Lau. VI, pp. 7–125. Laumonier regards the term *Bocage* as copied from that of *Silvae* (used by Statius), and that of *Selve* in Italian (introduction to VI, p. xiii).

them, *A Dieu, pour la famine*), but was otherwise all new. A quite different and much later group of poems was classified, in the sixth collected edition of the works of Ronsard, in 1584, under the title *Bocage royal* (the epithet being justified by the large proportion of poems addressed to members of the French royal family or to foreign sovereigns).[1] To the third and last of these poetical *bocages* Ronsard prefixed twenty-two lines of verse, opening with the following comparison:

> Comme un Seigneur praticq & soigneux du mesnage
> Regarde en sa forest ou dedans son bocage
> Mille arbres differents de fueilles et de fruict;
> L'un pour l'ouvrage est bon, l'autre indocile fuit
> La main de l'artizan: l'autre dur de racine
> Tantost va veoir la guerre, & tantost la marine:
> L'autre est gresle & chancelle, et l'autre spacieux
> Ses bras durs et fueillus envoye jusqu'aux Cieux:
> Ainsi dans ce Bocage on voit de toutes sortes
> D'arguments differents...[2]

It is tempting to imagine that the 'Seigneur praticq' whom Ronsard saw in his mind's eye inspecting the trees was his father with whom, some fifty years ago, he might often have been in the forest of Gâtine when the *sergent fieffé* walked or rode to confer with keepers and woodmen.

Family associations, and particularly filial affection, may have counted for something, in helping to develop his love of the woods. It was not, however, with a forester's eye that he himself beheld them.

For Ronsard, the discovery and fulfilment of his vocation as a poet was an experience he had undergone alone and in the forest. In his full maturity, he wrote of this experience in an autobiographical vein, in three important poems: the *Hymne de L'Autonne*, the *Complainte contre Fortune* and the *Elégie à Pierre l'Escot*. But it is already to be found in the earliest Odes. The Ode *A la forest de Gâtine* in its original form already has the haunting invocation to the forest, the alternating 8- and 6-

[1] Lau. XVIII, 1, pp. 64–105.   [2] Lau. XVIII, 1, p. 233, lines 1–10.

syllable lines of its quatrains illustrate already Ronsard's mastery of lyricism:

> Toi, qui au dous froid de tes bois
> Ravi d'esprit m'amuses,
> Toi, qui fais qu'à toutes les fois
> Me répondent les Muses.[1]

In the first Ode of his Book III Ronsard recalled, in similar terms, the initiation bestowed upon him in the woods by the Muse:

> Euterpe la sacrée
> M'a de mortel fait compagnon des Dieus.
>
> Aussi elle m'aime, & par les bois m'amuse,
> Me tient, m'embrasse, & quand je veil sonner,
> De m'accorder ses fleutes ne refuse...[2]

In the *Complainte contre Fortune*, the poem containing his 'Age of Gold' picture of the natives of the New World, Ronsard affects to describe his carefree life before the favour of the Cardinal de Châtillon had aroused his ambition; wandering now by the woods, now by the streams, now by the meadows, taught by the Nine Muses, learning every rock and cavern; no spring but he had drunk from it out of his hand, no valley so deep that he had not explored it in his solitary walks. In these solitudes Phoebus Apollo presented the poet with his lyre, Pan the forest god leaped to the sound of his pipes, and the gentle Dryads partnered by the *silvani* danced on the grass to the sound of his songs.[3] Apart from his encounters with the supernatural inhabitants of the woods, his wandering is not without affinities with the movements of the human beings in the Age of Gold which he described. In the *Elégie à Pierre l'Escot*, he claimed that his discovery of his vocation as a poet went back to such solitary expeditions in the forest, as a boy of twelve:

> Je n'avois pas douze ans qu'au profond des vallées,
> Dans les hautes forets des hommes reculées,
> Dans les antres segrets de frayeur tout couverts,
> Sans avoir soing de rien, je composois des vers...

---

[1] Lau. I, p. 244, lines 13–16 (*Odes*, 1550, II, xxiii).
[2] Lau. II, p. 4, lines 51–5.   [3] Lau. X, p. 20, lines 80–90.

and the company which appeared to dance to his music was even stranger, Dryads, Satyrs, Pans, and fauns which leapt as they danced like goats, joined the gentle company of 'fantastic fairies' which, with skirts flying free, circled about him.[1] The theme was used again in the *Hymne de l'Autonne*, with a more decidedly romantic emphasis, the 'midnight revels by a forest side' this time being specifically by moonlight, and the woods 'noires forests en fueillages voutées', while the wildness and mystery grows: 'Une vallée, un antre, en horreur obscurci, Un désert effroyable...'[2]

Joachim du Bellay wrote, in a poem *A Pierre de Ronsard* which has been ascribed on stylistic grounds to the period of his residence in Rome, 1555 or 1556:

> Qui vit doncques, Ronsard, plus que toy bienheureux,
> Plus aise & plus content? Or le dos plantureux
> De ton vineux Sabut, ores la teste peincte
> De Braye te retient, or ta Gastine saincte,
> Et les Nymphes du Loyr apres toy vont sonnant,
> Et Bellerie encor' va tes vers bouillonnant.
> Nymphes, heureuses vous, à qui la nuict aggree
> Mener soubs tel sonneur vostre danse sacree.
> Il hante voz forests sans crainte & sans souci,
> Voz antres, voz rochers, & vos fleuves aussi...[3]

Du Bellay's summary of Ronsard's existence in his native countryside thus begins with allusions to the local features celebrated in Ronsard's early odes, the vineyards of Sabut, the trees of the banks of the Braye and the forest of Gâtine, the river Loir, and the 'fontaine Bellerie', but reaches its climax with the nymphs of the forest dancing at night to his music, and with the words which become more and more the favourite symbols of Ronsard's landscape, 'forests', 'antres', 'rochers',

---

[1] *Ibid.* p. 304, lines 85–94.   [2] Lau. XII, pp. 47–8, lines 31–48.
[3] *Œuvres poétiques*, ed. H. Chamard, V, pp. 362–3, lines 23–32. First published in the posthumous collection edited by his friend Aubert in 1568. A Latin elegy, of which this is a French transposition, was published by Du Bellay among his *Poematum libri quatuor* on his return from Rome, in 1558: the Latin counterpart to the passage I have quoted above can be read in a foot-note to *A Pierre de Ronsard*, in Chamard's edition, V, pp. 362–3.

and 'fleuves'. It is hard to assess the exact significance of this interpretation, in view of the uncertainty surrounding the date of the poem, but Du Bellay certainly by 1558 clearly saw the trend of Ronsard's interests.

What feeling for the forest there was, among Ronsard's poet-contemporaries, tended to express itself in terms of the pastoral tradition. The largest areas over which pigs, sheep and cattle grazed were still woodland, and shepherds' songs and sports could be represented quite naturally against a background of sylvan scenery. As we have seen, Ronsard did not imagine the Age of Gold as a pastoral society at all, and (though he made use of the pastoral convention in his Eclogues, etc.) did not find this convention very congenial.

It would, however, have been open to him to evoke the forest in connection with hunting, the pastime above all of the princely and noble class. If he were determined to place his Age of Gold in a period before mankind kept flocks and herds, why did he not allow hunting—a stage of human development emphasised by all writers on the history of the human race, and which would have given scope for his familiarity with the forest and its lore?

At the period when he was interested in the Age of Gold, Ronsard's only poem on hunting was *La Chasse*: this was, like *Les Armes*, written as a form of thanks for a present from Jean Brinon (in this case, a dog) and was published in the same collection, the *Meslanges* of 1555. Some of the lines in this poem do express a pleasure in the forest in terms recalling those of *Les Armes*: describing the relaxation after the kill, he says:

> Quel plaisir esse encor de manger es bocages
> Du fromage & du lait & des fraises sauvages!
> Ou secoüer le fruit d'un pommeux arbrisseau,
> Ou se desalterer dans le prochain ruisseau.[1]

There is, however, no other connection between *La Chasse* and the Age of Gold theme.

The people of the Age of Gold, as he imagined them, are

[1] Lau. VI, p. 238, lines 115–18.

indeed forest-dwellers, but they are so innocent of the skill or foresight needed to make the simplest trap or weapon that they may be said to lack the means to hunt, even if the idea of eating meat were to enter their heads. They are truly at the very earliest known stage of human life, that of gathering, and Ronsard almost thinks of them as harmless animals themselves, though he never goes quite so far as to say so.[1]

Peace between man and the animal creation was (as we have seen) a traditional feature of the Age of Gold.[2] Though not explicitly mentioned by Ronsard, except in the *Bergerie* of 1565, the existence of this tradition both in poetry and art may have deterred him from allowing his Age of Gold people to slay animals for food or sport.

Ronsard's ideal seems furthermore to exclude any activity which required organisation or exertion, let alone exposure to hardship or danger: when his Age of Gold people were provided by Nature with fruits and nuts requiring only to be picked, why should they hunt?

Nor did he show any great fondness for hunting himself. *La Chasse* does not prove any more familiarity with the customs and jargon of the hunt than would be normal in any gentleman of the period. In commenting upon this poem that he was 'grand chasseur',[3] Laumonier may have had in mind the later poem called *Les Amours d'Eurymédon et de Callirée*,[4] in which, in the passage beginning 'C'estoit un Meleagre au mestier de chasser', he makes a considerable display of learning on the subject. It has, however, been demonstrated conclusively that, in this and similar passages of his later poetry, he drew

---

[1] The lines written on early man by Scèvole de Sainte-Marthe, quoted by Hélène Naïs, *Les animaux dans la poésie française de la Renaissance* (Paris, 1961), p. 575:

> Parmy les animaux despourveus de raison,
> Avec ces animaux ils passoient une vie
> Franche d'ambition, d'avarice et d'envie...

may be influenced by Ronsard's descriptions of the Age of Gold. Mlle Naïs herself comments pertinently: 'On a reconnu le thème de l'âge d'or, présenté ici sous une forme assez remarquable: la vie naturelle pour les hommes consiste à se rapprocher des animaux' (*ibid.* pp. 575–6).

[2] See above, p. 61. [3] Lau. VI, p. 231, n. 3.
[4] Lau. XVII, pp. 144–66.

heavily upon the *Venerie* of Jacques du Fouilloux for technical
terms, and did not—even so—always use them correctly.[1] The
Venerie was published in 1561, and was clearly a godsend to
Ronsard in writing poetry which would give pleasure to the
young Charles IX, whose passion for hunting was well known.
Les Amours d'Eurymédon et de Callirée, published in volume 1
(*Amours*) of the collected edition of his works in 1578, celebrated the love of Charles IX for the court beauty Anne
d'Acquaviva. While Ronsard attempted to give suitably
technical descriptions of Eurymédon's prowess as a hunter, he
also wrote a sonnet against hunting, supposed to be spoken by
the object of his passion, the nymph Callirée. Though solicitude
for the safety of Eurymédon (Charles IX) is her main consideration,[2] she also condemns hunting as an outrage to the
gods, and a cruel violation of the laws of nature, and an intrusion
into the silence of the woods. Callirée has the last word: this is
the concluding poem of the sequence:

> Celuy fut ennemy des Deitez puissantes,
> Et cruel viola de nature les lois,
> Qui le premier rompit le silence des bois,
> Et les Nymphes qui sont dans les arbres naissantes:
> Qui premier de limiers & de meutes pressantes,
> De piqueurs, de veneurs, de trompes & d'abois
> Donna par les forests un passetemps aux Rois
> De la course du sang des bestes innocentes.
> Je n'aime ny piqueurs, ny filets, ny veneurs,
> Ny meutes, ny forests, la cause de mes peurs:
> Je doute qu'Arthemis quelque sangler n'appelle
> Encontre Eurymedon, pour voir ses jours finis,
> Que le dueil ne me face une Venus nouvelle,
> Et la mort ne le face un nouvel Adonis.

The sentiments expressed in this sonnet may have been those
of Anne herself. That she would have thought of invoking the

---

[1] F. Remigereau, 'Ronsard sur les brisées de Du Fouilloux', *RSS*, XIX (1932–3),
46–95; M. Francon, '*Les Amours d'Eurymédon et de Callirée* de Ronsard et
La Venerie de J. du Fouilloux', *Studi Francesi*, XVII (1962), 275 ff.
[2] Lau. XVII, p. 165. Ronsard may have been thinking here of the poem of
Tibullus, 'Parce meo iuueni' (IV, iii). The idea of hunting being an outrage
to the natural world of the forest, however, seems to be his own.

Laws of Nature, the silence of the forest, and the nymphs which have their life and dwelling in the trees, is less probable. Ronsard may speak in her name: he also seems to speak in his own. He may have had mixed feelings about hunting. Like many other country gentlemen, he may have found pleasure in it which was made up of many elements besides that of sport: pleasure in the fresh air and in the exercise of riding, pleasure in the landscape of field and forest, pleasure in observing the birds and beasts whose destruction was the pretext for the outing. Ronsard was keenly sensitive to all of these. In particular, his awareness of animals, and his power to treat them poetically, is remarkable by any standards and exceptional among French poets of his century.[1]

That the forests were the 'house' of the wild creatures who peopled them was an idea, accordingly, very congenial to Ronsard. The starting-point was probably the phrase 'antiquas domos auium' in Book II of the *Georgics*, where Virgil describes how the birds fly out into the sky, forced to abandon their nests, as trees are cut down and the rich soil on which they grew is ploughed.[2] The expression 'frondiferasque domos auium' had already been used by Lucretius in the invocation to Venus at the beginning of *De Rerum Natura*. The passage from the *Georgics* was evidently in his mind when he composed the passage in *Elégie contre les bûcherons de Gâtine*[3] beginning,

> Forest, haute maison des oiseaux bocagers,
> Plus le Cerf solitaire et les Chevreuls legers
> Ne paistront sous ton ombre...

But the primeval woods had already been called in 1565,

> Haute maison des Sangliers escumeux,
> Et des grans Cerfs au large front rameux...[4]

[1] See Hélène Naïs, *op. cit.* chap. x, 'L'observation et l'art de la description' and chap. xi, 'Le lyrisme animalier'.
[2] *Georgics*, II, line 209.
[3] *Elégie*, 'Quiconque aura premier la main embesongnée' (1584), Lau. XVIII, I, p. 145, lines 27–9.
[4] *Elégie à la majesté de la Royne d'Angleterre*, 'Mon cœur esmeu de merveille se serre', Lau. XIII, p. 48, lines 223–4.

and a forest is described as 'Haute maison des oyseaux' in the *Hylas* of 1569.[1]

That remote period, when the forests were the 'house' of human beings too, was for a time a subject on which his imagination dwelt with pleasure. The aspect of the Age of Gold tradition which assigned it to a very early and simple society, though not at all necessarily to a wild state, allowed him to idealise that period and to identify it with the Age of Gold.

The way of life of the Age of Gold, as imagined by Ronsard, thus was determined by the forest setting, and by the lack of will or skill to tamper with this environment. Sociable, but not yet organised in families or tribes, nor looking to any fixed place as their home, the inhabitants wandered at will like a herd of grazing animals at large, their underlying concern being to seek the best fruits and roots, and the freshest water, in fine weather the best shade and in storms the best shelter, the sweetest scents and the fairest flowers. Any activities which would distinguish men from the animals are ignored: not only harmful, like the making of walls and weapons, but innocent like song and dance.

His interest in this state of nature, though it may have been prompted by the classics and affected by the New World, was neither archaeological nor anthropological. He was not interested in the practical problems of their existence, nor in the stages by which it changed (for good or evil) through the centuries into an ordered society and finally into a civilised one.

These were the human beings whom he imagined in order to people the forest, as in other moods he peopled it with Fauns and Fairies, or enjoyed its solitude alone, as Jean-Jacques Rousseau imagined the characters of *La Nouvelle Héloïse* in his solitary walks in the woods of Montmorency:

J'allois alors d'un pas plus tranquille chercher quelque lieu sauvage dans la forêt, quelque lieu désert où rien ne montrant la main des hommes n'annonçât la servitude et la domination, quelque asile où je pusse croire avoir pénétré le premier, et où nul tiers importun ne vînt s'interposer entre la nature et moi. C'était là qu'elle sembloit

---

[1] Lau. xv, p. 240, line 151.

déployer à mes yeux une magnificence toujours nouvelle... Mon imagination ne laissoit pas longtemps déserte la terre ainsi parée. Je la peuplois bientôt d'êtres selon mon cœur... Je me faisois un siècle d'or à ma fantaisie...[1]

Ronsard's starting-point was the legend of the Age of Gold as he read of it (in varying forms) in the poets of antiquity, in Plato, and in later writers. It did not occur to him to give it a Christian interpretation, by identifying it with the Garden of Eden in the past (as Henry Estienne did in the first two chapters of his *Apologie pour Hérodote* in 1566) or with Paradise in the future. He did not treat it in the mythological manner, except for the episode of Astraea in the *Hymne de la Justice*. Astraea herself is never the subject of an *Hymne*, whereas, in the visual arts, she inspired the greatest of all the pictures on the Age of Gold theme, Salvator Rosa's *The return of Astraea*,[2] some fifty-five years after Ronsard's death. Nor, for that matter, is there an *Hymne* to Saturn. On the other hand, he did not make an Age of Gold of his own, as a Romantic poet might have done, by idealising his own childhood, though childhood recollections had some part to play in shaping his image of the ideal world. Yet his fondness for the theme over a period of years, the distinctive features he impressed on it, and the eloquence with which he sang of it, show that he had made the legend part of his own imaginative landscape.

It expressed his romantic interest in the early history of mankind, his love of the forest, and his love of freedom. It recalled, too, certain passages in the poets who had treated the theme which was dear to him, and also passages (such as those in Lucretius) which had no connection with the theme except the connections which he made between them.

In so far as the Age of Gold meant simply his ideal of a happy existence for himself and for mankind in general, it was not a rational programme of a reformed society (like the *Siècle doré* of Guillaume Michel) but a daydream, as if the way he

[1] Letter to M. de Malesherbes, Montmorency, 26 January 1762.
[2] Kunsthistorisches Museum, Vienna (Kat. 1, 645). Poussin, curiously enough, never treated the Age of Gold, though he treated closely related themes.

spent his time on a fine day in the forest could be extended to an entire way of life. For a few hours one could wander or rest under the trees, eating berries or nuts and drinking from a sparkling stream, and watching the movements of the wild creatures and the shadows, until one had the illusion of being part of that world for ever.

It was a daydream which provided an escape into peace, in moments of disgust with unrequited love or unsatisfied ambition. His fondness for wine, women and song had already ample scope in the sonnets, songs and odes. What idealism he was capable of feeling needed other outlets than these. All his revulsion of sentiment against the society in which he lived (which in other moods he was ready to idolise), its greed and its artificialities, needed at times to voice itself in a world of carefree trust in nature and in his fellow-men. The Age of Gold was, for him, a society, but a society where each individual was always at peace with all the rest. Logically, passion was excluded. So was private property. Platonic influence may have encouraged him to picture, as an ideal world, a society free from desire to possess a particular person or particular objects. But he was inclined by nature to picture it so, in moods of discouragement with the fortunes of his career and his courtships.

'Le regret de l'âge d'or n'est que la transposition d'un rêve dans le passé. Car l'éloignement dans le temps et dans l'espace peut seul conférer aux choses le charme qui fait qu'on les désire ou qu'on les regrette', remarks Dora Frey in her study of Ronsard's Elegies. Nothing, therefore, can be more revealing than to see what a poet puts into his picture of the Age of Gold. Ronsard put into it much that was closest to his heart: he also gave it a violence of nostalgia for a free and simple life which was equally part of him, but which found other forms of expression in the later years of his career, when, at Saint-Cosme or at Croixval on the edge of the forest of Gâtine, his dream of freedom and of nearness to nature was in some measure realised.

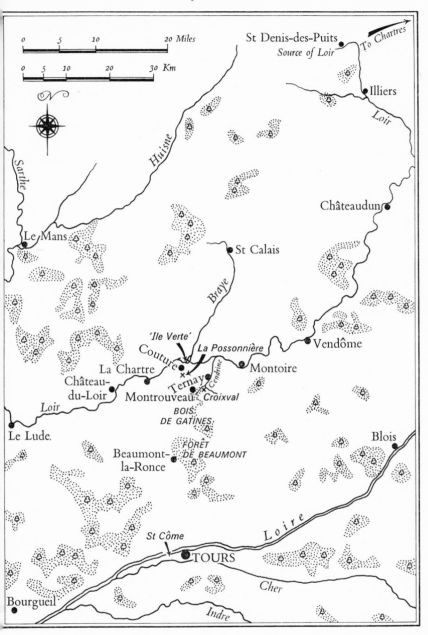

Map of the Ronsard country

13-2

Appendix to Chapter I

CHRONOLOGICAL TABLE OF THE PASSAGES OF
RONSARD'S POETRY RELATING TO THE
THEME OF THE AGE OF GOLD*

Year	Title	Lau. vol. and page
1549	Avant-entrée du Roi	I, 17–18
1550	Les quatre premiers livres des Odes...Ensemble son Bocage	
	A Dieu, pour la famine (Bocage, IX)	II, 186
	Avant-venue du printens (Odes, I, xxvii)	I, 152–4
	A Bouju, Angevin (Odes, IV, ii)	II, 88
1551	——	
1552	Cinquieme livre des Odes	
	A Madame Marguerite (Odes, V, iii)	III, 105
	A Claude de Ligneri (Odes, V, x)	III, 175
1553	Livret des Folastries	
	Folastrie, V	V, 35
	Les Amours nouvellement augmentées...Plus quelques Odes	
	A Mellin de Saint-Gelais	V, 169–70
	Les Isles Fortunées, à M-A. de Muret	V, 175–91
1554	Le Bocage	
	Epitaphe de Hugues Salel	VI, 34–5
1555	Les Meslanges	
	Ode à François Charbonnier, Angevin	VI, 201–2
	Les Armes, à Jean Brinon	VI, 204–5
	Les quatre premiers livres des Odes (3e éd.)	
	A Monsieur le Dauphin (Odes III, iii)	VII, 55

* (1) The date is that of publication. (2) The page-references are to the passages specifically mentioning this theme, except for the cases when the whole poem is concerned. (3) The *Epitaphe de Hugues Salel* and the *Elégie des Armairies* are placed in this table because they are considered for purposes of comparison, being on closely related themes.

Appendix to Chapter 1

Year	Title	Lau. vol. and page
	Les Hymnes	
	Hymne de la Justice	VIII, 50–72
	Le Temple de MM. le Connestable et des Chastillons	VIII, 77
	Hymne de l'Or	VIII, 186–8
1556	——	
1557	——	
1558	*Exhortation pour la Paix*	IX, 23
1559	*Chant pastoral sur les nopces du duc de Lorraine*	IX, 79
	Chant de liesse au Roy	IX, 132
	Second Livre des Meslanges	
	Complainte contre Fortune	X, 33–5
	Sonet xi, 'On dit qu'avec les loups, Bourdin, il faut urler'	X, 76–7
	Sonet xvii, *A Monseigneur le cardinal de Lorraine*	X, 82–3
1560	*Les Œuvres*	
	A André Thevet (*Odes*, V, xxi)	X, 270
	Elegie, 'Si j'estois à renaistre' (*Poèmes*, III, *A Robert de La Haye*)	X, 315–22
	Livre de Meslanges [music]	
	Prose preface by Ronsard	X, 2, 486
1561	——	
1562	——	
1563	*Responce aux injures et calomnies de je ne sçay quels predicans et ministres de Genève*	XI, 148
1564	*Les Trois livres du Recueil des nouvelles poésies*	
	Elegie au Seigneur Baillon	XII, 87–91
	Compleinte à la Royne mere du Roy	XII, 186
	Elegie des Armairies	XII, 240
	Eglogue, Daphnis et Thyrsis	XII, 155
1565	*Le Proces*	XIII, 26
	Elegies, Mascarades et Bergerie	
	Elegie à la Majesté de la royne d'Angleterre	XIII, 58–9

197

Year	Title	Lau. vol. and page
	Bergerie dédiée à la Majesté de la royne d'Escosse	XIII, 75–131
	Elegie à Monsieur de Foyx	XIII, 154
	Stances pour l'avant-venue de la royne d'Espaigne	XIII, 227
	Les Sereines	XIII, 233
	Sonet au Roy	XIII, 240
1566	——	
1567	——	
1568	——	
1569	——	
1570	——	
1571	[Scenario for the wedding-entry of Charles IX]	
1572	——	
1573	In J. Dorat, *Magnificentissimi spectaculi*	
	La Nymphe de France parle	XVII, 3, 415
1574	——	
1575	*Estreines au Roy Henry III, envoyées à sa Majesté au mois de decembre* [1574]	XVII, 1, 85
1576	——	
1577	——	
1578	*Les Œuvres*	
	Variant in line 105 of the *Elegie à Marie*	x, 243
	first published in *Les Œuvres* of 1560	(XVII, 2, 114)
	Les élémens ennemis de l'Hydre (probably composed in 1569)	XVII, 3, 408–9
1579	——	
1580	——	
1581	——	
1582	——	
1583	——	
1584	*Les Œuvres*	
	Discours, 'Doncques voici le jour'	XVIII, 1, 133
[1585	Death of Ronsard]	
1587	*Les Œuvres*	
	Les Hymnes	XVIII, 1, 263–4
1609	*Les Œuvres Caprice*	XVIII, 2, 322

Select Bibliography*

All material is recorded here which has contributed essentially to the book in one way or another, (except dictionaries, bibliographies and library catalogues).

Works to which the reader is referred in footnotes for further information on related subjects are not included, unless they come into this category, nor are classics of modern literature to which reference is made in passing.

CLASSICAL, MEDIEVAL AND RENAISSANCE SOURCES

(Renaissance texts are quoted from a modern critical edition, or, failing that, from the original edition or nearest to it available. In the latter case, the place of publication, publisher, year-date, and format are given, also the shelf-mark of the copy consulted.)

AGRICOLA (Georgius). *De re metallica* (1556), trans. H. C. and L. H. Hoover. New York, 1950.

ANON. *La magnifica entrata del re Henrico secondo fatta nella città di Lyone.* Lyone (G. Rouillio) 1549, 4°. BM 278.g.14 (1).

C'est la deduction du sumptueux ordre et magnifiques theatres dressés par les citoiens de Rouen à Henry second. Rouen (I. Le Prest pour R. le Hoy, R. and J. du Gord) 1551, 4°. BM 811. d.26.

ARATUS. Callimachus, Lycophron, Aratus, trans. of Aratus G. R. Mair (Loeb Classical Library). 1955.

BAÏF (Jean-Antoine de). *Œuvres en rime*, ed. Ch. Marty-Laveaux. 5 vols. Paris, 1878.

BEMBO (Pietro). *Gli Asolani* [1504], trans. Rudolf B. Gottfried (Indiana University Publications, Humanities Series, no. 31). 1954.

BINET (Claude). *La vie de Pierre de Ronsard* (1586), ed. P. Laumonier. Paris, 1910.

BODIN (Jean). *Methodus ad facilem historiarum cognitionem*, Parisiis (M. Juvenis) 1566, 4°. BM 580.g.2.

* For abbreviations see above, p. xiv.

Bibliography

BOETHIUS (Anicius Manlius Torquatus Severinus). *De consolatione.* Venetiis (hered. O. Scotus) 1524, fol. Bodl. Toynbee 3664. *The theoretical tractates; The Consolation of Philosophy,* trans. H. F. Stewart (Loeb Classical Library). 1936.

BOUCHET (Jean). *Triomphes du tres chrestien, tres puissant et invictissime roy de France François premier de ce nom, contenant la difference des Nobles,* Poitiers (De Marnef) 1550, fol. BN Rés. Ye 55.

BOUQUET (Simon). *Bref et sommaire recueil de ce qui a esté faict à la joyeuse entrée de Charles IX en sa cité de Paris,* Paris (D. du Pré pour O. Codoré) 1572, 4°. Bodl. Douce C.613.

BRUÉS (Guy de). *The Dialogues* (Paris, 1557) ed. with a study in renaissance scepticism and relativism by P. P. Morphos. (Johns Hopkins Studies in romance literatures and languages, extra vol. xxx). Baltimore, 1953.

CICERO (Marcus Tullius). *Artis Rhetoricae Libri II (De inventione rhetorica),* ed. A. Weidner. Berolini, 1878.

DU BELLAY (Joachim). *Œuvres poétiques,* ed. H. Chamard (STFM). 6 vols. Paris, 1908–31.

Poésies françaises et latines, ed. E. Courbet, 2 vols. Paris, 1918.

DU CHOUL (Jean). *De varia quercus historia,* Lugduni (G. Roville) 1555, 8°. Bodl. 8° C.44. Art. Seld.

DU PUYS (Rémy). *La triumphante entrée faicte sur le nouvel advenement de Charles, prince des Hespaignes, en la ville de Bruges,* Paris (G. de Gourmont) 1515, fol. BM C.44.g.11.

DU THIER (Jean). *Traicté fort plaisant des Louanges de la Folie, traduict d'Italien en François par feu messire Jean du Thier...* Lyon (B. Rigaud) 1567, 8°. BM C.66.d.8.

ERASMUS (Desiderius). Μωρίας ἐγκώμιον *id est, Stulticiae Laus, Opera,* Basileae (Froben) 1540, fol., IV, 353–89. Bodl. E.2.4.Th.

GELLO (Giovan-Baptista). *La Circe, nouvellement mise en Françoys par le seigneur du Parc.* Rouen (pour R. & J. du Gort frères) 1551, 16°. Bodl. Douce g.7.

GIAMBULLARI (Pier Francesco). *Apparato et feste nelle noze dello Illustrissimo Signor Duca di Firenze, e della Duchessa sua consorte, con le sue Stanze, Madriali, Comedia & Intermedii, in quelle recitati.* Fiorenza (Benedetto Giunta] 1539, 8°. Bodl. Mortara 339 (1).

GRIMAUDET (François). *Des monnoyes, augment et diminution du pris d'icelles,* Paris (M. le Jeune) 1576, 8°. BM 522.b.4 (1).

Bibliography

HARVEY (Gabriel). *Works*, ed. A. B. Grosart (Huth Library), 2 vols. 1884.

HEROËT (Antoine). *Œuvres poétiques*, ed. F. Gohin (STFM). 1943.

HESIOD. *The Works and Days, Theogony, Homeric Hymns and Homerica*, trans. H. G. Evelyn-White (Loeb Classical Library). 1954.

LA TOUR D'ALBÉNAS (Béranger de). *Le siècle d'or et autres vers divers*, Lyon (J. de Tournes and G. Gazeau) 1551. 8°. BM G. 17879.

LUCRETIUS CARUS (Titus). *De rerum natura libri sex*, ed. with Prolegomena, trans. and comm. by Cyril Bailey. 3 vols. Oxford (Clarendon Press), 1949.

MAGNY (Olivier de). *Les Amours* [1553], ed. E. Courbet. Paris, 1878. *Les Odes* [1559], ed. E. Courbet. 2 vols. Paris, 1876.

MALLEVILLE (Claude de). *In regias aquarum et silvarum constitutiones commentarius*, Parisiis (V. Sertenas) 1561, 8°. Bodl. M. 11. Jur. Seld.

MAROT (Clément). *Œuvres lyriques*, ed. C. A. Mayer. London (Athlone Press), 1964.

MARTYR ANGLERIUS (Peter). *De rebus oceanicis et orbe novo Decades tres*... Basel (Bebel) 1533, fol. Bodl. H.4.17.Art.
Extraict ou Recueil des isles nouvellement trouvées en la grand mer oceane... Paris (S. de Colines) 1532, 4°. BM C.55.c.29.

MEDICI (Lorenzo de'). *Opere*, a cura di Attilo Simioni (Scrittori d'Italia). 2 vols. Bari, 1913–14.

MICHEL (Guillaume). *Le siècle doré: contenant le temps de Paix, Amour, & Concorde*, Paris (G. Fesandat pour H. le Fevre) 1521, 4°. Bodl. Douce M.709.
De la justice et de ses espèces, ed. G. Aubert. Paris (J. Kerver) 1556, 8°. BN. R. 18719.

OTTO FRISINGENSIS. *Chronica sive Historia de duabus civitatibus*, ed. A. Hofmeister. Hannoverae and Lipsiae, 1912.

OVIDE MORALIZÉ. *Poème du commencement du XIVe siècle*, ed. C. de Boer (Verhandelingen der Kon.Akad.van Wetenschappen te Amsterdam: Afdeeling Letterkunde. Nieuwe Reeks, deel 15, 21, 30). Amsterdam, 1915, 1920, 1931.

OVIDIUS NASO (Publius). *Fasti*, trans. J. G. Frazer (Loeb Classical Library). 1931.
Heroides, trans. G. Showerman (Loeb Classical Library) 1914.
Metamorphoses, trans. J. J. Miller (Loeb Classical Library) 2 vols. 1916.

Bibliography

PAPE (Jacques de). *Elegiae Jacobi Papae Hyprensis,* edidit Jacobus Meyerus reprinted in *Recueil de chroniques, chartes et autres documents concernant l'histoire et les antiquités de la Flandre-Occidentale publié par la Société d'Emulation de Bruges,* 3me série, *Documents isolés, chartes et keuren.* Bruges, 1847.

PELETIER DU MANS (Jacques). *Les Œuvres Poétiques* (Paris [M. de Vascosan] 1547, 8°), reproduction photographique, ed. M. Françon. Rochecorbon, 1958.

PLATO. *Dialogues,* trans. B. Jowett, 4th ed., revised by order of the Jowett Copyright Trustees, 4 vols. Oxford University Press, 1953.

POLIZIANO (Angelo Ambrogini). *Le Stanze. L'Orfeo e le rime,* ed. A. Momigliano (Collezione di classici italiani). Torino, 1925.

POSTEL (Guillaume). *Les tresmerveilleuses victoires des femmes du nouveau monde. A la fin est adjoustée la doctrine du siecle doré.* Paris (J. Ruelle) 1553, 8°. BM 688.a.29.

PROPERTIUS (Sextus). trans. H. E. Butler (Loeb Classical Library). 1958.

RABELAIS (François). *Pantagruel,* ed. V.-L. Saulnier (TLF). Paris, 1946.

RAULIN (Joannes). *Epistolarum opus.* Luteciae (A. Ausurd pour J. Petit) 1521, 4°. Bodl. 4° R.7.Th.

ROMAN DE LA ROSE, LE, par Guillaume de Lorris et Jean de Meun, ed. E. Langlois (SATF). 5 vols. Paris, 1914–24.

RONSARD, (Pierre de). *Œuvres complètes,* ed. P. Laumonier (STFM, 2ᵉ éd.). 18 vols. (vols. XVII and XVIII, completed by I. Silver and R. Lebègue).
Paris, 1924–67.
   ed. G. Cohen (Pléiade). 2 vols. Paris, 1938.

SANNAZARO (Iacopo). *Opere,* ed. E. Carrara (Collezione di classici italiani). Turin, 1952.

SCHMIDT (A.-M.) ed. *Poètes du XVIᵉ siècle* (Pléiade). Paris, 1964.

SENECA (Lucius Annaeus). *Ad Lucilium Epistulae morales,* trans. R. M. Gunmere. 3 vols. (Loeb Classical Library). 1953.

TAHUREAU (Jacques). *Les premières poésies* (Sonnets, odes et mignardises), Poitiers (Les de Marnef and Bouchetz) 1554, 4°. BM 1073.d.32.

THEVET (André). *Les singularitez de la France antarctique,* Paris (héritiers de M. de la Porte) 1558, 4°. Bodl. Douce T.266.

TIBULLUS (Albius). trans. J. P. Postgate (Catullus, Tibullus and Pervigilium Veneris) (Loeb Classical Library). 1953.

Bibliography

TYARD (Pontus de). *Œuvres poétiques complètes*, ed. John C. Lapp (STFM). Paris, 1966.

VAUQUELIN DE LA FRESNAYE (Jean). *Les Foresteries* (1555), ed. M. Bensimon (TLF). Genève–Lille, 1956.

VIRGILIUS MARO (Publius). *Opera*, ed. F. A. Hirtzel. Oxford University Press, 1900.

MODERN WORKS AND ARTICLES

ADHÉMAR (J.). 'Ronsard et l'Ecole de Fontainebleau', *BHR*, xx (1958), 344–8.

ART EXHIBITION CATALOGUES:
London, Royal Academy of Arts. *Landscape in French Art* (Introduction, Bernard Dorival). 1949.

Manchester, City Art Gallery. *Between Renaissance and Baroque, 1520–1600*. 1965.

Nancy, Musée des Beaux Arts. *La forêt dans la peinture ancienne* (Preface, Denis Rouart). 1960.

ATKINSON (G.). *Les nouveaux horizons de la renaissance française.* Paris, 1935.

BALDASS (L. von). *Albrecht Altdorfer.* Zürich, 1941.

BOAS (G.). *Essays on primitivism and related ideas in the Middle Ages.* Baltimore (Johns Hopkins Press), 1948.

BURY (J. B.). *The idea of progress: an inquiry into its origins and growth.* London, 1924.

CARLYLE (A. J. and R. W.). *A history of medieval political theory in the West.* 6 vols. Edinburgh and London, 1903–36.

CASSIO (R.). 'La forêt de Gâtine au temps de Ronsard', *HR*, IV (1937), 274–85.

CHAMARD (H.). *Histoire de la Pléiade.* 4 vols. Paris, 1939–41.

CHARTROU (J.). *Les entrées solennelles et triomphales à la Renaissance (1484–1551).* Paris, 1928.

CHINARD (G.). *L'exotisme américain dans la littérature française au XVIe siècle.* Paris, 1911.

CLARK (Sir Kenneth). *Landscape into Art.* London, 1949.

CLEMENT (N. H.). 'Nature and the country in sixteenth and seventeenth century French poetry', *PMLA*, XLIV (1929), 1005–47.

CORNELIA (W. B.). *The classical sources of the nature references in Ronsard's poetry.* New York (Publications of the Institute of French Studies, Columbia University), 1934.

14-2

Bibliography

DEVÈZE (M.). *La vie de la forêt française au XVIe siècle* (Ecole pratique des hautes études, vie section, centre de recherches historiques: Les hommes et la terre, VI). 2 vols. Paris, 1961.

DIMIER (L.). *Le Primatice* (Les Maîtres du Moyen Age et de la Renaissance). Paris, 1928.

FAIRCHILD (H. N.). *The noble savage: a study in romantic naturalism.* New York, 1928.

FÊTES DE LA RENAISSANCE, LES, ed. J. Jacquot.
   I. Journées internationales d'études, Abbaye de Royaumont, 8–13 juillet 1955.
   II. *Fêtes et cérémonies au temps de Charles Quint.* IIe Congrès de l'Association Internationale des historiens de la Renaissance (2e section), Bruxelles, etc., 2–7 septembre 1957. Collection 'Le Chœur des Muses', 1956 et 1960.

FRAISSE (Simone). *Une conquête du rationalisme: l'influence de Lucrèce en France au XVIe siècle.* Paris, 1962.

FREY (Dora E.). *Le genre élégiaque dans l'œuvre de Ronsard.* Liège, 1939.

GOMBRICH (E. H.). 'Renaissance and Golden Age', *JWCI*, XXIV (1961), 306–9.

GRAF (A.). *Miti, leggende e superstizioni del Medio Evo*, 2 vols. Torino, 1892–3.

GRAF (E.). 'Ad aureae aetatis fabulam symbola', *Leipziger Studien zur classischen Philologie*, VIII (1885), 3–84.

GUY (H.). 'Pierre de Ronsard, peintre et interprète de la nature', *Bulletin de l'Académie Delphinale* (Grenoble), XV (1926), 151–64.

HALLOWELL (R. E.). *Ronsard and the conventional Roman elegy.* Urbana (Illinois University Press), 1954.

HULUBEI (Alice). *L'Eglogue en France au XVIe siècle 1515–1589.* 2 vols. Paris, 1938–9.

HUTTON (J.). 'Rhetorical doctrine and some poems of Ronsard', *The Rhetorical Idiom: Essays presented to H. A. Wichelns*, pp. 323–32. Ithaca, 1958.

JOHNSON (R.). 'The Promethean commonplace', *JWCI*, XXV (1962), 9–17.

LAUMONIER (P.). *Ronsard poète lyrique: Etude historique et littéraire* (2e édition). Paris, 1923.
Ronsard et sa province. Paris, 1924.

LEVIN (H.). 'The Golden Age and the Renaissance', *Literary Views: critical and historical essays*, ed. C. Camden, published for Rice University, pp. 1–14. Chicago University Press, 1964.

Bibliography

LIPSKER (Erika). *Der Mythos vom goldenen Zeitalter in den Schäfer-dichtungen Italiens, Spaniens und Frankreichs zur Zeit der Renaissance* (Inaugural-Dissertation). Universität zu Berlin, 1933.

LONGNON (H.). *Pierre de Ronsard, essai de biographie: les ancêtres, la jeunesse*. Paris, 1912.

LOVEJOY (A. O.) and BOAS (G.). *A documentary history of primitivism and related ideas*. Vol. I: *Primitivism and related ideas in antiquity*. Baltimore (Johns Hopkins Press), 1935.

MORRISON (Mary). 'Another book from Ronsard's library: a presentation copy of Lambin's Lucretius', *BHR*, XXV (1963), 561–6.

NAGLER (A. M.). *Theatre festivals of the Medici 1539–1637*. New Haven and London (Yale University Press), 1964.

NAÏS (Hélène). *Les animaux dans la poésie française de la renaissance: Science, Symbolique, Poésie*. Paris, 1961.

NOLHAC (P. de). *Ronsard et l'humanisme* (Bibliothèque de l'Ecole des Hautes Etudes, 227). Paris, 1921.

PANOFSKY (E.). *Studies in iconology: humanistic themes in the art of the renaissance*. New York, 1939.

PANOFSKY (E. and D.). *Pandora's Box: changing aspects of a mythological symbol*. London, 1956.

PARTURIER (E.). 'Quelques sources italiennes de Ronsard au XVe siècle: Politien et Laurent de' Medicis', *Revue de la Renaissance*, VI (1905), 1–21.

PATCH (H. R.). *The tradition of Boethius: a study of his importance in medieval culture*. New York, 1935.

PETRICONI (H.). 'Über die Idee des goldenen Zeitalters als Ursprung der Schäferdichtungen Sannazaros und Tassos', *Die Neueren Sprachen*, XXXVIII (1930), 265–83.

PHILLIPS (Margaret Mann). *The Adages of Erasmus: a study with translations*. Cambridge University Press, 1964.

POSSE (H.). *Lucas Cranach d. Ä.* Wien, 1942.

REMIGEREAU (F.). 'Ronsard sur les brisées de Du Fouilloux', *RSS*, XIX (1932–3), 46–95.

ROUPNEL (G.). *Histoire de la campagne française*. Paris, 1932.

SAYCE (R. A.). 'Ronsard and Mannerism: the Elégie à Janet', *L'Esprit Créateur*, VI (1966), 234–47.

SEZNEC (J.). *La survivance des dieux antiques*. London, 1940.

SILVER (I.). 'Pierre de Ronsard, Panegyrist, Pensioner and Satirist of the French court', *Romanic Review*, XLV (1954), 89–108.

Bibliography

SILVER (I.). *Ronsard and the hellenic renaissance in France*. 1: *Ronsard and the Greek epic*. St Louis (Washington University Press), 1961.

STORER (W. L.). *Virgil and Ronsard*. Paris, 1923.

TAYLER (E. W.). *Nature and Art in renaissance literature*. New York and London (Columbia University Press), 1964.

THOMAS (A.) and ROQUES (M.). 'Traductions françaises de la *Consolatio Philosophiae* de Boèce', *Histoire littéraire de la France* (Académie des Inscriptions et Belles-Lettres), XXXVII (1938), 419–88.

TROUSSON (R.). 'Le mythe de Prométhée et de Pandore chez Ronsard', *Bulletin Association Guillaume Budé* (1961), pp. 351–9. *Le thème de Prométhée dans la littérature européenne*, 2 vols. Geneva, 1964.

WEBER (H.). *La création poétique au XVIe siècle en France, de Maurice Scève à Agrippa d'Aubigné*. 2 vols. Paris, 1956.

WEINBERG (B.). 'Guillaume Michel, dit de Tours, the editor of the 1526 *Roman de la Rose*', *BHR*, XI (1949), 72–85.

YATES (Frances A.). 'Queen Elizabeth as Astraea', *JWCL*, X (1947), 27–82.

ZAVOLA (S.). 'The American Utopia of the sixteenth century', *Huntington Library Quarterly*, X (1947), 337–47.

Indices

Index

SUBJECT INDEX

Index

INDEX OF NAMES

Index

Calais, 97
Cassandre [Salviati], 98, 108, 163, 172, 173
Cateau-Cambrésis, treaty of, 26, 98
Cecil, Sir Robert, 42 n. 1, 43
Cendrine, brook, 44
Ceres, 15, 72, 97, 100, 101, 123, 164, 168, 169
Certon, Pierre, 32 n. 2
Cervantes, 107 n. 2
Chantilly, 168 n. 3
Charbonnier, François, 18, 31
Charlemagne, 47
Charles V, Emperor, 2, 5, 25, 108
Charles IX, King of France, ('Carlin'), 9, 37, 38, 40, 41, 45, 47, 85, 120 n. 1, 190
Charles, Duke of Angoulême, afterwards Duke of Orleans, third son of Francis I, 135
Châteaudun, 158, 159 n. 2
Cicero, 124, 125, 134 n. 2
Circe, 142
Clark, Sir Kenneth, 170
Claudin, 32 n. 2
Clouet, François, 108, 109
Clovis, 47
Cluny, 6 n. 2
Colie, Rosalie, 142 n. 1
Coligny, Gaspard de, 22
Coligny, Odet de, Cardinal of Châtillon, 19 n. 1, 22, 186
Colines, Simon de, 135 n. 3
Columbus, 15, 134, 135
Como, 116, 130
Coquillart, Guillaume, 81 n. 2
Cosimo, Piero di, 116
Couture, 44, 158, 160, 164, 165, 166
Cranach, Lucas, The Elder, 113, 118
Crespin, René, 34 n. 2
Crete, 66
Croixval, priory of, 44, 165, 181, 194
Cronus, 54, 60, 61, 63
Cubans, 135
Cuspinianus, 155
Cyclops, 108

Dante, 83–4
Demeter, 122
Denisot, Nicolas, 108
Des Autels, Guillaume, 105

Desportes, 128
Devèze, Michel, 183
Diana, Artemis, 85, 190
Dijon, 83
Dorat, Jean, 46, 95, 96, 122, 127
Dresden, 113 n. 1
Dryden, 136 n. 3
Du Bellay, Guillaume, 93
Du Bellay, Cardinal Jean, 98
Du Bellay, Joachim, 13 n. 1, 44, 45, 95, 97, 98, 103, 105, 145, 181, 187, 188
Du Cerceau, 168 n. 1
Du Choul, Jean, 77
Du Thier, Jean, 139, 140

Egypt, 122
Elizabeth I, Queen of England, 42, 43, 89
Empedocles, 59
Enghien, prince d', 83
England, 42, 96, 154
Epicurean, 124
Erasmus, 62, 139, 141
Estienne, Charles, 142
Estienne, Henry, 193
Europe, 1, 10, 14–15, 17, 76
Europeans, 27–8, 30, 131

Faunus, 182
Flanders, 1
Flora, Flore, 16
Flora, Joachim of, 152
Florence, 7, 115; Uffizi, 117
Foix, Paul de, 42, 43
Fontainebleau, 37, 41, 109, 112, 120, 168, 179
Forest, Jean, 119 n. 3
Fouilloux, Jacques du, 190
Fraisse, S., 128
France, 14, 21, 33, 42, 46, 47, 49, 97, 119, 120, 127, 145, 152, 154, 156, 178
France, Claude of, 26
France, Margaret of, daughter of Francis I, Duchess of Savoy, 11, 12, 44, 94, 95, 96, 153 n. 1
France, Margaret of, daughter of Henry II (= 'Margot'), 38
France, Renée of, daughter of Louis XII, Duchess of Ferrara, 6
Francis I, King of France, 5, 95, 110, 135, 148, 166

210

Index

Index

Martyr, Anglerius Peter (Pietro Martiro d'Anghera), 134–6, 140
Mary, Queen of Scots, 96, 178–9
Maximilian I, King of the Romans, 155
Mayenne, river, 158
Medici, Catherine de', 7, 38, 44, 46, 89, 139
Medici, Cosimo I de', 7, 115
Medici, Francesco de', 115
Medici, Giuliano de', 85
Medici, Lorenzo de', 86, 88, 105, 151
Merlin, 42
Meung, Jean de, 78, 79 n. 1, 81, 82, 86, 110; *Roman de la Rose*, 3, 49, 109
Michel, Guillaume, 3, 148–9, 193
Milton, John, 6, 56
Molière, 8 n. 1
Montmorency, Anne de, 22
Montoire, 44, 158
Montrouveau, 165, 184
More, Sir Thomas, 62
Morel, Guillaume, 56
Moulu, Pierre, 32 n. 2
Mouton, Jean, 32 n. 2
Munich, 119
Muret, Marc-Antoine, 14, 132
Muses, The, 27, 102, 104, 186

Neptune, 16
Nicander, 58
Nicolas, Simon, 49
Nicot, Jean, 143, 145, 147
Nolhac, Pierre de, 157

Olympus, 54
Orpheus, 123
Oslo, 113 n. 1
Osiris, 72, 122
Ovid, 13 n. 1, 53, 54, 56, 67, 70, 71, 75, 76, 77, 80, 82, 102, 111, 121, 128 n. 1, 130, 143, 173, 176, 177, 181, 182; Ovide Moralisé, 82, 83, 132 n. 3

Pales, 97
Pan, 100, 187
Pandora, 11, 21, 139
Pantagruel, 1
Paolo, Giovanni di, 110
Pape, Jacques de, 5
Paris, 9, 94, 145, 159 n. 2, 171
    Chambre des Comptes, 34 n. 2

Fontaine des Innocents, 46
Louvre, 24, 36, 46, 115 n. 1
Navarre, Collège de, 5
Porte aux Peintres, 45
Tuileries, 46
Parnassus, Parnasse, 44, 54, 96
Pascal, 155
Paschal, Pierre de, 102, 184
Pazzia, La (anon. work, attributed by some to V. Albergati), 139
Pegasus, Pégase, 44
Peletier du Mans, Jacques, 64, 92, 93, 94, 164 n. 2
Pesloe, François, 103
Philip V, King of France, 78
Philippe le Beau, Archduke, King of Castille, 2
Plato, 60, 61, 62, 90, 139, 144, 193
Pliny the Elder, 77
Poitiers, 106, 166, 167
Poland, 46
Poliziano, Angelo, 84, 85 n. 2, 86
Pomona, 97
Posidonius, 133
Postel, Guillaume, 152, 153
Poussin, 168, 193 n. 2
Priapus, 97
Primaticcio, 119, 168
Probus, 31 n. 3
Prometheus, 87, 122
Propertius, 53, 71
Protestant, *see* Huguenots
Pythagorean(s), 61, 70

Quiroga, Vasco de, Bishop of Michoacan, 136
Quixote, Don, 107

Rabelais, 1
Raulin, Jean, 5, 74 n. 2
Rembrandt, 170
Rembure, Seigneur de, 36
Remus, 66
Rhea, Rhée, 156
    son of, *see* Jupiter
    husband of, *see* Saturn
Richaffort, Jean, 32 n. 2
Richelet, Nicolas, 165 n. 2
Roman de la Rose, see Meung, Jean de
Rome, 187
Ronsard (or Ronsart), Claude (brother of the poet), 158; Loys de (father of the poet), 74, 93, 184–5

212

Index